Into the Inferno

Into

the

Inferno

THE MEMOIR OF
A JEWISH PARATROOPER
BEHIND NAZI LINES

✴

YOEL PALGI

Introduction by David Engel
Afterword by Phyllis Palgi

Rutgers University Press
New Brunswick, New Jersey, and London

Library of Congress Cataloging-in-Publication Data

Palgi, Yoel, 1918-
[Ruah gedolah ba'ah. English]
Into the inferno : memoir of a Jewish paratrooper behind Nazi lines /
Yoel Palgi.
p.   cm.
Includes bibliographical references.
ISBN 0-8135-3149-7 (alk. paper)
1. Palgi, Yoel, 1918- 2. World War, 1939–1945—Personal narratives,
Jewish. 3. Jews—Palestine—Biography. 4. World War, 1939–1945—
Jews—Rescue—Hungary. 5. World War, 1939–1945—Jewish
resistance—Hungary. I. Title.

D811.P25713 2002
940.54'81439—dc21   2002023699

British Cataloguing-in-Publication information is available from
the British Library.

Manufactured in the United States of America

To Ofra, Hagar, Daniella, and Avigail.
In remembrance of the Jewish Palestinian paratroopers,
Hannah Szenes and Peretz Goldstein,
and the almost one million Jews of Hungary
who perished at the hand
of the Nazi regime.

Contents

Acknowledgments

The sustained support and critical eyes, most notably of my daughters, Ilana Kaufman, Anat Palgi-Hecker, and their spouses, Ehud and Reuven enabled me to prepare this memoir for the English-language reader, originally written in Hebrew by my late husband, Yoel Palgi. It was a complex and frequently painful task as I once again became immersed in the crystalline images evoked during the year he spent behind Nazi lines. My editor, David Myers, also requested that I give my own perspective on Yoel's life, before and after that defining year, which I include as an afterword. I am grateful to David for bringing me to this illuminating experience, especially because I have been blessed with the help and encouragement of so many.

After Yoel and I first met, he turned his gaze to the future, so that his early life in Europe, where his parents and sister perished, became a closed book. To help me fill in these gaps, I talked to friends from his childhood. I wish to thank Yishai Shilo, Yosef Givol, and Bobbie Ayalon, who regaled me with stories of Yoel's originality, both in pranks and in his ideological contribution to the pioneer Zionist youth movement. From Moshe Alpan, an underground leader in wartime Budapest, I learned more about Yoel's role in their rescue schemes. I am grateful to Herta Goren, who spent hours with me vividly describing the background of that time, her own special experience, and her significant encounter with Yoel. Meno Ben-Ephraim, who himself parachuted into Romania, was most generous with information and advice. Yonah Rosen, who parachuted into Yugoslavia, was always available for inquiries. Architect Leo Goldner, a survivor from a labor camp, prepared a map of Yoel's clandestine journey from Yugoslavia to Budapest as a tribute to him.

Many colleagues from later in Yoel's life were most informative and told fascinating stories. My thanks go to Milton Lang, an American pilot, and Mordechai Ben Porat, both of whom were involved with Yoel in organizing the massive Iraqi and Yemenite airlifts, to Amatzia Arnon from the Israel Embassy in Dar es Salaam, and to Chaim Gordon and Rafi Reuveni from Kupat Holim Health Service. Chanoch Bartov also shared with me his experiences with Yoel during the Yom Kippur War.

Due to my undeveloped computer competence, I was dependent on high-level technical and secretarial assistance, which I received from Sylvia Weinberg, Norma Davidov, and Fortuna Cohen. Roz Langbart was extraordinary in responding to my frequent last-minute requests. Eva and Tory Weintraub graciously checked the Hungarian names.

I wrote Yoel's biographical sketch in an expansive spirit, which resulted in having to pare it down to half its original length. My special thanks to Ruth Nevo, Ghila Sharfstein, and Clair Wollach for helping me in this difficult task. So many assisted me in different and important ways, notably my sister, Chasya Pincus, Masha Mishkinski, Becky Davis, Yoshua Dorban, Aharon Doron, Shlomo Peled, David Toren, Yerach Shram, and Nomi and Yosef Chason.

I am sure that somebody's name has slipped my memory at this moment. Please forgive me!

My thanks to the translator, Reeva Rubin, who is a poet and who responded so beautifully to Yoel's poetic passages, and to the copy editor, Eric Schramm. I am also grateful to David Myers of Rutgers University Press, for being like the Rock of Gibraltar while we shared a common goal: to bring Yoel's memoir to the English-language reader.

Phyllis Palgi
Ramat HaSharon
April 2002

Previous Editions

In Hebrew, as *Ru'ach Gedolah Ba'ah*. Tel Aviv: HaKibbutz HaMe'uhad, 1946. 2nd edition, 1948. Revised edition, Tel Aviv: Am Oved, 1977. 2nd edition, 1978.

In Hungarian, as *". . . es jott a fergeteg."* Tel Aviv: Alexander Publishing, 1946 (out of print).

In Italian, as *Un vento Impetuoso Soffie*, translated by Rabbi Gustavo Castelbolognesi. Florence: Rinascimento Del Libro, ca. 1958. (Only 200 copies were printed; they are no longer available. They were to "honor the Rabbi and the fighter, Yoel Palgi, the greatest of all fighters.")

Various modified extracts have appeared in Hebrew and English from the first Hebrew edition. From the 1977 Hebrew edition, an extract is due to appear in *The Encyclopedia of the Holocaust* [Hebrew], edited by Dina Porat.

Introduction

In the epilogue to the 1977 version of his memoirs, presented here in English for the first time, Yoel Palgi spoke of the doubt that had pursued him thirty years earlier: Could he make people "whom fate had allowed to observe the Holocaust from a safe distance" understand the full extent of the catastrophe he had witnessed? In 1944 he had served as a secret emissary from Palestine hoping to aid the threatened Jews of Hungary; when he returned a year later he lacked an adequate vocabulary to convey "the mute heroism of masses of Jews who were caught in a situation with no solution . . . but who . . . retained their humanity through all the tortures of hell until their last breath." Still, he felt compelled to communicate a sense of that heroism, so that subsequent generations would not be tempted to place "the six million on the accused's bench" for going to their deaths "like sheep to the slaughter."

Palgi was not alone in his dilemma. The theme of the obligation to bear witness to a previously unimagined aspect of the human condition, despite the inability of human language to render that aspect imaginable, is a staple feature both of Holocaust testimonies and of the growing body of scholarly literature that analyzes them. But underlying this conundrum is a basic fact about any narrative:

no story can tell itself. A story can be transmitted only if a teller chooses specific words through which to represent it. The choice of words can be crucial: change a phrase here, an adjective there, and the narration can produce an altogether different effect. Thus, memoirists like Palgi, who relate their experiences consciously in order to evoke a specific response in their readers, invariably select their words with a mind to how they think their intended readers will receive them. The task of selection can be challenging.

It seems, moreover, that in the interval between his first efforts to relate his story and the completion of his final version more than thirty years later, Palgi learned another truth about memoirs: not only are they shaped simultaneously by the events remembered *and* by the act of narrating them to a specific audience for a specific purpose, but writers' perceptions of audiences' needs and expectations can change over time, depending upon the writers' ongoing experiences and those of the societies to which they belong. Memoirs are timebound because the memories that inform them may generate different stories depending on when they are told. Whereas in 1945 most of those with whom Palgi came into contact were not ready to absorb the message of his epilogue, by 1977 he could state it clearly and imbue it with moral force.

Not that Palgi remained silent for thirty years for fear he would not be understood. In fact, the first Hebrew edition of his memoir appeared in British mandatory Palestine in 1946.[1] Immediately it established its author as a hero of the Jewish state in the making. One reviewer extolled how the book "captivates . . . with an intense spellbinding power"; he called it a work "exemplifying the great spirit of humanity."[2] Palgi himself began a distinguished career in public service, largely on the strength of his wartime efforts. In Israel's War of Independence he trained the fledgling army's first paratroopers. He was elected to the first Knesset (Parliament) but did not take his seat, citing more pressing public responsibilities, including helping to establish Israel's national airline (El Al) and arranging the airlifts that brought the Jewish communities of Yemen and Iraq to the Jewish state. In Israel of the early 1950s, he stood out as the embodiment of the young state's most cherished values, and his memoir became standard reading for Israeli youth.

Less than a year before his death, however, he released a new version of the memoir, in which he stated that he had been compelled by his military superiors to present a false account of one especially tragic episode.[3] In the new edition he sought "to be as accurate as possible" and to relate the events of his mission with "the maximum degree of precision."[4] On the surface, the differences between the versions seemed minor (an epilogue was added, a chapter removed, some passages altered here and there), but their cumulative effect was substantial. Through changes in just a few words readers were presented with a radically different view of some of the central personalities and events in the baleful history of the Holocaust in Hungary. Thus even as Palgi's memoir relates a compelling story of human courage and sacrifice, it offers remarkable insight into the complex process by which memories are formed and passed on. For this reason it stands out among Holocaust testimonies and merits special attention.

Whatever their differences, both versions were built around a solid core of historical fact.

Palgi was born Emil Nuszbacher on February 17, 1918, in Transylvania, an ethnically mixed, bitterly contested border region then in the Hungarian portion of the Austro-Hungarian Empire.[5] Following Austria-Hungary's defeat in the First World War, the area was annexed to Romania. In August 1940, at the behest of Nazi Germany, the northern two-fifths of the province—including Nuszbacher's birthplace, Cluj (Kolozsvár in Hungarian, Klausenburg in German)—were returned to Hungarian rule, under which they remained to the end of the war.

Transylvania's 195,000 Jews had long identified linguistically and culturally with the middle-class Hungarian and German constituents of the region's population over the largely Romanian peasant majority—a fact that exposed the Jews to widespread hostility and suspicion under Romanian sovereignty during the interwar years.[6] Cut off after 1918 from their historic Austro-Hungarian connections and rejected as a foreign element by the Romanian rulers, many Transylvanian Jews, Emil Nuszbacher among them, were attracted to Jewish nationalism, especially to the young Zionist movement, which sought to establish Palestine (then governed by Britain) as the Jewish national homeland. Nuszbacher joined a Zionist youth labor movement at age fourteen. Seven years later, on the eve of the Second World War, he immigrated to Palestine, hebraized his name, and became a founding member of Kibbutz Maagan on the shores of the Sea of Galilee.[7]

The Zionist youth movement educated him in leadership and volunteerism. In that spirit he was one of almost 11,000 Palestinian Jews who enlisted in the British army during 1941, hoping simultaneously to fight the Nazis and to strengthen Jewish claims for sovereignty in Palestine once peace was restored.[8] Wearing a British uniform, he served for over two years with various supply and engineering companies in North Africa, until he was selected for the mission with which his name would become linked from then on.

That mission was part of a British operation in which special commando units worked behind enemy lines in Europe, establishing bases for wireless communication, conducting sabotage, rescuing downed Allied fliers and prisoners of war, and assisting anti-Nazi resistance movements. Palestinian Jews, many of whom knew the target countries intimately and were fluent in their languages, seemed to some British military and intelligence officials to be ideal recruits for such activities. In early 1943 discussions began between the British secret services in Cairo and Jewish political and military representatives about organizing a Palestinian Jewish commando force.[9] For their part the Jewish representatives were interested in the scheme because it offered an opportunity to establish direct contact with underground Jewish groups under Nazi rule and to aid Jews trying to escape or resist the German mass murder program, which at that time had reached its apogee. They hoped to send a force of up to 1,000 volunteers to countries within the Nazi orbit. British negotiators balked at such a large number, fearing, among other things, that Jewish commandos might eventually assist in a revolt against British rule in Palestine.[10] In spring 1943 British-Jewish agreement on a limited commando force was achieved, and fourteen Palestinian Jewish volunteers began training.[11] More, including Palgi, were added later in the year.

Palgi was selected for an operation in Hungary. Though still a German ally, the Hungarian regime, led by Regent Miklos Horthy, harbored doubts about the wisdom of its orientation and had begun making overtures to the West. Horthy and his prime minister, Miklos Kállay, also shielded Hungary's Jews from deportation to the Nazi killing centers. This policy made Hungary a relatively safe place for Jews in comparison with neighboring countries. Whereas the Germans and their allies had murdered some 85 to 90 percent of the Jews in Poland, the Baltic countries, Ukraine, Belarus, Slovakia, the Czech lands, Austria, and Germany proper between late 1941 and the middle of 1943, almost all Hungarian Jewry, numbering perhaps 750,000, was still alive when Palgi set out on his mission in early 1944. The Germans were angered, however, by the Hungarian leaders' seeming unreliability—because of both their foreign policy and their lenient treatment of Jews—and by 1943 threatened to take control of the Hungarian government and send the country's Jews to their deaths.[12] Thus, Britain and the Jewish Agency each had powerful reasons for wanting to place secret operatives in Hungary as soon as possible—Britain to strengthen Hungarian anti-Nazi activity, the Jewish Agency to help Hungarian Jews preserve their precarious security.

Doing so was no easy matter, however. Though Palgi pressed to be parachuted directly into Hungarian territory, British planners feared that such a "blind jump" would be unsuccessful because the Allies lacked direct connections with the Hungarian partisans who could have received the parachutists. Instead it was decided to send him and two comrades, Hannah Szenes and Peretz Goldstein, via Yugoslavia, where a pro-Allied partisan force of 250,000 under the command of Marshal Tito controlled the mountain regions of Croatia, Bosnia, and Montenegro, tying up more than ten German divisions.[13]

Yugoslavia had fallen under Nazi domination in April 1941; shortly thereafter the Germans partitioned it, taking territories for itself and giving others to Hungary, Bulgaria, and Italy; instituted military rule in Serbia and Montenegro; and established a puppet state in Croatia, Bosnia, and Herzegovina under the leadership of a right-wing paramilitary organization, the Ustaše (Insurgents). The pro-Nazi Croatian regime had quickly embarked upon a murderous campaign to rid the region of so-called foreign elements, including the relatively small Jewish population; in 1941–42 Croatian government forces, without German assistance, killed about two-thirds of the area's Jews, along with half of the local Serbs. In Serbia itself an anti-Nazi uprising in July 1941 had prompted the German occupiers to take revenge against the similarly small Jewish community, which was effectively obliterated by mid-1942. Thus Palgi and his companions felt little motivation to spend time in Yugoslavia and hoped to reach Hungary as quickly as possible. For the British, in contrast, Yugoslavia was an important theater of operations.

These differing British and Jewish interests contributed to a fateful delay. During the three months (March through June 1944) that the parachutists spent in Yugoslavia preparing to enter Hungary, Germany sent troops into the country, forcing Horthy to jettison Kállay and install a pro-Nazi government, which quickly organized the deportation of over 430,000 Jews to Auschwitz. By the time Palgi arrived in Hungary in mid-June, almost all Hungarian Jews outside of Budapest had already been sent to their deaths. Moreover, internal security measures were increased, leading to the penetration of many Hungarian underground resistance cells. Palgi and his companions were betrayed immediately upon entering the country; it was only a matter of time before Hungarian security forces located and arrested them.

The fate of the three parachutists then depended upon the vicissitudes of Hungarian internal politics and German-Hungarian relations. On July 7, 1944, shortly after Palgi had been taken into custody, Horthy, with the help of loyal army units, reasserted active control of the Hungarian government. Responding to pressure from the Vatican, the Red Cross, and the Swedish and U.S. governments, he ordered the deportation of Jews stopped, sparing the 200,000 remaining Jews of Budapest from the Auschwitz gas chambers. He also resumed attempts to withdraw from the German alliance. These moves angered Hungary's pro-Nazi elements, which were heavily represented in the internal security apparatus. The security apparatus understood, though, that in the deteriorating military situation, with Soviet troops advancing rapidly from the east and the British-American invasion force moving through France, German and Hungarian interests were not necessarily identical. A tug-of-war soon developed between the German and Hungarian security forces and even among rival factions within the two groups. Palgi experienced this tug-of-war firsthand as he was passed back and forth for months between Hungarian and German jailers, all of whom had different ideas about what should be done with him.

The stalemate was broken on October 15, when Horthy announced that he had concluded an armistice with the Allies. With German support, the radical right-wing Hungarian Arrow Cross Party staged a coup d'état; Horthy was arrested and the Arrow Cross leader, Ferenc Szálasi, installed as head of state. For the parachutists this turn of events was disastrous. A day before the coup they had seemed on the verge of being released.[14] Now they fell victim to an Arrow Cross campaign against the "Jewish Bolshevik enemy." Szenes was tried and executed; Palgi and Goldstein were deported. Goldstein perished; Palgi escaped and returned to Budapest, where he looked for ways to aid the city's Jews. There he fell into the dangerous and chaotic situation created by the Arrow Cross government's dubious legitimacy and tenuous hold on public order. From the day of the coup, party militias began shooting, incarcerating, ghettoizing, and deporting the remaining Budapest Jews; over the next three months more than 80,000 Jews were killed by Arrow Cross violence.[15] At the same time, Szálasi wanted desperately to achieve international recognition of his regime's right to govern. Thus he tried to cultivate favor among diplomats representing neutral states and the Vatican in the Hungarian capital by acknowledging their right to apply their countries' laws in properties they owned and permitting them to protect Jews whom they certified as potential emigrants to their countries.[16] In these circumstances Palgi was able to find shelter in the so-called Glass House maintained by the Swiss Embassy, where he established contact with a small underground Zionist resistance cell. With this group he helped defend the inhabitants of the Glass House and other protected buildings from Arrow Cross mobs (see Chapter 11), which the government itself had difficulty controlling. Though his initial hopes of catalyzing widespread rescue and resistance had come to naught, he still managed to play a role in aiding almost half of Budapest's Jews to remain alive (Chapters 11 and 12).

These were the historical elements out of which Palgi fashioned his memoir. He told his tale with artistry and verve. Nonetheless, its initial message was not exactly the one he later argued needed to be heard. In the first edition he did not refrain completely from judging the victims in a spirit like the one he rejected in 1977. In fact, his original version included an entire chapter, "On the Jews of Hungary," in which he excoriated the ideology of assimilation that in his view had induced the Jewish leadership not only to ignore the mortal danger ahead but to lull virtually the entire Jewish population into a false sense of security.[17] By doing so, those leaders had, he charged, "caused the deaths of tens and perhaps hundreds of thousands of Jews."[18] Such a statement was hardly likely to undermine the belief that Hungarian Jewish leaders were largely responsible for the fate that befell their community at Nazi and Hungarian hands—a belief Palgi criticized in his revised version.

Nor did the first edition explicitly repudiate the dichotomy between the duped many and the heroic few to which Palgi later took exception. In his initial presentation, the heroes were a small group of Zionist activists, mostly from Transylvania, "who took upon themselves the task of rescuing Jews under any and all conditions."[19] These activists formed an Aid and Rescue Committee that smuggled Jews from areas of great danger to areas of relatively greater safety. Before the March 1944 German invasion this operation, known by the Hebrew code name *Tiyul* (tour), moved mainly Polish and Slovakian Jews *into* Hungary; afterward it concentrated on transporting Hungarian Jews *out of* the country, mostly into Romania, from which Jews were not being deported.[20] Shortly following the overthrow of the Kállay government, however, a group within the committee, led by Rezső Kasztner, a lawyer and journalist from Cluj, suggested an additional approach—offering a substantial ransom to the German authorities in return for the safety of all Hungarian Jewry. Kasztner's thinking was that *Tiyul* could save only individual Jews, whereas negotiation and payment might save the entire community.[21] Some committee members, mostly younger people associated with the Zionist youth movements, disagreed, doubting that the Germans could ever be induced to renounce their murderous aims, no matter how great the bribe offered.

Nevertheless, a serious split within the committee never developed, and the youth leaders (Rafi Friedl, Peretz Revesz, and others who formed the resistance cell Palgi joined after his escape) cooperated with Kasztner and his colleagues throughout the war. In his original version Palgi noted the disagreement between the two groups, but, although he expressed greater sympathy for the youth leaders' position, he nonetheless included the negotiators, especially Kasztner, among the heroes.[22]

Indeed, one of Palgi's main concerns in 1946 seems to have been to explain to a Palestinian Jewish public eager for stories about "the few who had fought like lions" that both approaches taken by the Aid and Rescue Committee were more appropriate responses to the specific conditions in Hungary than an armed revolt à la the Warsaw Ghetto Uprising. He argued that several factors made flight preferable to fight for Hungarian Jews: the swiftness with which the deportations were carried out, the lack of any effective Hungarian underground, and the possibility of escape to a neighboring unoccupied country. In Poland, he noted, escape and rescue possibilities had been absent, and those who took up arms in the ghettos had not been trying to save lives but "to crown their deaths with the wreath of heroism."[23] Palestinian Jewish readers, for whom the valiant rebellion of the ghetto fighters and partisans served as virtually the only source of solace for their inability to prevent their people's destruction in Europe, were thus introduced to a new sort of hero— rescuers and negotiators instead of fighters. This, to be sure, represented a bold new departure in presenting the Holocaust to Palestinian Jews, but it did not arouse the radical new understanding of "the mute heroism of masses of Jews" for which he argued in the second edition.

Even the text of the 1977 version did not offer many illustrations of the broader concept of heroism set forth in the epilogue. Palgi did not revise his observations about the masses of Hungarian Jewry and their leaders. Instead, he eliminated the chapter in which he presented them altogether, thereby focusing entirely on his own assignment and its fate and reporting only what he had experienced or observed himself.[24] Actually, the principal change in the new version lay less in a reconsideration of the victims' behavior in the face of mortal danger than in a reevaluation of the actions of those who had tried to bribe the Germans into leaving Hungarian Jews in peace. In particular, through only a few changes, Rezső Kasztner appeared not as an unambiguous hero but as a deeply flawed source of adversity, whose exaggerated confidence in his ability to deal with the Germans and obsessive commitment to his rescue strategy were responsible for Palgi and Peretz Goldstein's incarceration and the ultimate failure of their mission.

Palgi's relationship with Kasztner had begun well before the war, when Kasztner was Palgi's counselor in the Zionist youth movement and a family friend. He was also one of the people who Palgi's superiors in Palestine had instructed him to contact upon arrival in Budapest. Clearly Palgi expected Kasztner to aid him in his goal. From Kasztner's perspective, though, Palgi could not have arrived at a worse time. For their own reasons, the Nazis, under Adolf Eichmann, were intrigued by the idea of selling Jews for ransom. Evidently Eichmann, and presumably some of his superiors in the SS, hoped to use negotiations over the fate of Hungarian Jewry as a cover for establishing direct contact with Britain and the United States, with whom they wished to explore the possibility of reaching a peace agreement that would exclude the Soviets.[25] Thus in May 1944 Kasztner dispatched a member of the Aid and Rescue Committee, Yoel Brand, to Istanbul with an offer to the Western allies, to be transmitted via the Jewish Agency (a body that represented the interests of world Jewry concerning Palestine before the British mandatory authorities). The offer proposed to exchange one million Jews for ten thousand trucks and other basic supplies provided by the British and U.S. governments. Though Brand arrived safely in the Turkish capital, he was unable to get his message to Jewish Agency leaders in Palestine quickly. Because of the delay, he did not return to Budapest within the allotted two weeks. Kasztner, worried that Eichmann would revoke his offer, then attempted a new stratagem: he explained that the Allies sought a sign of good faith and that if Germany would release a small group of Jews in return for cash payment, the larger "goods for blood" scheme would appear more credible. In response, Eichmann permitted Kasztner to select 1,684 Jews who, at the price of $1,000 per head (which Kasztner's colleagues raised and paid), would depart for a neutral country (preferably Spain). Kasztner shared the selection with several other Hungarian Jews, who tried to fill the available slots with a cross-section of Hungarian Jewry.[26] In mid-June the candidates were chosen, and on June 30 a train carried them not to Spain but to the Nazi exchange center at Bergen-Belsen, whence eventually they were brought to Switzerland. In the interval—while the candidates were being held in a transit camp on Columbus Street in Budapest, uncertain of the fate that awaited them—Palgi and Goldstein appeared at Kasztner's door.

Kasztner quickly learned that the Hungarian security forces knew that the two parachutists had contacted him, and he feared that the Germans, thinking he was collaborating with them, would retaliate by not permitting the rescue train to leave. In order to explain their presence without endangering the train, the parachutists agreed to Kasztner's suggestion that they report to the Gestapo as Jewish Agency emissaries sent to check on the seriousness of Brand's proposal. The gambit backfired, mainly because the Hungarian security forces already knew of their mission for the British, and Palgi and Goldstein were arrested. The cover of the Brand mission thus proved of no avail, and Kasztner, despite the close connections he had developed with Nazi leaders in the course of negotiations over the rescue train, was unable to secure their release. This circumstance may well have marred Palgi's attitude toward Kasztner. Even more, though, as he indicated in the 1977 epilogue, he was incensed that when Kasztner made a special trip to Cluj to select candidates for the rescue train, Palgi's parents and sister, whom Kasztner had known from his youth, were not chosen.

Whatever hostility he may have felt toward Kasztner, Palgi did not make it public at first; not only in the first edition of his memoir but in everything else he wrote at the time he had nothing but praise for the man he called "a magnificent human being . . . [who], although he could not prevent the tragedy, managed to reduce the extent of the calamity and slow its pace."[27] Behind the scenes, though, he made his grievances known to leaders of the Zionist movement. Specifically, he claimed that Kasztner effectively forced the parachutists to report to the Gestapo by informing the Germans in advance that they were coming and deliberately betrayed Goldstein in order to ensure the safe departure of the rescue train. Still, his 1946 readers heard him call the idea that the parachutists present themselves to the Gestapo a good one; he represented himself as an active partner in its formulation and attributed Goldstein's capture to an unfortunate miscalculation.[28] The 1977 version, in contrast, presented events as he then claimed they actually happened.

Why had Palgi initially disseminated what he later termed a "false account" of Kasztner's actions, and what moved him later to disavow that account publicly? In the 1977 epilogue he attributed the false version to instructions from his superiors and suggested that perhaps he might have let it stand indefinitely had it not been for a sensational trial concerning the events in Budapest that rocked Israel in the mid-1950s. In 1952 an elderly Viennese Jew living in Israel, Malkiel Grünwald, distributed a broadsheet accusing Kasztner of accepting bribes and of giving preference to his own relatives in filling the rescue train. Kasztner, who had survived the war and immigrated to Palestine in 1947, was employed by an Israeli government ministry, and an Israeli law made defamation of a public official a crime. Grünwald was accordingly indicted, brought to trial, and challenged to prove the truth of his accusations. However, his aggressive (many would say unscrupulous) attorney, Shmuel Tamir, quickly put the prosecution on the defensive, turning the trial into an indictment not only of Kasztner but of the Israeli political establishment that had welcomed him into its ranks. Tamir sought to portray Kasztner as a Nazi collaborator, a dealer with the devil who, in return for a chance to save those closest to him, had helped mislead the masses of Hungarian Jews regarding the fate that awaited them and stifled their ability to escape or resist. The prosecution called upon Palgi, a symbol of Jewish resistance, to speak well of Kasztner, certain that his "prestige was so great . . . it would smash the defense's attacks once and for all." [29]

Under direct examination Palgi did not depart from the favorable representation of Kasztner he had presented publicly hitherto. [30] Nonetheless, defense attorney Tamir discovered small discrepancies between his testimony and his writings, and in cross examination he pursued them with a vengeance, seeking to impugn Palgi's credibility. He twisted Palgi's words to make it appear as though he had gone to the Gestapo at Kasztner's suggestion to declare his willingness to collaborate and had betrayed Goldstein when his companion balked at the idea. By the time Tamir finished he had induced Palgi to reveal that his original description of how Goldstein had been captured was untrue. Palgi now declared under oath that "technically" it was Kasztner who had "turned [Goldstein] over to the enemy," explaining that "I did not write the true version of Goldstein's arrest . . . in order to protect Kasztner and to protect the entire episode." He also admitted that his memoirs contained numerous inaccuracies. He did not believe, however, that he should be called to task for inconsistency of detail, claiming that his memoir was "a novel, not history," in which he was entitled to some measure of invention. [31]

The end of Palgi's epilogue suggests that he felt deeply hurt by the trial: he had endangered his life on behalf of his people, but now, because he had returned and not perished, he was being judged harshly for his efforts—tarred, ironically, by association with Kasztner, whom he had dutifully represented as a hero despite his own private misgivings about the propriety of his former friend's wartime behavior. The status of his book suffered as well: his publisher, about to reissue the memoir in a third edition, [32] severed connections with him, stating that if ever asked why it had taken such a step, it would "seek forgiveness from the public" for the "deception" in which it had unknowingly taken part by presenting Palgi's "novel" as a factual account of events. [33] The trial judge exonerated Grünwald on the premise that Kasztner had "sold his soul to the devil."[34] The verdict turned Kasztner into a target for public opprobrium, until, on March 3, 1957, he was shot and mortally wounded outside his Tel Aviv home. Even though ten months later Israel's Supreme Court overturned the trial court's verdict on all but a single count, for more than twenty years thereafter few people were prepared to speak publicly in Kasztner's defense.

How could Palgi correct the record as he perceived it? Whatever obligation he might have felt previously to help preserve Kasztner's good name was now obviated, both because Kasztner's good name had all but vanished and because he had already revealed damaging information at the trial. Thus he was now free to tell his story without restraint, as he saw fit. On the other hand, it appears that he was troubled by the discrepancies of detail between what he had written immediately after his return from his mission and what he recalled in court years later. Two years after the trial he collected his thoughts in writing, not intending them for publication. He wondered about the trustworthiness of his memory and about how his perceptions of the historical situation might have been affected by the thought that Kasztner could have saved his family but did not. Since the trial, he wrote, he had begun "to ask questions, to rummage through archives, to check his memory against documents," with a mind to getting the facts straight in order to assess Kasztner fairly.[35] His search culminated with the publication of the 1977 edition.

How well did Palgi succeed in building a narrative that reflected not only his personal truth but a truth that others would be compelled to accept?

Most historians of the Holocaust in Hungary have regarded Palgi as a generally reliable witness; a minority have been skeptical.[36] Even the former, however, have hesitated to endorse unequivocally the details of his account of how he came to appear before the Gestapo and how Goldstein was captured.[37] Independent documentary confirmation for most of the specifics of Palgi's story (as opposed to the general historical core) has yet to be found, and other testimonies offer different versions of some events, especially of Goldstein's capture. On this question Kasztner, for one, claimed that following Palgi's arrest and Goldstein's disappearance, Hungarian counterintelligence detained Kasztner (along with Hansi Brand, Yoel Brand's wife, herself a member of the Aid and Rescue

Committee) and threatened that if Goldstein's whereabouts were not revealed, Palgi would be executed. According to Kasztner, he and Mrs. Brand went to Goldstein's hiding place in the Columbus camp and offered him the choice of whether to turn himself in: "It took him only a few minutes to decide, 'I will report [to the Gestapo].'"[38] Hansi Brand corroborated the gist of this version elsewhere.[39] Although, to be sure, their testimony was self-serving,[40] they testified to actions they themselves had taken, whereas Palgi based his version on what he claimed Goldstein later told him in prison. Thus on the basis of testimony alone it seems impossible to determine the exact nature of Kasztner's role in Goldstein's arrest. There are no grounds (beyond a subjective sense of the veracity of the various witnesses) for regarding Palgi's story in the second edition as more or less reliable than competing accounts.

The case is different regarding his own appearance before the Gestapo; here there is a document that lends credence to Palgi's testimony in the second edition. As Palgi related in his epilogue, he and Kasztner faced each other before a panel of inquiry in December 1946, and the panel declined to charge Kasztner with any wrongdoing. The panel's report stated clearly, however, that Kasztner had informed the German authorities of the parachutists' presence in Budapest *before* consulting with Palgi about this course.[41] It is unlikely that this document would have included such a statement had the testimonies of Kasztner and Palgi not been in substantial agreement. But such nontestimonial evidence is exceptional; comparable independent documentation for Palgi's assertion that Kasztner was summoned before the panel at Palgi's suggestion and denied a position with the World Jewish Congress as a result of his charges has not been adduced to date. So far it can be proven only that as early as December 1945 Kasztner requested a public hearing to answer accusations that he understood Palgi to have made privately and that Palgi was generally interested in "clarifying some matters."[42]

Future archival discoveries may eventually resolve these and other ambiguities of nuance and detail.[43] In a larger sense, too, comparing Palgi's narrative to other documents helps shed light on central concerns of the humanities today—the interaction between history and memory, the similarities and differences between history writing and fiction, the problems inherent in the materials used to reconstruct the reality of a bygone era, the uncertainty present in any historical description, and the ways in which accounts of many historical events (not only the Holocaust) are repeatedly rewritten with the passage of time.

But in the final analysis, *Into the Inferno* offers much more than material for an academic case study. Whether read as fact or fiction, the book invites readers to confront the prodigious challenges the author faced when, at age twenty-six, he was suddenly thrust into a perilous situation for which he could never have been adequately prepared. This young man volunteered, against overwhelming odds, to rescue his people from slaughter—no more, no less. To do so he was forced to operate in a world where ordinary rules of human conduct had been suspended, where the line between resistance and collaboration was often murky, and where moral choices were hardly ever clear-cut. In the end his mission could not help but fail.[14] No wonder he returned with haunting memories, demanding time, effort, and courage to work through. His story may have changed between its first and second telling, and parts of it may be open to question and debate. Still, it retains the power to inspire. Readers will be richly rewarded for their reading.

David Engel
Greenberg Professor of Holocaust Studies
New York University

Notes to Introduction

1. Y. Palgi, *Ru'ah gedolah ba'ah: Korot tsanhan ivri* (Tel Aviv, 1946) (henceforth 1st ed.).
2. *Devar haShavu'a*, December 12, 1946, quoted in Y. Weitz, *HaIsh sheNirtsah pe'amayim: Hayav, mishpato uMoto shel Dr. Yisra'el Kasztner* (Jerusalem, 1995), 48.
3. Palgi, *Ru'ah gedolah ba'ah* (Tel Aviv, 1977).
4. The quoted words are from written communications by Phyllis Palgi, Yoel's widow, August 30, 2000, and September 20, 2000.
5. The principal ethnic groups were Romanians (56 percent according to the Hungarian census of 1910), Hungarians (28 percent), German-speaking Saxons (9 percent), and Jews (4 percent). There were smaller Slovak, Ruthenian, Serbian, and Armenian minorities. H. Seton-Watson, *Eastern Europe between the Wars 1918–1941* (3rd ed.) (Cambridge, 1962), 297; R. Vago, "Yehudei Transylvania—bein integratsiyah leYihud," in R. Vago and L. Rotman, eds., *Toledot Yehudei Romania*, vol. 3 (Tel Aviv, 1996), 184.

6. In the Hungarian census of 1910, 73 percent of Transylvania's Jews listed Hungarian as their mother tongue. German was widely used as a second language. Under Romanian rule many Jewish children learned Romanian in school, but Hungarian remained the Jewish community's dominant vehicle of communication. In the 1930 Romanian census, 58 percent of the region's Jews listed Yiddish as their mother tongue, perhaps hoping thereby to diminish their identification with the Hungarian population in the eyes of the Romanian authorities. Vago, "Yehudei Transylvania," 184–193. Employing the Hungarian spelling of its German surname, Nuszbacher's family typified Transylvanian Jewry's linguistic orientation. Palgi himself was a native Hungarian speaker and knew German well.

7. Palgi is derived from the Hebrew *peleg*, which, like the German *Bach* (as in Nuszbacher), means "brook" or "stream."

8. Y. Bauer, *From Diplomacy to Resistance: A History of Jewish Palestine 1939–1945* (Philadelphia, 1970), 94.

9. Palgi represented the British as acquiescing reluctantly to a longstanding Jewish demand. Actually, though, it appears that British-Jewish disagreements involved the number of Jewish commandos, their deployment, and their relationship to the British army, not the idea of sending them. Eventually, thirty-two parachutists were dispatched. See Y. Gelber, "The Mission of the Jewish Parachutists from Palestine in Europe in World War II," *Studies in Zionism* 7 (1986): 52–58; D. Porat, *Hanhagah beMilkud: HaYishuv nochah haSho'ah 1942–1945* (Tel Aviv, 1986), 407–412.

10. Bauer, *From Diplomacy to Resistance*, 94.

11. R. H. Lawson supervised the project for the British side, and Enzo Sereni for the Jewish Agency. Sereni eventually went into action as a commando and was replaced by Zvi Yehieli. Lawson was an officer in A Force, a British military intelligence unit commanded in the eastern Mediterranean region by Col. Tony Symonds. Symonds, Lawson, Sereni, and Yehieli all are mentioned by Palgi.

12. R. L. Braham, "The Rightists, Horthy, and the Germans: Factors underlying the Destruction of Hungarian Jewry," in B. Vago and G. L. Mosse, eds., *Jews and Non-Jews in Eastern Europe 1918–1945* (New York and Toronto, 1974), 141–142.

13. German and Ustaše forces still controlled, among other areas, the Drava Valley, which Palgi had to cross in order to reach Hungary.

14. According to one report the Hungarian Defense Ministry had agreed to their release on October 14. R. Braham, *The Politics of Genocide: The Holocaust in Hungary* (2nd ed.) (New York, 1993), 2:1167.

15. L. Karsai, "The Last Phase of the Hungarian Holocaust: The Szálasi

Regime and the Jews," in R. L. Braham and S. Miller, eds., *The Nazis' Last Victims: The Holocaust in Hungary* (Detroit, 1998), 103–116.

16. This was the context in which Raoul Wallenberg and other neutral diplomats carried on their rescue activities. For details see A. Handler, *A Man for All Connections: Raoul Wallenberg and the Hungarian State Apparatus, 1944–1945* (Westport and London, 1996), 90–109.
17. Palgi, 1st ed., 228–240.
18. Ibid., 232.
19. Ibid., 231.
20. A. Cohen, "The Dilemma of Rescue or Revolt," in Braham and Miller, *Holocaust's Last Victims*, 124–129.
21. R. Kasztner, *Din veHeshbon shel Va'adat haHatsalah haYehudit be-Budapest 1942–1945* (n.p., n.d.), 74.
22. Palgi, 1st ed., 235–236, 382.
23. Ibid., 232–233.
24. According to Phyllis Palgi, "The overriding consideration not to repeat this chapter in 1977 was editorial. It was not really integrated into the flow of writing in the 1946 edition but was considered necessary as a background for the mission." In her view, Palgi had wanted even in 1946 to awaken empathy for Hungarian Jews who had gone to their deaths, but he realized in 1977 "that his message did not really get across" (written communication from Phyllis Palgi, n.d.). Still, it should be borne in mind that Palgi had had virtually no contact with Hungarian Jews during the period of their deportation and could not testify personally about how their leaders evaluated the Nazi threat. What Hungarian Jewish leaders understood about that threat, what they communicated to the rest of Hungarian Jewry, and why they acted as they did remain matters of intense controversy among survivors and historians today. For an overview see R. L. Braham, "What Did They Know and When?" in Y. Bauer and N. Rotenstreich, eds., *The Holocaust as History* (New York, 1981), 109–131.
25. Y. Bauer, *Jews for Sale: Nazi-Jewish Negotiations, 1933–1945* (New Haven, 1994), 145–195.
26. On the selection process see D. Dinur, *Kasztner: Giluyim hadashim al haIsh uFo'alo* (Haifa, 1987), 37–39.
27. Y. Palgi, "LeVo Yisra'el Kasztner," *Davar*, December 11, 1947, 812. In this article Palgi affirmed the negotiation strategy, contrasting Kasztner with those "moralists who kept their hands clean of contact with the Germans but with their superior morality saved not a single Jew from the Holocaust."
28. Palgi, 1st ed., 158–159, 257–260.
29. Quoted in Weitz, *HaIsh sheNirtsah pe'amayim*, 134.

30. Witness his conclusion: "If you ask me in which direction I lean, whether Kasztner was a traitor or a hero, I think that calling him a traitor is blasphemous. As to whether he was a hero, I don't know what a hero is. If a person endangers his life for the sake of others, to save someone else's life, that is heroism. As far as I am concerned, I think that in those days [endangering one's life for the sake of others] was a Jew's elementary obligation, and I think that Kasztner lived up to it." Quoted in ibid., 135.

31. Sh. Rosenfeld, *Tik pelili 124: Mishpat Grünwald-Kasztner* (Tel Aviv, 1955), 130–131.

32. A second edition, under the same title as the first, appeared in 1948.

33. There is no public apology on record. In a letter to Palgi written in July 1955, an official of the publisher, Menahem Dorman, explained the thinking behind the decision: "I do not say that what you initially submitted for publication constituted 'legal testimony,' but it is a long way from there to a 'novel.'. . . A person who is the only remaining witness to matters in which human life is at stake is obligated to be scrupulously accurate." Quoted in Weitz, *HaIsh shenirtsah pe'amayim*, 139–140. According to Phyllis Palgi, Dorman "was deeply hurt because he thought that Yoel had not trusted him enough to tell him the 'state secret' about the censored version" (written communication from Phyllis Palgi, n.d.). The 1977 "renovated edition" (*mahadurah mehudeshet*) was brought out by a different publisher, the prestigious house Am Oved. In explaining the decision to publish the new version, the editor for Am Oved, Ahuvia Malkin, wrote: "At the time I thought that Hakibbutz Hameuhad Press [the publisher of the 1946 version] had made an unfortunate mistake in dropping the book. . . . Thus, when Yoel proposed that I bring out his book a second time, I gladly accepted his proposal, because I thought that this is the true testimony of a person in possession of the facts, not a fictional story (even though he said what he said under pressure of questioning)" (written communication from Ahuvia Malkin, May 3, 2000).

34. In the event, Kasztner's relations with the parachutists played a secondary role in the verdict, which placed greater stress on the fact that after the war Kasztner testified on behalf of several Nazis with whom he had been connected and even boasted that he had been instrumental in securing the acquittal of at least one senior SS official. Weitz, *HaIsh sheNirtsah pe'amayim*, 68–76, 242–251.

35. Quoted in ibid., 140.

36. An example of the former is A. Cohen, *HaMahteret haHalutsit be-Hungariyah 1942–1945* (Tel Aviv, 1984), esp. 149–155; of the latter, R. L. Braham, *The Politics of Genocide: The Holocaust in Hungary* (New York, 1994), esp. 1166.

37. Cohen, *HaMahteret haHalutsit,* 154, took a tacitly neutral position: "Kasztner raised the astounding idea that Yoel Palgi should report to Eichmann as a representative of . . . the Jewish Agency." He stated that Palgi agreed to Kasztner's suggestion (saying his agreement represented "more than [an act of] courage; it was tantamount to a voluntary human sacrifice for the sake of the passengers on the rescue train"), but he offered no opinion about whether Palgi's agreement had been forced by Kasztner's previous contacts with the Gestapo. Regarding Goldstein's capture, Cohen preferred Kasztner's version of events to Palgi's. On that version see below.

38. Kasztner, *Din veHeshbon,* 112. Regarding the earlier decision leading to Palgi's appearance before the Gestapo, Kasztner's testimony was ambiguous: "[Neither Palgi nor I] had any information about Goldstein's whereabouts, and because we feared that he had [already] been arrested, we approached [SS Captain] Otto Klages, claiming that the two [parachutists] were working for [the Rescue Committee] and asking his intervention." Kasztner, *Din veHeshbon,* 111.

39. A. Weissberg, *Desperate Mission: Joel Brand's Story* (New York, 1958), 245.

40. Hansi Brand had become romantically involved with Kasztner and generally supported his version of events.

41. "Berur beInyan Rezső Kasztner," s.d., HaKibbutz HaMe'uhad Archives, Record Group 15, Box 172, File 2, Document 6. The panel stated that "it may be that the announcement to the authorities . . . came too *soon.* Perhaps this was a *mistake,* but it is not the basis for any charge [of wrongdoing]" (emphasis in the original).

42. Kasztner to E. Dobkin and Dobkin to Kasztner, Jewish Agency for Palestine, December 22, 1945, Central Zionist Archives, S6/1651. Searches in the archives of the World Jewish Congress have not yet turned up evidence of an unwillingness to hire Kasztner because of allegations concerning his behavior regarding the parachutists.

43. Historians would no doubt like to know if any notes were taken by the parachutists' Hungarian and German interrogators and whether such notes survived; if they did, much more of Palgi's memoir could be corroborated. Hungarian archives have yet to yield such information, however.

44. Many hold that the mission of the parachutists in all the countries where Palestinian Jewish commandos operated (Austria, Bulgaria, Czechoslovakia, France, Italy, Romania, and Yugoslavia, in addition to Hungary) should not be counted a failure, even if they did not fulfill their initial goal of organizing mass Jewish escape and resistance. According to one evaluation, the parachutists "took care of thousands of refugees from other countries . . . ; they were involved in preparing

Jewish immigration to Palestine . . . and played a decisive role in organizing it toward the end of the war; they formed a barrier against the
attraction of communism, which appeared in the form of the liberating,
long-awaited Red Army; and they fought shoulder to shoulder with
the Yugoslav and Slovak partisans, becoming key figures among the
Jews who joined those partisan units" (Porat, *Hanhagah beMilkud*,
416). Others stress the psychological importance of the mission: it let
European Jews know that they had not been abandoned by their fellow
Jews abroad, and it provided Palestinian Jews with a sense that they had
made a serious effort to help the threatened Jews of Europe.

Into the Inferno

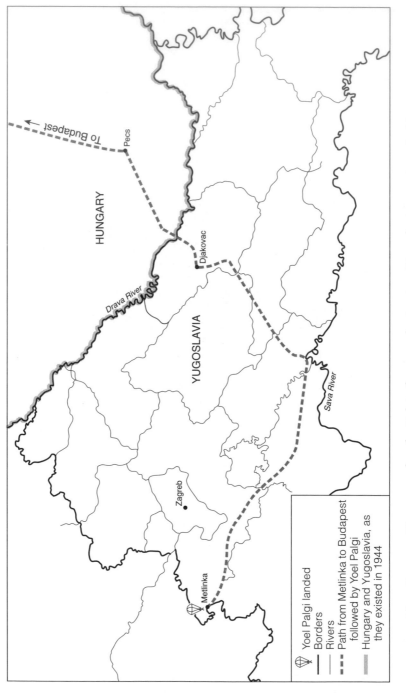

Map: *Route to Hungary taken by Palgi after parachuting into Yugoslavian territory in May 1944.*

Chapter I

Between the Lines

OUR CAR SKIMMED ALONG THE DESERT ROAD under a sky overcast with leaden clouds. The cold seeped into my bones and I was assailed by an unpleasant, on-edge sensation. Things had begun badly. Could it be true that coming events cast their shadows before them? I was ashamed of the superstition, acquired on the battlefield, and tried to fight it. Unsuccessfully.

We approached Tel Aviv in a depressing downpour. Disjointed, disconcerting thoughts nibbled at my mind. Here I was, on my way to the parachutist training school. Tomorrow or the day after I'd be making my first jump. As in a childhood nightmare of falling, I could see the chute failing to open. I knew that I would never be able to disclose to anyone my fears, nor could I give up now. I was no longer my own master. The disappointment and shame would not be mine alone. Feverishly, I repeated to myself, "It won't open, it won't open but I must jump. I will jump no matter what. . . ."

The car made its way through the Tel Aviv streets splattering mud on the pedestrians. Everything was gray, unwelcoming. I countered with my own indifference, as though I were in a foreign city.

I had a half-hour break before going up north to the training school and went to see Zvi.

At Davar House, the rundown premises of the daily paper that gave its name to the building, the pungent smell of printers' ink penetrated my nostrils. People were walking in and out of the editorial offices, the sound of their footsteps swallowed up in the clatter of the presses.

I climbed up a narrow stairway to a little room on the roof. A girl in a RAF uniform was sitting there in the dusk-shadowed light, cross-legged behind a small table. I asked for Zvi. "He'll be back soon," she said. Lighting a cigarette, I looked surreptitiously in her direction. She was tall, fine-featured with blue eyes and wavy dark brown hair. The blue-gray of her uniform enhanced the color of her eyes. There was something winning about her.

Zvi came in. Surprised to see me, he showered me with questions: How did I get here? When would I be moving on?

The girl eyed me curiously, then suddenly sprang to her feet and, with a smile lighting her face, asked, "Are you Yoel?" I looked back. I knew. She was the one! At once all the oppressiveness of that day lifted. "And you are Hannah?" Neither of us waited for the answer. I clasped her hands warmly. Without words, we knew we were united by a deep bond—the alliance of comrades-in-arms, front-line fighters.

She spoke first: "I have a lot to ask you. Will you be staying in Tel Aviv tonight?" I remembered the car waiting for me outside. "No," I blurted. "I'm going to jump."

She must have noticed the tremor in my voice. "I've done it already. It's not so bad. It can even be exciting. I'll never forget Nahalal from the air." She spoke simply, as though parachuting was the most natural thing in the world. I was abashed. If she could jump, so could I. If she had overcome her fear, I would have to overcome mine.

I went off in high spirits, knowing that Hannah Szenes, the gifted young girl about whom I had already heard so much, would be with me on the long journey ahead.

The rain pounded on the roof of the car, drenching the windows. Lawson, back erect and hair meticulously combed to cover his bald spot, was sitting in front of me. An officer in the British Intelligence and a RAF Wing Commander, he was my immediate superior. I felt like talking, but Lawson was British. Though Jewish, he struck me as foreign and remote. I was afraid he would interpret my apprehensions as wavering and drop me from the operation. So I said nothing.

I was very tired. As I leaned back in my seat, the events of the previous days returned to me.

It had started about three weeks earlier, in mid-December 1943, when I got leave. For two and a half years I had been moved from place to place in the Western Desert; it was close to a year since I had last been home. On my way up from the Libyan Desert I stopped in Cairo, where the British had their Middle Eastern Headquarters, to see Yonah Rosen and Peretz Goldstein. Friends from early youth, we had immigrated to Palestine together, and with others from our youth movement, established Kibbutz Maagan, on the Sea of Galilee. Yonah gave me a letter to deliver in person when I got to Tel Aviv. That was the first time I climbed the stairway to the little room on the roof of Davar House. When I reached it, I asked for Zvi Yehieli. A small man of about forty-five said, "That's me." I gave him the letter. "Wait, don't run off," he said, as I turned to leave. "When are you going back to Egypt?"

"In two weeks."

"Drop in and see me before you go. We'll have a talk. By the way, what's your name?" I told him. "You! I've been looking for you for weeks!" Where did he get my name? What did he want? "Are you from Romania?" he asked.

"Yes, that is, from Transylvania."

"Do you speak Hungarian?"

"Yes, it's my mother tongue."

"Are you ready to take on a tough, dangerous job?"

At the word "dangerous" my spine tingled. I had almost given up waiting for the chance. For months I had known that Yonah and Peretz had volunteered from the ranks of the Palmach for missions behind enemy lines. I wanted to join them but I had already enlisted in the British Army, and His Majesty for some reason refused to release me from water transportation and airstrip construction in the Western Desert. I reapplied later for a transfer to the intelligence corps after I heard that two Palestinian Jewish parachutists had been caught on Romanian soil, but was again turned down.

"It isn't feasible to send Palestinian paratroopers at the present time," I was told. My blood boiled. It was now January 1944. Jews were being slaughtered, the Warsaw Ghetto uprising against the

Germans had been crushed, reinforcements had not been sent from Palestine, and no words of encouragement were reaching the few who fought the last battle to save those still alive in the ghetto. And all the British could say was, "It isn't feasible."

As part of the propaganda program, Radio Berlin proclaimed that the German and Italian air forces had razed Haifa and Tel Aviv to the ground. Would the Jews in Europe have the heart to hang on without knowing that the Jewish settlement in Palestine still existed and that thousands of Palestinian Jews were at the front, volunteers under the Jewish flag? I had no doubt that they would resist the Nazis if only they had someone to lead them, if they could see some point to fighting—a chance of rescue or at least revenge.

It was February 1944; the murderous hand of the Nazis had not yet reached the Hungarian Jews. But any day now the radio would announce the German conquest of Hungary. If we didn't get there in time, that Jewish community would be lost too, ignominiously and without a fight, like the ones before them. Among them too, only a few would have died martyrs, fighting a final battle.

Gripped by a sense of urgency, I felt I had to get to them, warn them, arouse them. On sleepless nights I would see a million Jews rising en masse to oppose their would-be murderers, with myself leading them.

"Where's Petah Tikvah?" Lawson suddenly asked.

I shook myself free of tangled thoughts, wiped the window, and looked at the road. "Another kilometer."

"I was there many years ago, at the end of World War I," he mused, "when we took Palestine from the Turks. I was young then, a mere foot soldier. The first man to march into the village. I still remember the family I was billeted with. They had a little girl, Sarah, with a head full of blonde curls. She must be about thirty now."

Englishman though he was, it was good that Lawson, the liaison between British Intelligence and the Palestinian parachutists, was Jewish. We had undertaken a double mission for the British and for ourselves—and there could be a conflict of interest. We needed someone on our side.

The idea of sending Jewish agents behind enemy lines was developed in the Political Section of the Jewish Agency[1] and in the Hagana.[2] The idea was to make contact with the Jews of Europe, to bring encouraging news of a fighting Jewish Palestine, and to establish or lead a resistance movement. It seemed possible because the Jewish community in Palestine had, at the time, a large pool of young men and women born and raised in what had become Hitler's Europe. They knew the languages and customs, were familiar with the geographic and political conditions of occupied Europe, and might be able to make their way behind the lines without attracting attention. But the only way we could implement the scheme was with the cooperation of the British. There was no way that the Hagana by itself could train, equip, and send agents into enemy territory, or stay in touch with them once they got there. We had to persuade the Allies that we could contribute to the war effort in Europe, that we would advance their cause if they allowed us to advance our own.

For years the British vetoed every proposal that the Jewish Agency put before them. Then, in 1943, when the Allies were in great need of loyal saboteurs throughout occupied Europe, the British finally gave in to the pressure, though somewhat half-heartedly, as it turned out.

The operations would serve a dual purpose. We would help rescue Allied airmen who had been taken prisoner and we would rescue Jews. Lawson was responsible at H.Q. for the actual escape operation of all British airmen who had been struck down behind enemy lines.

Naturally we identified with the Allied aims, and would carry out our assignments for them faithfully. But there was always the disturbing question of whether they would show as much understanding for our concerns. So it was good that a Jew, like Lawson, was the intermediary. In those blood-soaked days, no Jew would be able to remain unmoved by the cry of despair rising from Hitler's hell.

✳ ✳ ✳ ✳ ✳

We were airborne. Four of us were on the bench: Abba Berdichev, Dov Berger-Harari, Shaike Dan, and me. We were wearing overalls, parachutes strapped to our torsos, and, on our heads, helmets padded with thick rubber. The man who had worn the helmet before me had written on it: "Don't follow me, I'm crazy!" Dov, a rather ponderous fellow who looked like a peasant but was, in fact, a cultured and refined man, smiled as he read the warning.

The instructor tried to create a relaxed atmosphere, as though jumping out of the sky were a perfectly ordinary act. "Look how beautiful it is!" We looked. The agricultural settlement Nahalal lay spread out below. But there was no time for appreciating its beauty because just then we got the signal to prepare for the jump. We smiled forced smiles. No one wanted to admit to a thudding heart. I felt ill. My hands shook and my teeth were chattering. For a split second I thought, why not say I'm sick and will jump tomorrow?

The red light went on and we crowded around the open door. I tightened my muscles to conceal my trembling and made myself stop thinking. I couldn't take my eyes off the red light. Suddenly, it went out, replaced by a green light. A roared "GO!" hit my ears; my trained hands and feet performed, apparently of their own accord. I jumped! The air hit me and my heart melted completely, I floated in space, empty of feeling and thought. Maybe this is how a dying man feels during his last moments.

The thin cord trailing after me from the plane was the only connection between me and reality. I yanked the chute from its bag and tore it loose. I was hovering between two worlds, liberated, my own master, alone in the void. As I glided in the air, the houses looked like matchboxes, the people like insects. The tremendous weight I had felt, the fear of death, vanished and happiness filled me. Warm blood coursed through my limbs, and I saw things clearly again. The wind turned me around a little and I saw Dov waving from a distance. I shouted with joy. I had jumped!

Training at the parachute school had been hard. Fear preceded each jump. Even guys with a hundred jumps behind them trembled before the one to come. Then training came to an end, and days and nights of intense preparation began. There were secret meetings with British Intelligence agents and with Jews who had managed to escape the inferno and enter Palestine despite the British mandatory prohibitions on Jewish immigration to Palestine. It was meetings with these escapees and "illegal immigrants" that provided whatever up-to-date information we would have before going back to the countries in which we were born. No mention was made of the absurd situation in which the British military was eagerly using the information gathered from the very people in Palestine whom their own government tried to keep out of that country. Although we had left Europe only a few years before, the war had thrown everything into flux; we had a lot to learn about what life was like there now. Also, they gave us names and addresses—trustworthy contacts who could help us in our mission. Zvi Yehieli, in charge of departure on behalf of the Hagana, also made sure to arrange informal talks with the leaders of the Yishuv,[3] Eliahu Golomb, Berl Katznelson, David Ben-Gurion, Golda Meir, and David Remez. We had two burning questions for them: what is our mission, our major task, and what is your final word, your blessing for the road? We met them at their homes and in places such as the secret headquarters of the Hagana in the basement of the General Federation of Trade Union building (the Histadrut). To these questions, we received these answers: "Teach Jews to fight," said Golomb. "Make Jews understand that Palestine, the Land of Israel, is their country and their haven," said Ben-Gurion. Golda Meir, the strong woman, wept. She knew that not all of us would come back. "Save Jews," said Katznelson, "the rest—later. If no Jews survive, the Land of Israel and the Zionist enterprise will perish too." These meetings gave us a vital sense of direction and purpose, but they also made us uneasy. We were dogged by the feeling that no one involved in the operation fully grasped the danger to each and every one of us if our identities or intentions ever reached enemy ears. We feared that our people were not being careful enough. One of us, I don't remember who, happened to come across some figurines of three mythical monkeys in a Dizengoff Street gift shop. We bought a dozen, and at each meeting left one of them on the table as a warning: hear nothing! see nothing! say nothing! On the remaining statuettes, we carved our names as a memento.

Writing these lines now, I look at those three monkeys, still in my possession, and at my friends' signatures. Of the five who signed, only two are alive.

As our departure date neared, we took advantage of every spare moment to imbibe the atmosphere of Palestine. We went to the theater, visited new settlements, spoke with friends. We wanted to hear, to see, to fuel ourselves for the long journey ahead. We also wanted to fix in our minds a clear, vivid image of Palestine to bring to the Jews of Europe.

We tried not to think of what lay ahead, but weren't always successful. Hannah confided to me that she was worried about her mother. Her brother Gyuri was due to come to Palestine, and her mother would be left on her own in Budapest.

In fact, a day before we were to leave for Cairo British H.Q., we were informed that he had arrived aboard the *S.S. Nyasa*. Hannah was excited, as tearful as a little girl, so unlike the sturdy young woman we knew. We left for the port of Haifa at once, only to find out when we got there that her brother was among those imprisoned at Atlit, where the British interned the "illegal" immigrants. Luckily we managed to get him released and put off our departure by twenty-four hours so Hannah could spend some time with him. She apologized for holding us back: "Who knows when I'll see him again."

February 4, 1944. Departure day. We were ready, but not one of us dared admit how hard it was to part. There was no way of knowing if we would ever see the country again, or our friends and families. We said our good-byes without embraces, without explanations. It was imperative to avoid questions.

The car sped south, crossing Judea, past the white houses of the Jewish settlements that became sparser, past the Arab villages that became denser. As we cleared the desert road to Egypt, we began to feel the gravity of the hour. We traveled the rest of the journey in a mood of forced hilarity.

Chapter 2

On the Threshold

DAYS AND NIGHTS OF STORMY DEBATE awaited us in Cairo. The question of the hour was how to get into the target countries. Should we all jump into partisan-held territory in Yugoslavia and make our way from there, in separate teams, to our destinations? Or should each team parachute directly into the country "allotted" to it, a "blind jump," it was called, when there would be no contacts to meet us when we landed nor any flares nor ground markers to show the pilots where to drop us? I favored the blind jump. It was true that in so doing we would go straight into enemy held territory, but if we weren't caught during the jump, our chances of making it to the target city were good. Though the actual jump into partisan territory was safe, and friends would be waiting for us, most of Yugoslavia was in enemy hands and Tito's partisans were only in control in the mountains. We would have to steal over the border and cross hundreds of kilometers to Budapest. We didn't know what the conditions were in Hungary, nor did we know whether the documents we carried would still be valid when we finally got there.

Before we could agree among ourselves, the British vetoed the blind jump on the astonishing grounds that the pilots could not be relied upon to drop us on target. To bring their point home, they reported that on the eve of the Jewish New Year, they dropped two Palestinian parachutists over Romania into a city some sixty kilometers off target. Both were captured.

Billeted together in an apartment in the center of Cairo, we continued to argue the point. I vehemently held my ground, urging that we parachute into the Tihany Peninsula near the lake at Balaton, not far from Budapest. It had the double advantage of being easy to identify, even at night, when the water glittered, and of being a resort area that attracted soldiers from all the Axis nations. If we jumped wearing uniforms and army raincoats, there was a chance we wouldn't draw any attention.

I made another point: the drop into Yugoslavia depended on coordination with the British military detachment there, and they were in no hurry to let us know whether the road was clear or when we could leave for Hungary. There was reason to fear that we might be forced to stay in Yugoslavia for a while.

At the height of the debate, reinforcements arrived for our group in Cairo. One of them, Enzo Sereni, added his voice to the blind jump plan, declaring with characteristic decisiveness: "It's the shortest route and thus the right one. Even if it's dangerous, with imagination and daring, we can take the enemy by surprise."

None of us knew at the time that Enzo, considerably older than the rest of us in our twenties, was also going. Apparently, he had felt free to choose the most dangerous plan because he had already committed himself.

In the end, the British agreed to a compromise: One team would leave for Yugoslavia, the rest would stay in Cairo for the meanwhile. If our doubts regarding Yugoslavia turned out to be correct, then two men would parachute into Hungary and (assuming they weren't caught) would help the ones in Yugoslavia to join up with them.

But our departure was put off, day after day, week after week. "No planes," the British said. Our total dependence on them was very frustrating. Precious time was slipping through our fingers and tension was rising in the group. Finally, at the beginning of March, we were informed that we would be on our way in a few days.

At the last minute, Yonah, Peretz, and Reuven Dafni, a Yugoslav by birth, joined us. Yonah and Peretz had been waiting for two and a half years since they had first volunteered for missions in occupied territory, and could hardly contain their elation that they at last would have the chance to jump, even with novices like us. All that was left was the final decision about who would go where, and with whom.

Originally Yonah was supposed to make the blind jump into Hungary with me. I was glad, because Yonah was practical and down to earth, and could think his way through complicated situations with a minimum of fuss. He had his own unique sense of what could be done to make the lot of his comrades easier. Peretz, the youngest of our group, a captivating personality with a friendly smile and refined manner, questioned the decision. He argued that the route was too dangerous for Yonah, who was married and the father of a little girl, and that he himself ought to be my partner.

When the assignments were finalized, Peretz prevailed. He and I would make the blind jump into Hungary; Shaike Dan and Dov Berger-Harari would parachute into Romania.

Hannah wanted to join Peretz and me, but our cover story in case we were caught, that we were airmen jumping from a damaged plane, couldn't include a woman. So, after some protest, she had to give in, and joined the group that was to parachute into Yugoslavia.

From Yugoslavia, Hannah and Yonah were to make their way to Hungary. Abba Berdichev would head for Romania. Reuven Dafni was to stay in Yugoslavia, along with Major John Eden, nephew of the British foreign minister. Dafni's task: to set up a base for other agents from Palestine and, more important, to take care of the refugees that we hoped to smuggle out of Hungary, making sure that they reached safety. Enzo Sereni was to fly to Italy, where he would remain.

Enzo and the Yugoslav group left first. With the five of them gone, only Shaike, Dov, Peretz, and I were left in what suddenly seemed like an empty apartment. It was a difficult time. We were extremely worried about the Yugoslav group, and anxious not much less about our own departure; it would take another two weeks before we would know whether we would be following them or making a blind jump into Hungary. Bored and irritable, we spent hours glued to the radio, listening to Budapest and Bucharest.

On March 19, 1944, we detected an odd note in the Budapest broadcast. Nothing was said explicitly, but we understood that the Nazi invasion of Hungary had begun. What we had so feared had come to pass. We were too late. Tomorrow or the day after,

anti-Jewish decrees would be announced; Jews would be confined
to ghettos; the expulsions and extermination would start. Our
hopes of organizing escape and self-defense before the Nazi invasion were dashed. Now we would have to operate under Nazi rule.
The only bright spot was that two or three days of chaos could be
expected before the conquest was completed, giving us a one-time
chance for a blind jump. I phoned the commander of Force A in
British Intelligence to whom we had been assigned. "You have to get
them to let us go now!" I insisted. "I'll shake up Zvi Yehieli," he answered. "I don't want to decide anything without him."

We waited. We hung around for hours, smoking cigarette after
cigarette; nightmare scenes passed through our minds. It was late,
but something could still be done. Everything depended on those
few hours. But Zvi didn't come. It took him four days to reach
Cairo. He had been held up by a curfew the British clamped on Tel
Aviv following a series of anti-British activities by the two dissident
Jewish underground movements, Lehi[4] and the Irgun.[5] By the time
Zvi reached Cairo, the Nazi takeover of Hungary was complete.
Yugoslavia was our only option. Shaike and Dov would stay behind
in Egypt until conditions were right for them to leave for Romania.

It was hard, that parting. The sustaining sense that we were out
to do great things had faded; the possibilities had diminished, the
dangers had mounted. The invasion of Hungary was a turning
point. Still, we all kept up a front. Shaike, Dov, and Zvi didn't want
to discourage us, and we didn't want to depress them. We knew how
difficult it was to stay behind, to stare somberly at people who were
going, perhaps never to return. At the air field, I felt especially sorry
for Zvi. Despite the night chill, beads of perspiration covered his
face. He clasped our hands in a strong, firm grip, but I couldn't help
feeling that we should be bolstering his spirits, not the other way
around.

Peretz and I took off at dawn. Our first stop was Bari, in the
south of Italy, by that time in British hands. Flying low, our plane
touched down on the loose ground of an airfield, slowed and
wobbled in the direction of a huge barn. Our traveling companions,
a British brigadier and major, casually took out their pipes and filled
them while watching us, clearly wondering what our business was.
Peretz and I folded our blankets, took off our overalls, collected our
gear, shouldered our submachine guns, and got ready to leave the

plane. Two men were waiting for us next to it. One, a tall British officer, greeted us with a wave of the hand. The other, in civilian clothes, kissed us with Mediterranean effusiveness. It was Enzo. Short and bespectacled, he ran in and out among the baggage, giving orders in Italian to the porters, explaining something in English to the British officer, speaking Hebrew to us. We understood little of his flow of words, but were delighted to see Enzo, dashing about, full of energy and enthusiasm.

At last all the packages were loaded into a car and we were on our way to Bari. As we drove along bomb-pitted roads I wanted to hear the news. What were we going to do? When would we be continuing on our way to Yugoslavia? Enzo neither answered nor listened. He was busy pointing to the passersby, children, young girls—"Look, Italians!" He couldn't calm himself. Italy was the country where he was born, where he had grown up, the country he loved and hated—hating its regime, loving its people. From the moment we arrived, he gave us no rest. No sooner had we shaken off the dust of travel than he dragged us through the streets, to churches, to the beach, down winding alleys, saying each time we passed a girl, "See! Marvelous! A nobleman's daughter!"

I enjoyed teasing Enzo. "Your aristocratic girls go about the city barefoot, selling themselves for a can of preserves," I needled him. His mood changed, becoming serious. "This nation has been destroyed by the fascists," he said. "But it will revive yet. The Italians are an ancient, cultured people, almost like us." As he spoke, he took the cigarettes out of my pocket and doled them out to people in the street. Then he made us buy candy and give it to the children.

"You have to have heart," he instructed. "Without heart you won't get anywhere. If you don't feel the next man's suffering, you won't feel the suffering of your own people."

Enzo was like mercury, enthusing, explaining, arguing, without letup. He rarely carried identification papers, and walked into command posts, airports, and military camps with such self-assurance that nobody stopped him. If a guard dared ask what he was doing there, he would fix the poor man with such a penetrating stare that he became confused and apologetic. The British brass grumbled that Enzo in civilian clothes went about undisturbed while they, officers in uniform, were made to produce their papers. It was something of a game for Enzo, but there was a lesson in

Palgi on the eve of mission departure, 1944.

it for us. "Self-confidence is what counts, not documents," Enzo explained. I followed his every move and listened to his every word, feeling lucky and privileged to have met this extraordinary man.

Finally I managed to draw his attention away from his beloved Italy to give him the orders I had been instructed by Cairo to relay to him: "You must return to Palestine immediately."

"Out of the question!" he snapped.

"You must. H.Q. suspects that you intend to get to the North." Northern Italy was under Nazi control.

"What of it? Isn't it our duty to rescue the few surviving Jews there?"

I tried to tell him that there were no more Jews in the north and that anyway he wasn't authorized to act on his own. "H.Q. doesn't know what's going on," he asserted. He maintained he had reliable information—there were Jews in the north and he had to go there.

"What about authority, Enzo, discipline?"

"Discipline? I listen to my own discipline!" He put his hand on his heart.

Enzo was not a man to send others on missions that he wouldn't go on himself; nor would he let anyone else tell him what to do. At forty he was already a legend, a man who balked at nothing. Now he knew we were setting out on a long, dangerous road and he wouldn't rest unless he could go too. I let him know what I was thinking.

"Nonsense!" he said. But I knew I had hit home.

"Look, I have a letter from my little boy," he said suddenly. "He writes: 'Daddy, even if you die, the main thing is to be brave!' But I won't die," he said, "I'm going to live."

That evening we were told we would be on our way the next day at nightfall. It was the first night of Passover, the Seder meal. Enzo dashed about, then presented us with a parcel.

"This package has everything you need for the Seder. A Passover meal in the plane, over enemy territory, just before you jump! That's going to be one of the stories in the book I'll write about this operation."

"Maybe it should be my book," I said. "After all, it'll be our Seder."

"No, I want to write it."

I hugged him and laughed. "OK, Enzo. I give in. I'll have bigger things than that to write about."

The discussion turned out to be superfluous. Our departure was delayed on account of weather conditions. Peretz and I joined Enzo in celebrating the first night of Passover with a Palestine Jewish transport unit stationed near Bari.

The next day we were grouped together to be driven to the airport. We were an odd bunch. In addition to Peretz and myself, there were two others. One was a Scottish officer—thin, bespectacled, gray-faced with expressionless eyes, carrying a revolver on his belt and a dagger on his thigh. He introduced himself as Captain Mac-Coy. I assumed that the "Mac" was bona fide, the rest fiction. We too were using borrowed identities. The other passenger was a gaunt, undersized young man, with black eyes and dark hair. If he hadn't been in uniform, I would have taken him for a boy. His name, Grandeville, which was French or English, also struck me as assumed. It didn't suit him at all. Despite an impeccable English accent, he didn't seem British born. I had the feeling that he would become a friend.

The four of us were bound by a single purpose. Despite the seriousness of the occasion, Peretz and I couldn't suppress our joy in the revolvers on our belts, the shining officers' insignia on our shoulders, and the submachine guns in our hands. We knew there was a struggle ahead and peril, but we were filled with hope. I could sense my muscles tightening and my pulse accelerating in anticipation. The delays were over. It was time to act. Enzo was standing next to the car. He asked us with a smile, "Aren't you angry that I'm not coming? Some of our soldiers at one of the camps are having a second Passover celebration, and I want to go."

I gave him my hand. He held it and with his free hand pulled my head down to kiss me on the cheek.

"Don't disgrace me! See you back at home!" he called as the car moved off in the direction of the airfield.

We sped along the southern coastal highway. Villages, towns, orchards, and fields flew by. The landscape reminded me of home. My eyes wandered between the fields to my right and the quiet blue sea to my left. Beyond lay Europe, conquered, mysterious, and dark. I was about to plunge into that darkness and would have to find my way through it. I had absolute faith in the justice of our cause and knew it was imperative that I go. I gripped my submachine gun. From now on it would have to be my good companion, my defender.

Mac, breaking the ice, politely offered cigarettes. A conversation started up. Passing quickly over the preliminaries—the fine weather and if we would be flying the same day—we began talking about what lay ahead.

"I know those bastards, the partisans!" Mac said. "They're good chaps, but you have to keep an eye on them. They overestimate themselves—as if they're the only ones fighting the Germans. This is the third time I'm going into Yugoslavia. I was there in two big attacks in the south and escaped to Italy."

"Why are you going back? Aren't two operations enough?"

"They're bastards, but I like them. It's better out there than doing staff work at home. I'd rather be in the forests, blowing up bridges, doing something."

Mac didn't look very bright. He had started to study engineering, he told us, but never finished and went to work as a draftsman instead. When the war broke out, he joined the army and did well. His plans were to return to Scotland when the fighting was over, complete his studies with money he saved from his army pay, marry, and raise a family. His work in special operations would give him something to tell his children and grandchildren, he said.

Young Grandeville didn't say much, only now and then interjecting some remark that made us laugh. He was derisive and biting, but never crude. The Scot didn't always get his jokes. I whispered to Peretz: "I bet that boy is one of ours."

We reached the airfield and immediately went to the storeroom to check our equipment. Fifteen large metal containers had been prepared for us; they stood side by side like soldiers on parade. They had enough food in them for months, tens of thousands of cigarettes, weapons, ammunition, clothes, and gifts. Each container was attached to a parachute and would be dropped for the partisans and for us.

"For God's sake," I exclaimed, "how will we carry all this? There must be nearly four tons here!"

"By truck," the British quartermaster assured me.

"Truck? Do the partisans have trucks?"

"What do you think?"

"Trucks!?" queried MacCoy. "I heard the partisans are doing well, but I didn't know they'd come this far!"

Then we went to another storeroom to collect our parachutes. Each chute had a numbered tag with the date and the name of the person who had folded it. Should a chute fail to open, the folder would be held responsible. It was not particularly gratifying to know that the negligent party would be properly punished in the event of a mishap.

The quartermaster suggested that we each choose a parachute according to the shade we like best or by our lucky numbers. When he discovered we were from Palestine, he said: "I've equipped hundreds of parachutists for the road, but I've only come across one woman parachutist. She was from Palestine and the first person I ever saw setting out to jump behind enemy lines really unafraid."

The gear was loaded onto a waiting Halifax bomber. After a last-minute check, the plane was ready for takeoff, ready to infiltrate Hitler's European stronghold. I was proud that this powerful plane and its crew were making a special flight for us, and as I stood under its wide wings I felt that even though I would now be on my own, its power would back me up.

When everything was ready, we received written instructions:

Supper at 19:30 at headquarters.
Free till 21:30.
Report to office at 21:45, leave for airfield.
Take-off in Halifax or 917 at 22:00.
Signed: The Commander.

At supper, one of the British officers said that Italian parachutists had taken off on a mission to northern Italy five times, and each time had refused to jump. "They aren't too eager to risk their lives," he said. "They volunteer only for the money and good food they get in training."

I felt the blood rush to my face. Is that what they thought of us? That we were also in it for what we could get out of it for ourselves?

"We don't accept any salary," I spluttered out, "even though we're entitled to officers' army pay." The officers fell silent. They probably didn't believe us. One of them wanted to know why. I explained that our goal was to save Jews from extermination and taking money was out of place in that endeavor.

They weren't convinced but began talking about Palestine and the Jewish question. To a man, they believed that Palestine was being developed through the exploitation of Arab laborers. They knew nothing or chose not to know about Kibbutzim, Jewish agricultural pioneering work, and the reclamation of wasteland. One young officer seemed to express the consensus: "Maybe you're exceptions—but I know Jews in England, and if you want to tell us that they're going to go out to Palestine and make the wilderness grow with their own hands, I'll laugh in your face. They'll go only if they're chased out, and they'll exploit the poor Arab there the way they exploit the British worker."

It was hard for me to find the right words in a foreign language. Angry and depressed, I went outside with Peretz. It was getting dark. A myriad of stars glimmered overhead. Suddenly the roar of engines split the air and a heavy bomber passed very low, followed by another, and another. We lifted ourselves onto a fence, our eyes following the two small lights on the wingtips until they merged with the stars and disappeared over the horizon. In a little while we would also be airborne and the lights of our plane would disappear like that, among the stars.

I felt a touch on my shoulder. It was the youngster with the black eyes, Sergeant Grandeville. "I wanted to tell you," he said, "that I'm a Jew."

"I thought so. I sensed it."

He told me a little about himself. He had escaped from Austria as a boy and worked on a farm in England. He was hoping to obtain British citizenship. He wasn't deluding himself. There were plenty of anti-Semites in England but it was the most civilized nation on earth. He would be happy to be part of it. With Judaism he had no connection but our stories about the extermination camps shocked him and made him feel sudden identification with the Jewish people.

"We'll try to be friends," I said, "but you should know, we're here on a dual mission. First to rescue our own people, and second, to hasten the end of the war. And since you are a Jew, I'm entrusting you with the first mission too."

"I'll help as much as I can," he answered in a whisper.

At departure time he came to the airfield. The heavy bombers were still taking off.

"There's going to be a raid somewhere; over a hundred planes have taken off," I observed.

"No, they don't go on raids from here," I was told. "They're going to Poland: a hundred and twenty planes carrying paratroopers and propaganda material."[6]

"Poland?" I was astonished. So they were going to Poland. Where had the planes come from? All those months the ghetto fighters didn't warrant even one plane. The Jewish community of Palestine hadn't been allowed to send even one person with a message of hope to the Jewish resistance that had been so brutally crushed. Of the hundreds of parachutists who would be dropped tonight, not one would be a Palestinian Jew. In the forests of Europe the Jewish partisans would continue to wait—if they were still there, that is.

Silently, we buckled our chutes. I waved aside the bottle of cognac that was offered to me. Some of the parachutists drank to calm their nerves. I wanted to be fully alert.

We told the pilot to take the plane up a thousand feet—the optimal height under the circumstances. It would give us enough time to take a good look at the ground and fix on a hiding place in case of trouble, without unnecessarily drawing out the time in the air over Yugoslavia where we could be spotted by the enemy.

We climbed into the plane.

Chapter 3

In the Yugoslavian Forests

✳ ONE BY ONE, THE GREAT ENGINES came alive, and before we had time to seat ourselves, we felt the aircraft move over the runway, pause briefly, and suddenly fling itself into the takeoff.

Everyone settled himself in his corner. We wore heavy overalls with numerous zippered pockets full of miscellaneous items: weapons, ammunition, a signaling light, first-aid kit, plenty of money, papers, and much else. We had peculiar hats on our heads, and on our backs were our parachutes in their big, heavy bags. It was difficult to sit like that for any length of time, anticipating the moment of the jump; nevertheless, I dozed off. They woke me with sandwiches and steaming black coffee.

"We're approaching the target," said the jumpmaster, an Australian officer. "Prepare to jump!"

I drew back the black curtain. The moon had just risen. Below—an abyss, a black, formless sea. Were we over a friendly or an enemy zone? We had no idea. It was hard to establish, the commanding officers had explained, because the partisans were here one day and there the next. Areas held by the partisans bordered on

German-held territory and mistakes were possible. The crew members were busy: they were arranging the bundles and containers in lines, attaching the parachutes to special railings, removing the round covering from the jump hatch. The red light over the opening was on: the signal that we were to sit at the opening, legs dangling in the air and hands gripping the edge, both to prevent an accidental fall and to give a strong shove at the right moment. The Australian attached our belts to the railing, but a lively sense of self-preservation made everyone check for himself.

Everyone sat in tense expectation. The Australian went from man to man, giving the thumbs-up sign for encouragement. We fixed our eyes on the red light.

Suddenly the light changed: the red went off and the green came on. The Australian roared with all his strength: "Go!" and Mac and Grandeville vanished into the yawning darkness below. Again the red light—it was our turn. Not half a second had passed when the green flashed on and the Australian's roar was in my ears, together with the increased rumble of the engines. I felt as if I was dropping endlessly into the void. It flashed through my mind: It's all over. The chute hasn't opened. But just then I felt a slight swaying. I shot a glance upward and saw that the chute had graciously opened and was swiftly filling out and that, through the ring at its center, a lone star in the sky of occupied Yugoslavia was greeting me.

A land of mountains and valleys stretched below me. The mountains were silvery in the moonlight, the valleys black. The cold wind pulled me above a spacious country as I sank. After the pre-jump tension, it was a wonderful sensation to sink freely beneath the big white canopy. At once I reminded myself that I was in serious danger: the wind was carrying me away, who knew where. The pilot had apparently been wary of flying low over the mountains. His promise to drop us from a thousand feet was meaningless. We had been at least five thousand feet up at the time of the jump.

I turned my head to right and left, trying to spot Peretz, but saw nothing. Maybe he hadn't jumped. Maybe the wind had carried him far from here? He was lighter than I.

The descent seemed to last forever. Seconds seemed like hours. My sense of well-being had passed and I was no longer enjoying the magnificent view. The approaching ground had a hostile look: mountains, rifts, rocks. Suddenly I noticed that I was about to land in a deep, narrow ditch. I would break my legs if I fell into it. I was apprehensive and tugged at the cords of my chute to get away from the ditch, but I could feel that I wasn't succeeding. My helplessness made me desperate. I thought: I have a revolver. If the Germans come I'll fight, keeping the last bullet for myself. Suddenly . . . solid ground! The ditch was far away.

Vigorously I unstrapped the chute. I folded it quickly so that the white silk wouldn't provide a marker for the enemy. I found a hiding place in a bush, hid the chute, and climbed a hill to survey the terrain. The plane circled overhead, veered to the left, and disappeared over the horizon.

A sense of loneliness engulfed me. I was on my own in an unknown country. The last link with the world I had come from had snapped and I didn't yet know the world I was now poised to enter. I was bewildered, straining my ears and eyes in the darkness, searching for a signal from my comrades. I saw nothing.

I knew it was unwise to signal; I was too exposed. But it was hard to be alone. I took the flashlight from my pocket and, despite the danger, began to flash signals in all directions, receiving no answer. I went back and took cover in my hiding place and surveyed the surroundings to see if anyone had been alerted by the light. Indeed—I saw an approaching figure. I lay still and drew my revolver. I let the figure come close. It was a man, who halted and looked around. I noticed that he was wearing a uniform and had a rifle slung on his shoulder. After a moment's silence, when he had turned to go—apparently he hadn't detected me—I called out to him: "Halt! Throw down your rifle!"

I shouted in Hebrew. I didn't know any Slavic languages, and had I called out in German, the man—if he was a partisan—would most likely have shot me.

He dropped his gun and raised his hands. I left my hiding place and cautiously approached him; then I pushed the barrel against his ribs. I saw a red star on his hat.

He began speaking in a torrent of words I didn't understand. I uttered the single Slavic phrase I knew: "*Ni ponyamayis!*" (I don't understand).

The partisan fell on my neck and, kissing me effusively, shouted: "*Tovarish Russki! Tovarish Russki!*" (Russian comrade).

This time I understood. They were happy to receive the Russians here. We would see if he would also be happy to hear I was English. I said: "*Ni Russki—Anglizi!*" He was not pleased. Politely, he took the chute from me and by gestures and incomprehensible words indicated that he would lead me to the camp.

We climbed a steep slope among rocks and bushes from which the snow hadn't yet melted. I walked behind the partisan. It was worth keeping an eye on him, I thought, who knows? When we reached the top, I saw a campfire near a log hut that was well covered with branches. A group of people were sitting on stumps of wood around the campfire. They made a strange gathering: one, who had three silver stars on his sleeve, was splendidly dressed in a pale gray uniform with shiny buttons and bands of soft, dark brown cloth at the collar and cuffs—this was the Gestapo uniform; another wore rags, the remains of some folk costume; yet another wore the uniform of a German soldier; a few were in Italian, Yugoslavian, and other uniforms. Two signs indicated that they belonged to the same organization. The first was their identical headgear—a small hat somewhat similar to the American army hat, with a five-pointed star placed on the forehead, between the eyes. The second common feature was the way they sat—cross-legged, with the rifle between their legs and leaning against the right shoulder. Even the one who was sleeping with loud snores hung onto his rifle as if his life's hope was invested in it.

Suddenly I heard Mac's voice and saw him standing next to the fire, rubbing his hands. "It's chilly here!" he addressed me, as though we had just risen from the dinner table and stepped out for a breath of air.

"What about the others?" I asked.

"They'll be OK!" he said.

The partisans surveyed me from head to toe. I was aware of their thorough examination. I jumped to attention and saluted crisply, as I had been taught. They all rose to their feet and returned the salute with their own: a clenched fist raised to the temple. They chorused, "*Smrt fascizmu!*" (Death to the fascists). Mac, who knew local manners, answered: "*Sloboda narodnu!*" (Freedom for the people). He immediately explained that these two words were as good as a passport signed by Marshal Tito himself.

At the end of the ceremony I felt I was among close friends. I unzipped the flight overalls and all my hidden stores tumbled to the ground. At once I opened a pack of cigarettes and offered them around. The nearest partisan first reached over and examined my revolver before taking the cigarettes, which then made the rounds, together with my revolver.

"Weapons come first with them, I see!" I commented to Mac.

"It's what we fight with," retorted a lad with three stars.

We looked at him in surprise and asked simultaneously: "You know English?"

"Yes," he told us, "when I was a boy my father went to America to seek his fortune. He made a bit of money, bought a plot of land when he came back here, and became a farmer. I spent ten years of my childhood there, overseas, and I still remember some English."

We asked him to send some men to look for Peretz and Grandeville, who hadn't turned up yet. He calmed us down and said that a chain of soldiers had been organized in the forest as soon as the plane was sighted. A few weeks before, he said, there had been a girl with a group of parachutists. She was light and the wind had carried her a long way off, almost to German lines, about seven kilometers from here, so this time they had taken special precautions.

He had barely finished his story when Grandeville appeared, followed by Peretz. Despite the early morning chill, both were perspiring profusely and breathing heavily. Excited, they told us what had happened to them: they had fallen into a forest and been left dangling in the trees. Peretz was only about a meter above the ground, but he had trouble freeing himself from his chute. Finally he succeeded in cutting through the cords and dropped safely onto Yugoslavian soil, soon both of them were free.

The partisans went in search of the containers scattered over the area. We asked the commander when a car would come to fetch us and our equipment. He looked at us in amazement. He seemed on the point of making a sharp retort, but he controlled himself and replied: "There'll be some carts coming in a while. You can go down to the town and I'll take care of the packages—I'll send them after you."

Mac swore softly. "The sons of bitches will steal everything! But we had better not argue. They're good chaps, but they've got itchy fingers and they keep them on the trigger."

Suddenly, as though to confirm his words, shots cut the air. The sound came from the forest, not far away. We jumped and loaded our rifles. "Germans?" asked Mac in a whisper.

"No," the commander replied calmly. "Peasants. When a plane passes overhead, the villagers come and try to steal some of the goods and our sentries shoot at them. The Germans will come later, but by then they won't find us here." We collected our belongings and turned to leave.

We walked heavily, overloaded and tired. A partisan carrying only a rifle walked ahead of us. Now and then he stopped and looked back, as though asking: Can't you hurry up?! We climbed mountains and walked along ridges. There were still occasional traces of snow and ice. I crouched a few times as we walked, taking handfuls of snow to enjoy the way it melted in my hands, despite the cold. I hadn't seen snow for such a long time.

The first rays of light slowly appeared. A gray light lay on the heights and a mist like milk rolled down to the valleys. The landscape assumed a tangible form. Deep valleys gaped beneath our feet, jungles became visible, here and there small squares of ploughed land could be seen, with white, thatch-roofed houses among them, emitting thin threads of smoke from their chimneys.

We soon saw a vast country before us. Mountains, whose peaks were decked with white ruffs of cloud, reminded me of history book illustrations of the kings of England. Paths carpeted with grass, indicating that people rarely set foot on them, twisted down into the deep gorges. It was wild, mighty country and we were like grasshoppers in it. As the sun rose, its beams pierced the morning mists and the valley came to life in all its many colors.

"Zumberak!" The partisan pointed with a gesture that seemed to embrace the world. I unfolded a map to discover where we were. Zumberak—I found it. This was the general name for the whole mountain district here. "Metlinka!" The partisan pointed again, this time to a village below us. It was marked as a town on the map. Apparently our concepts of town and village differed.

We came to the "town." A group of partisans were standing in front of a two-story building that apparently served as both headquarters and barracks. Their uniforms were from every army in Europe. There was a woman among them. I had seen our own girls with guns in their hands, but still it was strange to see this blonde girl, a child, really, in the partisan ranks. Her face showed that she wasn't a village girl. Her hair, tumbling from under the partisan hat, stirred in the light morning breeze. She held a submachine gun in her slender hand. Her body was engulfed by what had once been an

SS uniform; attached to her belt, which was decorated with a German eagle and Hitler's motto *"Gott mit uns"* (God is with us), was a cluster of hand grenades, embellishing her outlandish costume. The officer in charge of the parade ordered "Attention!" and saluted. Saluting and marching in step, we passed along the line as though we had been sent to review a parade of Marshal Tito's forces.

We were received at headquarters by a partisan major who spoke perfect German. He took us to the village tavern. The sound of a marvelous chorus of passionate but tender singing came from inside. It broke off when we entered and there was perfect silence. The gathering rose, shouldered arms, and saluted. At a sign from the major, they sat down but didn't carry on singing. We urged them to continue; at first there was no response, but soon their attention wandered from us and in no time they were singing again and drinking the light mountain wine. This wine slips down the throat like water, and only on standing up did one realize its potency, with the sensation that lead had been poured into one's bones. The head remained clear, but the legs adopted evil ways, ignoring commands. We opened our breakfast with a brandy, in order to begin the day well. We ate cornmeal porridge steeped in pork fat and washed it down with more wine to quench our thirst.

Some of those at the table left to stand guard and others, whom they had relieved, came in, but the singing and drinking never stopped for a moment. We asked them to translate some of the songs. They were about hatred of the Germans, love of the homeland, and the revered name of Comrade Tito, which recurred in every refrain. We were each presented with a fine gift: an autographed picture of the marshal. Mac advised us to guard the picture closely; it was an important document in these parts and could be a lifesaver on occasion. There was only one song they refused to translate. I listened carefully and understood that it was about King Peter of Yugoslavia, who had fled to London. When the chorus came round, everyone burst out laughing—apparently the song wasn't in praise of the king. He had recently performed the daring feat of marriage, and the song expressed their contempt and anger at the king who could find time to enjoy the charms of his Greek princess while the nation was fighting a bloody war in the mountains and forests.

After the meal, lodgings were arranged for us. Peretz and I mounted creaking wooden steps in the house of a storekeeper who had an interest in cows—the staircase was adorned with pictures of prize-winning Dutch cows. On the first floor there was a closed shop. No merchant and no goods. There were made beds in the room, hot water in a pitcher, and towels laid on the backs of chairs.

Having washed, we wanted to meet our host. We went into an adjoining room and there found a girl of about eighteen, blushing and embarrassed. We chuckled, realizing that she must have been peeping through the keyhole to catch a glimpse of the honored guests. We saluted with the cry of "Death to fascism!" and set about trying to find a common language. It turned out that she spoke fairly good German. We introduced ourselves by our English names, which concealed our birth defect: Jewishness. She opened her eyes as wide as they could go. To her, we were like creatures of another world, like gods from on high. She stammered her name: Marta. Excusing herself, she went into another room and immediately emerged with her parents. More handshakes, salutes, and all the rest. When the owner of the house said his name, I was astonished. I asked him to repeat it. "Fuchs," said he. I had not made a mistake. Fate had brought us to a Jewish house. I restrained my emotions with difficulty. Peretz was unaware of what was happening. He was deep in Marta's blue eyes and golden curls. When we were outside, in the street, I told him our hosts were Jews. That was when we first tasted the strangeness of being anonymous emissaries of the Jewish people, pretending to be gentiles, as if denying our own kind. We decided that without revealing our identities, we would tell them about Palestine, as though we had been there as tourists and had found the country most attractive.

At partisan headquarters in Metlika they informed us that Major John Eden would be arriving that night and that we would be on our way the next day. John was a member of a prestigious family. His uncle was foreign minister in the British War Cabinet. We had long since decided that when we arrived in Yugoslavia we would try to cultivate the friendship of this relative of a politician who, to a considerable extent, held the fate of the Jewish people and the Jewish homeland in his hands.

In the meantime, the oxcart had arrived, laden with our containers: not a thing was lost or stolen. We filled our pockets with good things: chocolate, cigarettes, soap—all so hard to come by in Yugoslavia—and returned to our lodgings. Marta, wearing an embroidered dress that was certainly her best, was blushing again. Our hosts at first politely refused the presents we offered, but agreed to accept them after much persuasion. They deluged us with questions about far away England and we told them whatever we knew from hearsay and reading and the fruits of our own imagination. Later, we asked about the partisans and their attitude to the local inhabitants, but they were evasive. Apparently they observed the rule that "silence safeguards wisdom." We inquired about the German conquerors and saw terror in their eyes. They spoke about the difficult situation they had been in for years now, the insecurity about what tomorrow would bring, and expressed their fear that the partisans would withdraw and that the town would again be overrun by the Nazis.

I asked an innocent question: "Is it true what they say, that the Germans kill Jews without mercy?"

"There are no more Jews in Yugoslavia," declared the father.

"And you, aren't you Jews?" I asked the difficult question quickly.

"No, that is, yes, my father was a Jew. But me and my family—no! But the Germans don't differentiate between us and real Jews."

Marta blushed deeply and said something to her father, who reacted sharply, mouthing the word "*Zhid.*" It was now my turn to feel the blood rush to my face. I stood up, mumbled something, and started to leave. Peretz did likewise. Marta rose to accompany us and extended her hand. I pretended not to notice and took my leave with a salute. I no longer saw the sea's depths in her eyes, and gold no longer glinted in her hair. Her cheeks reddened as though from the slap I had dealt her in my thoughts.

John arrived in the evening. Tall, thin, but strong, he was typically English, with fair skin and blue eyes. He was dusty and grimy and carried a rucksack and his submachine gun. After shaking hands warmly with us, he lay on the couch and told us that en route from the high command headquarters in Slovenia to regional headquarters where we now were, he and his interpreter had been attacked by the Ustaše—a local military organization on the lines of the Nazi SS—which was under the German High Command. They had run for their lives while returning fire. He also told us that Hannah, Reuven, Abba, and Yonah had gone east a fortnight earlier. He had information that the German army had carried out extensive

mopping-up operations against the partisans in the country stretching from Zumberak northward, and the army had cut off the area
from the Hungarian border. It was therefore impossible to put the
Cairo plan into operation.

Hearing this, I was furious that we hadn't been told in time to
prevent us from jumping into what was nothing but a blind alley.
John tried to mollify me, saying with a rather arrogant gesture: "You
understand nothing about this matter. The partisans are fantastic
people, they know everything and can do anything. The general
told me that we'll be leaving tomorrow and in five days we'll be in
Koprivnica, which is northeast of us on the Hungarian border. The
first group also took that route and are most probably in Budapest
by now."

We had a good time that night with the local officers in the
colonel's dim, narrow room. In as good a mood as his officers, thanks
to the tart wine, he joined them in telling tales of heroism: they
had trapped a tank with their bare hands and had immediately fired
its cannon. Owing to the petrol shortage, they used oxen to tow
their tanks to the battle front and only then would they start up the
engines. They conquered an airfield where scores of planes were
parked, and set them on fire. Finally, we were also obliged to tell
something. I told them how, dressed as a bedouin, I had appeared
beside an armored car, killed the German crew with a gun hidden in
my robe, and driven in the same vehicle to our own lines. Everyone
was astonished at my daring. My comrades were astonished at my
daring imagination.

In the morning we were provided with a rickety cart harnessed
to two toothless horses. The truck we had been promised remained
a figment of the Italian quartermaster's imagination. We took only
necessary equipment: a few clothes, weapons, ammunition, transmitters, some cigarettes, cognac, and the small container of personal
papers meant for the main part of our mission—the operation in
Hungary. This container had a self-destruct device activated by a
cord. All the rest we left as a gift to the partisans.

Ten partisans accompanied us as escort-guides. We were promised a stronger escort when we came into German-controlled territory. We made a grand exit from the town: in the lead, a squad of
armed partisans, behind them, the five of us—the English major,
the Scottish captain, the Austrian-Jewish sergeant, and the two of
us—the kibbutzniks from Palestine. The cart was behind us, and

bringing up the rear was a platoon of partisans as a guard of honor to the outskirts of town.

That was the beginning of a period of wandering in the Zumberak mountains from early morning till nightfall, from valley to mountain and from mountain to ravine. "Ascent for the purpose of descent, descent for the purpose of ascent," I hummed endlessly. We stopped at villages, drank the good wine from the welcoming farmers. Now and then we encountered obstacles that brought the horses to a standstill. Until they moved again, we were forced to push the cart. From the high mountaintops we surveyed the broad valley held by the enemy. Through binoculars we could see Karlovac, the center of German military rule in Yugoslavia, and Zagreb, the capital of Croatia—a state established under German auspices in the conquered zone of Yugoslavia.

When we reached the last range of hills, we heard the hum of a plane. We hurriedly scattered and took cover, but the pilot had apparently spotted us and dropped altitude. We could have hit him, but nobody fired. Perhaps, after all, he hadn't detected us? It was a sophisticated scout plane, excelling at low-speed performance—"*Storch*," the Germans called it, the Stork. Storks are a bad omen. It looked as though they were searching for us, and maybe they had even managed to photograph us. The Nazi spy chain apparently worked well within the ranks of the partisans too. The Germans had a great interest in finding out all about the British officers and their destinations.

Not many hours passed before the Stork turned up again. Once more, we took cover. We hoped that this time the pilot hadn't seen us nor discovered the direction we were taking. Toward evening we came to the last partisan outpost, a small village at the edge of the Zumberak range, overlooking the Sava River. We saw the winding white road, the gleaming railway tracks and, in the distance, the two main Croatian towns—Zagreb and Karlovac. Only a few kilometers separated us from the first German outpost. Through the binoculars we tracked what was going on in a big building flying the Nazi flag. We could make out moving figures. We took care not to be discovered, since it was most likely that the enemy was also keeping an eye on the village through binoculars, and we were liable to receive a hail of shells from mortars and field cannons.

I heard music with singing, and a spectacular sight unfolded: a troop of some five hundred armed partisans, marching three abreast,

Palgi (left) with mission companion Peretz Goldstein, 1944.

followed by horse-drawn artillery. At the head of the column, astride a white mare, rode a short, broad-shouldered man. Five hundred partisans in one battalion—it was a tremendous force. A battalion like that could operate over an extensive area and harass large, well-armed units.

The five of us stood at attention before the passing column of troops, who saluted as they drew abreast. The commander stopped, jumped off his mare, saluted, and informed us that he had come with his men to see us safely past enemy lines. He was responsible for our lives, and as long as we were under his protection we had to take orders from him alone—if not, he would be free of all responsibility for us.

We were accommodated overnight in a peasant's house. His daughter, a robust young woman, looked at me with her luminous eyes as if to say, "Later, after dark . . ." To our dismay the father remained with us, pacing the floor and spitting to the left and right. We tried without success to explain that it was impolite of him to spit on the floor we were to sleep on. In the midst of this, an agitated partisan came with a message that we were to follow him with all our belongings. Regretfully, I thought: the peasant's daughter was most attractive. We quickly climbed a high hill. The partisan offered no explanations as to where we were going or why. We were apprehensive: was he to be trusted? Maybe the partisans were plotting something? I checked my gun. Soon we learned that German and Ustaše forces were closing in on the village. Apparently the Stork had spotted us after all, and perhaps the partisans' display march had drawn the Germans' attention. We had been pulled out just before the circle closed. In the weak light of dusk, we saw the enemy approach the village, close the circle, and take up its position. A battle broke out. It was possible to distinguish between German and partisan fire: a burst from the partisans never exceeded two bullets, whereas the Germans, revealing their nervousness, let go with long volleys. The partisans stinted on their ammunition, but I had no doubt that the two partisan bullets equaled the Germans' prolonged bursts.

The Germans didn't press their attack. They had been surprised, it seemed, by the vigorous resistance. They hadn't expected such a considerable partisan force, and now found themselves in confusion as they awaited orders while sending a hail of fire, using all the weapons they had. From the hilltop we watched the partisans' movements.

Some stormed the Germans, throwing grenades, while others infiltrated through a break in the lines to attack the enemy from the rear. We felt that we should also go into action. We ignored our partisan who ordered us to lie low. We advanced toward the enemy's positions and directed strong machine-gun fire at them. The surprise was timely; the enemy began to retreat. Retreat turned to flight, leaving many dead and wounded behind. The brigade then commenced a general attack. The partisans returned from the battle late at night, tired but full of excitement and with a haul of weapons. When the brigade had mustered, the commander informed us that we were to leave at once, since our position and route had been discovered. The road would be closed to us from now on and the Germans would be rallying their forces to guard the railway line in the zone opposite the village in an effort to erase their recent disgrace. Therefore, we had to go up to the north at once, only crossing German-held territory tens of kilometers from the village.

At a swift pace we headed in the direction of Zagreb, whose lights winked at us in the distance. After five hours of quick walking, we turned east and entered the forest. We advanced over the uneven ground among the tree trunks with difficulty. They wrapped the horses' hooves in sacking, but the cart came to a halt ever so often and we were forced to drag it to get it past obstacles. The brigade advanced according to the rules. Groups of scouts and others carrying heavy artillery on tripods walked in front and at the sides, one providing cover while the other tracked, then changing roles. Everyone had a bullet in the breech, ready for battle. I was very tired, and the American submachine gun seemed intolerably heavy. I moved my legs instinctively, my mind devoid of thought. Everything around me passed before my eyes like a film. I would fall asleep as I walked, only to be awakened by a horse bumping into me from behind. The forest was absolutely dark. There was neither moon nor stars. Nobody uttered a sound. We knew that anyone who lit a cigarette would be a dead man. When the cart hit a tree, or when someone stumbled and his gun struck a stone, it sounded like a tremendous explosion, as if the entire forest had been alarmed and the enemy would immediately show himself.

Suddenly we found ourselves out of the forest, next to a white road stretching into the distance. Two lights were approaching. The command to lie down was given. We lay in silence waiting for the car that came slowly along the road, shedding a powerful light. "Armored car," the whisper passed down the line. We lay in a ditch, each man gripping a grenade in his right hand, ready at any moment to throw it. At last the armored car came abreast and passed us.

The Germans turned on their searchlight, and its sweeping beam streaked past without revealing the many men lying in the bushes, their hearts thumping. When the armored car had gone, we continued walking.

We reached the railway line. I thought we would cross this danger point quickly, but it wasn't so. Large groups of partisans scattered and took up positions, while one group began to unload shells and explosives from the cart. Feverish activity ensued. Our group was ordered to move on, but we couldn't restrain our curiosity and stayed where we were. With brisk, calculated movements, the partisans were hiding dynamite under the tracks for the length of a kilometer and attaching detonators. We stood a few hundred meters back and took cover. Silence. The only sound was a train in the distance, growing louder by the minute, and, as though in response, a nightingale lovingly trilling in the forest behind us. I clutched the submachine gun when the train's whistle sounded and the nightingale's song stopped. The anticipation was so intense that my muscles froze. The long train crawled heavily forward. Suddenly—tremendous explosions, the thunder of overturning engine and carriages, and the clang of iron on iron filled the air. For an instant there was only deathly silence, but cries and curses and roars of pain were soon heard and then more explosions, machine gun, submachine gun, and rifle fire erupting in a satanic uproar. The partisans burst from the forest, swarmed furiously over the train, and, by the light of a burning carriage, began to loot. Within minutes the two carts were loaded to capacity and many partisans were helping the horses pull the load. The order to retreat was given and we left almost at a run.

We continued more confidently once we were in the forest. The forest was the partisans' ally, their home. Dawn broke, the sun came out, and we were still dragging our feet helplessly; even though we were now in a partisan-controlled sector, we knew the enemy wouldn't let the night's disgrace go by without response. A battle could be expected, and our brigade was in no condition to face it. New, fresh forces were now streaming to meet the enemy, but we had to continue on our long, exhausting way. The brigade was slowly dispersing until we found ourselves with only our ten-man escort. We reached regional headquarters in a small village of no more than ten families, where we were served a meal fit for a king that nobody was able to eat. Dirty and sweaty, I fell onto the bed I was given and a deep sleep overcame me.

After such a night, the rest was welcome. The partisans took good care of us. We were given a comfortable room, the food was rich, and there was no lack of wine. No sooner were our eyes open than we were served strong slivovitz—a plum brandy—"to start the day right." It was a national tradition, they told us. And, to tell the truth, after two or three glasses one's mood was considerably improved. After breakfast we went for a walk in the forest. Like the partisans, we carried our weapons everywhere and we indulged in a bit of bird hunting. It was also good shooting practice. When we returned to the village we set up our transmitters. Actually, there was no need for this, but we knew it gave us status in the eyes of the partisans when they saw us through the window wearing our earphones and busy at our mysterious occupation.

When a squadron of Allied planes flew over the village a few days later, and Zagreb was bombed for the first time, we followed the raid through binoculars, standing on a hilltop. We rose immeasurably in their esteem, since they were all sure we had guided the bombers. Our lodgings became the focus of interest. The girls grew bold—with some encouragement from us—and came to our rooms. John devoured them with his eyes, curses escaping his lips in his Oxford accent. He was thoroughly vexed with the partisan law that anyone making love to a partisan girl was taking his life in his hands. So, at any rate, we had been told in our briefing in Italy. We all took the power of this law very seriously even though rumor had it that as far as Englishmen were concerned, it wasn't too strictly enforced. Peretz and I understood that both the partisans and the English weren't too keen on over-intimate relations between the "armies" for fear of espionage, but the death sentence would not be imposed except in cases of rape. Therefore, we could regard ourselves as being above the law, but John quaked at the thought.

One partisan girl used to visit us often. A city girl, she had been to France and England. We were wary of her, in case she would discover that our English wasn't fluent. In fact, she once overheard us exchange a few words in Hebrew and exclaimed: "What language were you talking? You aren't English!"

My blood froze. I was afraid her discovery would reach enemy ears. I had an inspiration and blurted: "Welsh! We're Welshmen!" and began to tell her about Wales, my "homeland."

"I never imagined Welsh was so different from English," she said.

Our days of recuperation began to drag out. When we felt we were strong enough to continue, it emerged that the rest period hadn't been granted us out of consideration for our fatigue. The enemy had opened a massive offensive in the area, and the partisans advised us to stay put. But we were impatient and sick of being idle. On the sixth day, a small man with a long nose came into our room. He wore the rank of colonel. Not introducing himself, he greeted us and surveyed the room like an officer inspecting barracks, then turned to leave. I asked whether he would join us for supper.

"No!" replied the colonel, "but we'll be seeing each other some other time. I'm also going to your destination."

"Now?" we queried. "But there's a siege!"

"There's no siege for me in this country!" He chuckled and left the room.

I questioned the partisans about him, without success. All I learned was his nickname: Colonel Ilia. I knew this wasn't his real name, since all the partisan officers went by assumed names. I didn't know then that our fate would be tied up with this Colonel Ilia. The brief meeting with him had opened our eyes: there were people to whom the siege did not apply. It became clear that only one thing was important to the partisans: no harm should befall us while we were their responsibility. They wouldn't help us put our plans into effect as long as there was any danger to our lives.

It should be noted that only Peretz and I questioned this. The other three wouldn't flinch from danger, but their attitude to their task was different. They were ready to carry out their superiors' orders, but were quite content when no orders came.

Peretz and I went to the commander and asked him to explain why he was delaying us, seeing that Colonel Ilia was allowed freedom of movement. He explained that Colonel Ilia went only with his aide, they were both light-footed, knew their country well, and could always evade the enemy, whereas we were heavily loaded, clumsy, and in need of a strong escort.

I expressed the wish to make my way alone with one guide. The rest could follow with the baggage when conditions improved. Reluctantly, he agreed.

I laid my plan before the rest of our small group: I would move ahead and join the first group, who must surely have crossed the border by now, and maybe I would also succeed in helping them to make their way to Budapest. I was sure the plan would be accepted and was astonished when John said: "It's a good idea, someone must go, but it won't be you. It'll be me."

"Why?" I demanded. "You don't speak Hungarian!"

"I'm the superior officer," he countered, "and besides, what makes you think the first group has crossed the border? I've received information that they're still hanging around the border area and not getting anywhere. I'll see to it that they cross. I know your lot, when the time comes for action, you drop out!"

I was left with my mouth agape. I shook with agitation and anger. I tried to restrain myself. Leaning against the wall, I said in a quiet but unsteady voice: "You bastard! You know very well that we've come to save our brothers from the furnaces and gas chambers. You, the great Empire, weren't prepared to help; you weren't prepared to let us have even one plane to get us there. If we could, we would have done everything ourselves without any help from you. But you insisted we operate as your agents, because you haven't that many who are able and willing to do the job. It's your fault that our departure was delayed till Hungary was conquered by the Germans, and now you've got the nerve to sling mud at us!"

The room was totally silent. I let my glance move over everyone there. Peretz's eyes flashed like lightning. Mac lay on his back staring at the ceiling. Grandeville lowered his eyes and reddened.

John was chalk white. He had gone too far, and any additional word was likely to cause an explosion. After a long, oppressive silence, he answered: "You Jews have a way of always exaggerating. I don't believe those tales of extermination. But it's just as well you've shown your true face. I've always known you Palestine Jews were hostile to us."

Mac felt it was time to intervene: "I don't like Jews either. They profit from war at our expense. But to exterminate them—no, sir. And you've made a good impression on me. You aren't like other Jews. I respect you."

Grandeville stood up and left the room. I didn't answer. With trembling fingers I dismantled my submachine gun and began oiling the parts. Peretz also began cleaning his gun. Who knows, maybe we would need our weapons in strange and unexpected circumstances.

From then on, we severed all contact with John. We were five men in one room, and the tension was intolerable. Grandeville and Mac acted as go-betweens. Mac would pass on what we said to John, and what he said to us, like a children's game. But nothing was mentioned about the situation to the partisans; it was tacitly agreed that they should remain ignorant of what was transpiring in our group.

My plan was dropped, but John continued to negotiate with the commander of the district, and one day he announced: "Tomorrow we'll be leaving with ten partisans, but we'll have to carry our belongings on our backs."

We packed only what was most necessary: the two transmitters, some cigarettes, parachute cloth for wrapping ourselves at night (pure silk it was, and warm and light), shaving and toilet kit, the document container, and a bag of gold coins.

We left the village stealthily, early in the morning. We knew from experience that even this quiet little place was rife with espionage and counter-espionage. In the end the enemy would be informed where we were headed, but we hoped our departure, like that of thieves in the night, would buy us some time.

We proceeded quietly, not entering villages. We concealed our hats so that nobody would identify us as English. We weren't worried about the uniforms—many partisans wore British uniforms. Our hardships had long since rubbed away traces of the immaculate British officer.

We walked in the forest. It was early May, but spring was late. Rivulets of melted snow flowed over the ground and the paths were covered in rotting leaves. We trudged through swampy mud. The dark was terrifying and I bumped into bushes and trees, injuring my hands and face. I was separated more than once and lost my way, only locating the column with great difficulty, so that from then on I walked with my hand on the knapsack of the man in front of me. I was very tired. I felt a great desire to lie down, to sleep. Smoking was forbidden. I remembered I had some pep pills, but decided to do without them. I knew we still had a long way ahead of us and when the influence of the pills wore off, I would be very weak. The brandy I swallowed from time to time didn't quench my thirst, but the disturbing shuddering passed and I felt a return of strength.

I checked our direction on my compass and realized we were wandering around the forest like a ship lost on the ocean wastes. It was as if the four points of the compass had changed places. I wanted some explanation of this, but was sunk in apathy. I knew there was no point in arguing with the partisans—we were in their hands. I understood that map and compass couldn't measure against the villager's natural sense. He alone could reach the destination in the gloom of the forest, laying a tree trunk over the river to enable us to cross without getting wet to the hips, for example.

The increasing cold and the water seeping into my shoes were making themselves felt. I began to cough and choke, forced to halt a few times. When a fit of coughing took me, I stuffed my hat into my mouth so as not to be heard. In addition, an old knee injury sustained in a practice jump was bothering me. I carried on walking. In that forest you had to keep moving or you were finished. The knapsack, so light when we had started out, now seemed full of lead. Even the submachine gun, my companion, to which I was deeply attached, weighed me down. At times we would come to a clearing, and then when I could see John's faint outline ahead of me in the darkness, my anger would smolder: that Jew-hater was to blame for everything! Because of him we had to walk with the heavy load on our backs. I had a powerful urge to press the trigger. Nobody would be able to prove it had been done on purpose. Bastards like that should be wiped out! I was shocked at myself and shook myself awake: for God's sake! I was feverish; perhaps I could lie down without their noticing. I had emergency rations, a map, a compass, ammunition. In a day or two, I would continue. Yes, that would be best, just a few steps to the side, then to sink down and wait till the last of them had passed me.

I had run out of strength. My eyes were streaming. I felt as if the cord binding me to the world had been severed. I sank to the ground and the man behind me stumbled. I opened my eyes and took another hefty swallow of brandy. The partisans wanted to make it easier for me by carrying my load. It really did weigh me down, but I did not want to lose face. I walked on. After a time we emerged from the forest and the sound of powerfully rushing water struck my ears. It was the River Sava. We walked along the bank until we came to a bombed-out bridge with only its supports rising out of the water. The crossing was difficult and complicated. We advanced at a crawl over a narrow plank we laid between one pole and the next, with each unplanned movement likely to end with a fall into the abyss. The gun, which I had hung around my neck, slipped and got tangled with my legs. By a miracle I managed to grab the sides of the plank and by desperate effort succeeded in pulling myself right side up again, covered in icy perspiration and with my heart pounding. When I came to the other side, shaking with the effort, I turned to look at the men coming after me and I saw Peretz suddenly slip and drop into the abyss. We all rushed to his aid, but as it happened, he had fallen where it wasn't deep, and apart from a few scratches he was unharmed.

We could hear bursts of machine-gun fire in the distance, growing more distinct as we advanced. Then we saw iron tracks in the space between two forests. It was the Zagreb-Belgrade line, part of the main Berlin-Istanbul line—the key to the conquest of Greece and perhaps the entire Middle East. Now the meaning of the shots was understood: concrete outposts were placed at intervals of one kilometer along the railway tracks. German soldiers were keeping up a steady rain of blind fire to deter acts of sabotage. At a crawl, we approached the ditch that ran beside the track. We waited for the next volley and then immediately crawled across the tracks to lower ourselves into the ditch on the opposite side. Before we could get away from there, a long train arrived, transporting troops, armored cars, and anti-aircraft guns. We crouched in the ditch, biting our lips: an opportunity like this, and we weren't doing a thing! We continued to crawl until we reached the forest. Once again, the wearying march began.

We were welcomed on the other side of the Sava by soft, spacious, cultivated countryside. The landscape showed signs of human design. In the east, there was already an indication of dawn.

We were very tired. The squad commander, a pleasant youngster, consoled us with the news that we would be reaching the village in an hour and would rest the whole day. A copy of Engels's "Anti-Duhring" protruded from his pocket and I smiled to myself: it was from this book that I had absorbed the basis of Socialist theory in my youth.

Tonight we would cross the great river for the second time. It was the most serious obstacle in our path.

We rested awhile before entering the village. The sky was overcast and it began to rain. I lay under a bush and immediately fell asleep. Half an hour later they woke me. They had found out that an "action" was being carried out by the fascist Ustaše military in the village. They were confiscating cows and pigs. Two peasants who had resisted were murdered, together with their families. There was no point in talking about food and shelter now. We would have to wait until the Ustaše left the village.

We began to scout around for cover, but the Ustaše were everywhere in the vicinity. They were looking for something—either us, or animals hidden by the peasants. The rain didn't let up for a moment and we were trembling with cold and fatigue. At times I thought I couldn't bear any more and would collapse. We heard sporadic shots. We knew the fascists were murdering innocent, defenseless people, while we hid here with weapons in our hands. There was no point in engaging in a battle with our meager strength. This wasn't our task. This wasn't why we had jumped into Yugoslavia.

Toward evening we noticed that a large platoon, some on horseback, was drawing away from the village, laden with booty. Despite the terror the village had suffered that day, women appeared with baskets full of fine food: fresh eggs, cheese, cutlets, good bread, and jugs of milk. After a twenty-four-hour fast we ate our fill and soon warmed up. I felt a renewal of strength.

We continued our journey. When we came to the river, we found that the Germans had sunk all the boats to cut off communications between the partisan forces on either side. But the partisans had forestalled them: they had filled a few boats with water and had sunk them close to the riverbank. As the need arose, they would pull up a boat and prepare it for use. In spite of the darkness, we found one of these boats. We discovered that here, too, as along the railway track, the Germans shot in all directions to scare off would-be border crossers. We sat in the boat with our heads down, guarding against stray bullets.

We succeeded in crossing the river and came to a village. One of the partisans tapped lightly at the window of an inn. The innkeeper, a friend of the partisans, immediately opened the door and let us in. When he saw us, the English, he was frantic with joy at having us under his roof. He prepared Yugoslavian-style omelets: one-third eggs, one-third butter, and one-third pork. He brought jugs of brandy and good wine from his cellar. We went on our way in high spirits after this feast.

We encountered an annoying phenomenon: the partisans' lack of any sense of time. We were told we would reach our destination at midnight, but dawn was already breaking and we still had a long way to go and had to hurry in order to find cover.

We reached another village and before the peasants awoke, we sneaked into a barn. We stretched out on the straw and after thirty-six hours of wandering, slept the sleep of the just.

At nightfall we were on the road again. We crossed the great plain of the Sava. This time the walk was pleasant, with only the pain of my knee troubling me, badly. At one of the villages we were joined by a woman who was a language teacher at a high school in Zagreb, and a girl of about twelve, whose parents had been murdered. They were both heading for the partisan territory: the teacher had heard that the children weren't being taught in partisan areas owing to a teacher shortage and she wanted to contribute her skills. The girl wanted to fulfill her desire to kill one German with her bare hands. With childlike innocence, she asked: "Isn't it true that they give children hand grenades, too, and children are also allowed to kill a German?"

"That's right," one of the partisans answered.

Another rest, under a tree in a field. As with all the many night rest stops, the commander walking in front gave the signal to halt, and we immediately lay down to regain strength.

After a short consultation, the commander announced that he would go on with a few men to inspect the situation in the next village. If the village was clean, we could cross the railway tracks that ran through the village and spare ourselves a long walk and much danger. We were to follow him in half an hour.

The rest refreshed us. After the arranged time lapse we rose and approached the village. One of the partisans sounded an owl's hoot, but there was no reply. We were momentarily confused, but decided to press on. Again the partisan sounded the owl's hoot, without response. The partisans cursed the commander. They assumed the "bastard-son-of-a-bitch" had gone into one of the houses and had a drop too many.

We advanced toward the serene village. On either side of the road the peasants' houses gleamed white in the darkness, surrounded by orchards. The peasants here were obviously well-off. "This village doesn't like partisans," we had been told earlier. However, when there were no soldiers, there was nothing to fear from the inhabitants. They were afraid of the partisans. In any case, it was best to be careful. Therefore, we moved with our weapons at the ready. A boy leading two horses gaped at the silent line of men.

It was a large village. We had walked for more than half an hour and still had not reached the tracks. Light streamed from the windows of one of the houses. When we were alongside the house, the partisan walking in the lead halted and stood stock-still for a second, then gave the signal to run. Running in a crouch, I managed to get a look inside the house. It was a bar full of German and Circassian soldiers sitting around drinking at their ease. Their hats and coats hanging on the walls, and especially their weapons lying casually around, indicated that they hadn't the slightest fear that partisans were coming. Possibly they relied on their sentries, who were neglecting their duty.

We crossed the tracks, running through gardens and fields until we came to a deep ditch at a crossroad, where we lay flat. Two of the partisans went to see what had become of the commander. We crouched in the ditch, tense with expectation, not moving a muscle, till they returned with the commander. It emerged that he had returned to warn us that the village was crawling with enemy soldiers. Somehow, we hadn't met. While he was berating his men, three Circassians on horseback appeared. We flattened ourselves on the ground. These, apparently, were the sentries we hadn't come across earlier.

It was easier to walk after the long rest and we were heartened by the success of our last escapade. The commander again promised us that we would be arriving soon, almost immediately. Nobody paid attention to his promises. Someone jokingly remarked: "Say anything you like, just don't say 'immediately.' Because your 'immediately' means another day's walk. Why not call it by its right name? You have to multiply one partisan kilometer by five or ten."

We reached a large village at dawn. We sat down at the outskirts while two partisans went to get carts from the villagers. In the morning, we continued toward Cazma, where regional headquarters were situated. We were once more in a partisan-controlled zone, but we had to hurry to avoid being hit by Circassian cannon fire— who amused themselves by shaking up the district in the mornings.

We were given a celebrity welcome in Cazma. The whole town turned out to see the five Englishmen from the other side of the Sava. The three youngest members of the group—all of us Jews— hurried to improve our appearance so as to make an impression on the partisan girls, particularly on one who had stolen all our hearts. John and Mac flung themselves into chairs, tired and disheveled. After we had eaten they informed us that we still had another ten kilometers to go before reaching headquarters, where our arrival was already known. We had hardly launched a conversation with the beauty—who carried four grenades in her belt—when we were on the move again.

We continued on our way with excitement. We were doubly happy! We had succeeded in our daring march and we had a few days of rest ahead of us. Peretz and I were full of speculations about what had happened to the group that had gone ahead of us. Would we meet? The partisans told us there was a British general at headquarters. We thought it was the famous General Maclean, head of the British contingent at Tito's headquarters and our commanding officer for as long as we would be in Yugoslavia, and we were anticipating a meeting with him. We knew that his headquarters was in the Vosnian mountains in the south—had he really come north? While we were still considering this, three riders galloped over to us. As they approached, we noticed that two were wearing British uniforms. The third rode a fine white horse. We stopped and, jumping to attention, saluted smartly. When the dust raised by the horses' hooves settled, there before us stood . . . Reuven and Yonah! We looked at one another and burst out laughing.

We situated ourselves in a tiny village, Donji Miklous. There was an even tinier village on top of the hill, Gornji Miklous, to which we climbed daily to set up our transmitters.

We had the use of two rooms. In one, at the end of the village, John, Mac, and Grandeville were accommodated, while the Palestinian contingent settled in the other, smaller room. A wide, rustic bed was given to Peretz and me, since we were exhausted from our journey. A folding bed, used earlier by Hannah, was temporarily given to Reuven. Abba and Yonah slept on the floor. When Hannah later returned from a patrol of the northern border zone under partisan control, a place would be found for Reuven to sleep on the floor, squeezed in with the others. The peasant family crowded in the kitchen. In order not to disturb the family, we came and went via the window. It was pretty crowded, but the mood was merry.

As we entered the village, John addressed me directly for the first time since our clash: "I'm sorry for what I said. You proved on the journey that I had underestimated you."

I had no choice but to offer him my hand. By his standards the disagreement was over. But I knew that a man didn't change his nature that easily, and there were likely to be other clashes between us. My fears were soon borne out.

Reuven had succeeded in establishing friendly relations with the partisans. But things were spoiled by John, whose manners were strange to the partisans; also, he patronized them. The partisans were sensitive to such behavior and paid him back in the same coin, unfortunately lumping us together with him. From now on friendship was out of the question and relations became formal. They trusted only Reuven, because of their common language. He was a good talker and knew how to communicate with them. John didn't like this. How was it that he wasn't the main intermediary with the partisans? Out of this stemmed disagreements, minor ones at first, but more serious later, and the air became charged. Even with Mac, John didn't know how to maintain good relations. He insisted that Mac should obey his orders, although Mac was answerable only to his commander in Italy. He had come on another mission and was absolutely independent. The crisis reached its peak when John tried to put down Reuven, the only one of us directly under his command. We reached the conclusion that it was impossible to work with him and notified our chief in Cairo that we weren't prepared to carry on unless John was removed.

This all took place in Hannah's absence. When she returned from her survey of the border zone, a real storm broke loose. She disagreed with our conclusions. This argument, she said, could jeopardize the whole operation. It was a personal disagreement between Reuven and John. The British would favor the Britisher, the more so since he was a major and from such a well-connected family. There were other differences between Hannah and Reuven: Reuven believed in the partisans' goodwill, whereas Hannah had her doubts. She had come back from the border with a negative impression. The partisans said it wasn't possible to cross the Hungarian border. She claimed that whether this was so, or whether the partisans were simply not interested in helping us, we should rely on our own resources. She demanded this emphatically. We hadn't come here "on condition," that is, to cross the border only if everything was guaranteed beforehand. We hadn't the right to spare ourselves. Reuven strongly objected to this point of view: if the operation had no chance of success, we shouldn't go to our destruction.

There were two sides to the coin. On the one hand, it was impossible to sit with our hands folded while the Germans brutalized a million Jews. We couldn't have that on our conscience. It would be better never to return than to return having failed. On the other hand, had we the right to endanger ourselves when there was no hope of carrying out the mission? Had we come only so that the Palestinian Jewish community could discharge their obligations, saying, "We sent people and they fell in the line of duty"? No, we had no wish to be mere sacrificial objects. Our purpose was to help and not to sacrifice ourselves. We didn't aspire to become symbols without actually going into action.

The discussion began to harm our relationship. At times it seemed we had lost the distinction between caution and fear. Finally, Hannah insisted that everyone be given the right to act according to their own conscience. She refused to accept anyone's authority in a matter that could affect her peace of mind for the rest of her life.

Then, one sunny day as we were walking along the village street, Hannah in our midst, a young fellow stopped us and offered his hand, first to Hannah and then to the rest of us, introducing himself simply: Dobszyn.

Behind him, I saw someone familiar: the mysterious Colonel Ilia, who had dropped into our room during one of the stops on our march. I greeted Colonel Ilia, and he introduced himself to the others.

I then examined Dobszyn curiously. He was a handsome youngster, with the face of an educated person. The gleam in his eye and his sharp, confident movements revealed a store of inner strength. His conversation was lively. He knew English but refrained from speaking it, preferring to have us stammer in his language, with Reuven's assistance. There was no badge of rank on his sleeve. I thought: one of the partisans' political commissars.

Dobszyn told us he planned to visit us before he left. We returned to our room wondering who the man was. Meanwhile, I told them about my previous strange meeting with Colonel Ilia.

We made tea and put out our remaining chocolates in preparation for our guests. Reuven went to find out who they were and returned with the information that young Dobszyn was the commander-in-chief of the partisan armies in northern Yugoslavia. He had been a student in Prague and taken part in the Spanish Civil War. Ilia was the commander of an independent force, a sort of army within an army, a sabotage and commando patrol, and was also a hero of the Spanish Civil War. Prior to that he had been a miner in America, an explosives expert who had worked all his life at that trade. When he was young, he had done so to earn a living, and in the last ten years, in the name of liberty.

We greeted both of them with respect. It was a great honor to be in the company of one of the partisans' top saboteurs, and to provide hospitality to the youngest general in the world.

As soon as they arrived, they came to the point: they knew that we wanted to get to Hungary. Ilia also wanted to go there with a group of saboteurs, but they lacked the necessary explosives for the operation. They had a suggestion: if we would acquire explosives for them, they would undertake to get us over the border.

Perhaps we could have resented this give-and-take plan. They should have helped us without any conditions, but we knew how severely short they were of weapons and explosives. We knew that had they been provided with enough equipment, they would have been able to strike the enemy even more effectively. When I saw how they valued every bullet, I remembered the wealth of ammunition lying around in the Western Desert of North Africa. This blackmail was morally justified from their point of view.

Ilia, apparently, felt the need to explain his strange suggestion. He drew out a typed sheet of paper and read a summary of the operations carried out by the organization under his command during the preceding three months: some 1,200 acts of sabotage against railway lines; 840 trains blown up; over 400 strikes against bridges, factories, and 3 airfields; the destruction of more than 50 tanks, scores of cannons, and so on. According to his estimate, had they sent the partisans one-hundredth of the explosives that the Allies were wasting on the pointless bombing of Yugoslavia, he and his people would have achieved a hundred times those results, while cutting down on airforce casualties.

We agreed with his opinion. The general said: "I suggest you leave at once. Go in the direction of the Papuk Mountains. When you get there, contact the communications officer. I have friends over the border; on my orders they'll get you across."

After they had had their tea, they took leave of us. Two officers with four horses were waiting for them in front of the house. They jumped into the saddles and were soon swallowed in the cloud of dust raised by their horses' hooves. The glint of the submachine guns slung across their backs could be seen for a moment longer and then they disappeared completely.

I thought them the most romantic and interesting people I had ever met.

When our excitement subsided, we agreed—the wiser for experience—that we should not rely on promises. It would be wrong for all of us to go to the Papuk Mountains. We would split into two groups and look for different routes. If one group succeeded, the other would follow in their tracks.

It was decided that Peretz and John would stay behind to wait for the planes that would drop the explosives we had promised to Dobszyn. We would also request new transmitters because ours had been damaged on the journey. I was to take the direction of the Papuk Mountains, and Peretz would follow after the transmitters arrived. Abba had decided to join us for a stretch of the road, and Hannah, Yonah, and Reuven were to turn north-westward.

The nine days in Miklous had been beneficial for my knee that was so troublesome on the march.

We decided that we would leave on May 13, 1944.

So Yonah, Peretz, and I, the three from Kibbutz Maagan, were about to separate, each to take his own path in the forests of Yugoslavia. We were apprehensive—who could tell whether we would ever see each other again? We weren't merely members of the same kibbutz; we had come from the same town, were part of the same youth movement, and were childhood friends. All three of us wanted to spend a little more time with each other. We went for a walk together. On the way we came across a cart with a girl in it. She was delighted to see us and began talking to us in English. I invited her to visit us, forgetting we were soon to leave.

When she was gone, Peretz and Yonah breathed more freely: poor fellows, their English was even shakier than mine. Yonah confessed: "That girl's a problem. Actually, she's been chasing me all the time we've been here, while I've been trying to give her the slip before she could find out that I don't know English. Once, when I couldn't get away, I told her I had sworn never to talk any language but German, till I was fluent. She said she was keen on perfecting her English, so we agreed that she would speak to me in English and I would speak German to her. But I was afraid I would get into a mess."

We decided then and there that we would each take on one

language: I would speak English, Yonah German, and Peretz French. (We all knew Serbo-Croatian mixtures in local use, some better than others.) This made sense, since it was a known fact that Englishmen weren't usually masters of many languages. We always aroused amazement at knowing "every" language.

We came to Cazma and strolled around to our hearts' content. We heard stories about the last battle, when the town had been taken. Seven hundred Germans and Ustaše had been killed, with the loss of about two hundred partisans. As we wandered around the little town, a large flight of bombers suddenly surged overhead, glinting in the sunlight. We stood watching the display. Flight after flight of bombers ("flying fortresses") passed. We counted almost a thousand planes. It was a magnificent sight. Had it not been for the cheering crowd, we would have thrown our hats in the air and run wild with joy, but we had to put up a cool front and utter a few re-strained phrases; after all, we were British officers. One of the planes suddenly emitted a stream of smoke and went into a screaming dive. The crowd was distressed, running about in panic. We stood stunned, waiting for the crew to jump. When we saw the first chute open on the horizon, we breathed in relief. We hoped the crew would come to no harm, but there was nothing we could do, as they had jumped far from partisan territory. Only then did we become aware that a girl had clasped Yonah's arm, trembling with fear. He soothed her in Croatian and German. She was Viennese and had been a partisan for over a year. According to our agreement, it was Yonah's turn to do the talking, and he faithfully translated for us what she said, and for her he translated our words into German. We walked some of the way with her, enjoying the translation game as Yonah smoothly did his act. When we prepared to leave her, our Viennese asked us to wait while she fetched her rucksack—she was going our way.

We crossed a field, walking through wildflowers and along winding paths. Peretz and I began to regret that we "didn't know" German, as she and Yonah walked arm in arm ahead of us, with us "foreigners" trudging along in their wake, only able to enjoy the conversation in translation. We took some comfort in teasing Yonah now and then about his wife and his daughter Ruthie.

Suddenly, the charming Viennese said: "Listen, there's a path into the forest. Let's go into the trees and leave these clods to take the road. Agreed?"

It's just as well we were behind them, because we couldn't control ourselves, splitting our sides with laughter. We enjoyed the sight of Yonah's red face. He stammered something or other, dragging us along with them. We were in a happy mood.

Seeing that her love plans had been foiled, the Viennese became serious. She told us how she had become a partisan: she had been living with her husband's parents in Zagreb. The Ustaše killed the parents and she and her husband had escaped by a miracle. They fled to the forest and joined the partisans. Her husband fell in battle a few weeks later, and she had been in a fighting unit ever since. She concluded her story, saying: "The Germans and fascists are killing millions of people. They have murdered three million Serbs."

"And millions of Jews!" Yonah exclaimed.

"I don't like Jews," said the beautiful Viennese offhandedly.

I felt my face flush.

We walked on in silence. She wasn't even aware that we weren't making a sound as she explained why she didn't like Jews. I didn't have the heart to meet my friends' eyes. The three of us kept up appearances, but each one was ashamed of being able to do so.

We parted from the Viennese partisan with somber thoughts. Why did everyone hate us? What would become of the survivors if freedom fighters, who hated the fascists, were of one mind with Nazis concerning the Jews?

When we got back, we told our friends about the Viennese, but Reuven had a far more serious story to tell. Some Croatian peasants collaborated with the Germans under their leader, Maček, whose propagandists were spreading the rumor among the local peasants that the partisans had the support only of the Russians, the Communists, whereas the English were behind Maček. Therefore the partisan general, Matačic, had to display the Englishmen to his people as concrete proof that Maček's people were lying. The Palestinian group responded willingly and took part in a massive First of May gathering. Hannah even delivered a speech in Croatian. "Go and tell it at home," General Matačic called out in his speech. "On whose side are the English: ours or the enemy's?" And he pointed to the Palestinians, again crying out: "Look and see where the English are, in Zagreb, or here with us?"

Apparently this damaged Maček's standing in the area; his propagandists looked for a way out. Our landlord, a well-off peasant, furiously told us that the rotten fascists in Bjelovar—a nearby town under Nazi control—were saying that the English in Miklous were nothing but filthy Jews.

We didn't know whether the Germans had identified us, or whether this was a shot in the dark that had hit home, but we decided to get out of there as soon as we could.

That very day we received a transmission telling us that planes were due the same night, and that they would drop men and the explosives we had requested. We waited impatiently for them. We went to the designated field after dark. A thin rain was falling and our feet sank into the mud, but we were in good spirits. All six of us turned out as if we were on parade, wearing revolvers and a variety of hats. Our procession impressed the people we passed. In the middle, Hannah marched—the first woman parachutist—increasing the partisans' respect for the British army. Her gray-blue uniform had a steely shine, and her blue eyes glowed. The heaviness lifted from our hearts, and all hesitation melted: tomorrow we would be on our way! And how pleasant it would be tonight—people would arrive from the big world beyond and we would sit companionably together all night. Partisans we encountered stood stiffly to attention and saluted our group, but their eyes were on the girl who, with a polite smile and an energetic wave, returned their greeting.

A broad clearing stretched not far from the village. It was an ideal place for a parachute landing. A platoon of partisans were busily unloading logs and straw from a cart, and preparing beacon fires to mark the boundaries of the area to prevent the planes from dropping the people and material on the roofs of the village. We marked a huge "D" on the ground—the prearranged signal to the pilots.

The feverish activity came to an end and the hours of waiting began. The thin rain persisted and the night chill intensified. A fire was lit. People wrapped themselves in their coats, collars up, and huddled around it. Flames licked hungrily at the logs, giving a pleasant warmth. Someone began to hum and was joined by another, and yet another, until a powerful chorus swelled to fill the night's stillness. It was a sorrowful song, in which the nation mourned its fate. Like its language and its song, this was a wonderful, tender nation. Even its loves and hates seemed to be wrapped in tenderness. Its emotions were deep and stormy, yet delicate and subtle. As they sat around the fire, singing together, the true face of the people was revealed. There was a beautiful harmony of contrasting and blending voices, without a conductor and without the allocation of parts, everyone finding the right place, both in the singing and in life.

"If only it is granted to us to sit in Hungary with our own people, listening to the songs of our country sung by our Jewish freedom-fighters," said Hannah, and I saw tears glistening in the corners of her eyes.

"Our own fighters?" she continued. "Listen to the partisans' song: it's loaded with searing pain, yet they are fighting for freedom on their own soil. This people's blood will be spilled for its own country, in its own country. If one of them falls, his own soil will embrace him, his wildflowers will be his monument. Their song weeps, but it also rejoices in the day their freedom will come. And we? What will we be fighting for? We're like hunted animals, and the devil laughs at our dying tremor. . . ."

I entwined her arm in mine, and we slipped away from the circle of partisans. "What will we say to those Jews we'll still find there?" she asked. "What will we promise them? Freedom? A new world? Recompense for their suffering? A victim's indemnity? We have no news for them. Only the demand that they struggle, take vengeance, and die with honor. Unclean soil will drink the blood of our fallen, unclean soil will be fertilized by the bodies of our fallen—to bear a crop of gold for the offspring of our murderers! The songs of Jewish partisans will echo, the shout of millions, but unsoftened by the joyful cry of hope and belief in victory."

"Don't you believe in the establishment of Israel?" I asked.

"My heart tells me that we're not going to rescue Jews anymore. We're going to pay our final respects to the remaining few on their way to execution. And even if thousands are rescued, tens of thousands, will they have the strength to start a new war for the nation's life?

"I also feel that the remains of Hungarian Jewry face the same fate as the others, elsewhere. That's why we have to act without weighing the cost or consequences. I'm sorry that in the heat of the argument I hurt the rest of you, but I had to. We must act at once. My impatience isn't because of my mother. Of course, I'm terrified to think of what might happen to her. But we have to rescue others as well as those close to us. We dare not leave it until it's too late. If Hitler succeeds in destroying the whole of European Jewry, we have no future in Palestine either. The Jewish settlement there will wither without the impetus of immigration and development. If we collapse this time, another two thousand years could go by before the emergence of another group of pioneers with enough strength to begin again. I don't know what I've done to deserve this sacred task, but I do know that having begun, there's no turning back for me. Should I save myself? For what—for whom? We won't be condemned even if we fail, but we will be judged by our consciences. Would we be able to live with it? I have to go. And if I die, it won't have been in vain. Perhaps the Jews will hear a rumor that an agent from Palestine tried to reach them and died in the attempt, and hearts in the forests and ghettos will quicken with the thought: We have to hang on, they haven't abandoned us, they haven't forgotten us, maybe rescue is near. Faith can work miracles. I have to go, there's no other way. I don't want to die. No, I want to live. I expect a lot from life, but I have to repurchase my right to life."

The moon set; the partisans put out the fire. The planes hadn't come. Perhaps tomorrow.

I held Hannah's hands: "Wherever you go, I go, too!"

We sat up late in the room, discussing final arrangements. We decided to meet in Budapest at the Great Synagogue after the Sabbath Eve service. And if there was no longer any organized Jewish prayer in Budapest, we would meet at the Church of the Coronation on Sunday.

We rose early. We had far to go that day.

On May 13, early in the morning, Abba and I set out accompanied by a partisan. The whole group stood in front of the house to say good-bye to us: Hannah, Reuven, Yonah, Peretz, Grandeville, Mac, and John. Hannah and Reuven were busy securing equipment on a horse. They were to leave at noon. After a long, warm embrace, we shouldered our guns and started marching along the uneven road. At the turning, I looked back: they were all standing there, still following us with their eyes. I waved, calling, "See you in Budapest!" Hannah, giving a thumbs-up sign, repeated: "See you in Budapest!"

We reached the forest and walked for many hours. Occasionally I glanced at the compass. Our guide, a man of the forest, looked derisively at this sophisticated instrument. He didn't believe that a compass was preferable to a sense of direction. Several times, we crossed the railway tracks belonging to the big, wealthy timber company that worked the Yugoslavian forests. The partisan told us that the partisan government had confiscated the holdings of the foreign—Dutch—company and that, in the future, all branches of industry would be the property of the people.

In the evening, we came to the last district before Nazi-held territory. We continued under cover of night. Our guide this time was the partisans' courier. We didn't know exactly where the enemy was situated. The Germans had attacked the Papuk Mountains with a huge force, in order to drive out the partisans completely. They had no control over the whole of the plain unless they held these mountains. In an attempt to disrupt the partisan network, they had penetrated to the heart of the mountains, with a force of some 60,000 German, Ustaše, and Circassian soldiers. The attack had lasted longer than usual, and although there was news that a retreat was in progress, it wasn't clear how far the partisans had advanced in the wake of the enemy. The local commissar knew nothing of the orders not to let us proceed unless the road was safe, and we didn't want to lose even one day. We went by way of villages that weren't hostile to us, although they weren't under partisan control. They were large, rich villages that paid their dues to both sides. In a few of these villages there were peasants who had spent some time in America, returning home to buy land when they had saved a little money. At heart they missed big, rich America, where they had failed to find a home. These "Americans" welcomed us with boundless enthusiasm.

We were in a fine mood after the plentiful food and drink with which we were welcomed in no-man's-land. Slowly and cautiously we advanced, knowing that anyone we met could well be an enemy. When we were close to the tracks, we were surprised to see the courier walk straight up to the sentry-post. We were afraid this was a betrayal. But the courier explained that the sentries guarding that stretch of line were partisan sympathizers and gave them help. When we walked into the guardroom, the guards' eyes flew open, making us burst out laughing at their astonishment. They hadn't expected a visit from British officers.

We made good time from the railway track marking the border of German-controlled territory. We didn't stop at any more villages. Our hearts shook when the village dogs scented us in the distance. We stopped only at isolated farms for information. However, we approached a house in one of the big villages, since we had no possibility of circumventing it and were forced to cut through. The village spread over several kilometers. One of us stayed on the other side of the fence on guard and the other took cover in the yard. The courier flattened himself under the window and tapped on the pane with his gun. We were all ready to return fire and get out of there should we encounter the enemy. We held our breath as we listened to an argument between the peasant and his wife as to whether they should open the window. Finally the partisan whispered his name and the window was opened. We heard a hoarse, trembling voice. After a brief exchange, the door opened and we were invited in. We refused, having learned that we were on the heels of the enemy and should be extremely careful.

We hugged the walls, waiting to check whether the road was clear. After a long wait, we heard the creak of a door and the sound of an old woman coughing. The courier went over to her with cat-like movements and clapped his hand over her mouth. The woman struggled, but calmed down when she heard what the partisan was whispering. She went to the gate, looked from side to side, and gestured to us that everything was in order. We crossed the road silently and went into the opposite yard and out again to be swallowed by the forest darkness. There were still Germans in the village that night.

The road had become steep and walking was getting increasingly difficult. We toiled up the mountain and reached the top at dawn. According to the information we had received, a platoon of partisans had set up camp in the village there. Nevertheless, we hid and waited. A sentry appeared, a Tito hat on his head. When we stood up, he aimed his rifle at us. The courier immediately gave the password and we were welcomed as friends.

Worn out, we went into the village school that housed the platoon. Men and women partisans lay horribly crowded on the crude floorboards. Some were fast asleep, others tossed and turned, breathing heavily and scratching themselves. There was no air in the room and the stench was awful. I looked at these people in their tattered clothes and torn shoes. They slept with hand grenades in their belts, clutching their guns—precious possession, true friend—and I was filled with respect for them. These were people who knew whom to hate, who the enemy was, people who didn't surrender to the strongest human drive: to stay alive! They were ready to sacrifice their lives at any moment.

The officer who was awakened on our arrival gave his orders

half asleep. Another partisan, swaying with fatigue, led us to a peasant's house where, he said, we would find a bed.

We knocked on the door and entered. Outside it was already first light, but the room was dark. I switched on my flashlight and was shocked at the sight that met my eyes: a narrow room filled with fragments of furniture and feathers from ripped bedding, beans strewn all over the floor, a shattered sewing machine. I flinched and cried: "What's this?" I was answered by a weeping voice from the darkness of the next room: "They murdered my wife, they killed the cow, they slaughtered the chickens, stole my pig, burned the barn, set fire to the hay, looted and destroyed my house. What will I do? What will I do?"

"Fascist culture!" our escort spat. Then he turned to us and said: "Hurry up and go to sleep. A day to rest and we carry on tonight."

We cleared a space on the floor, spread a blanket, and lay down without undressing, without the strength even to remove our shoes.

Not an hour had gone by when they woke us: we had to leave immediately—the enemy was coming back. The partisans had decided not to hold the village. We were instantly ready and left with the platoon. The peasant was still lying on his bed, quietly sobbing. He no longer cared about anything; what more could the Germans do to him?

The retreat was swift. We climbed mountains and went into valleys. We stopped only to drink water and refill our canteens. Old peasants and women stood at their gates and asked tremulously whether the Germans were really coming back. They returned to their houses in despair when the partisans answered, "Yes."

"How long?" sobbed an old woman.

Now and then a partisan would turn into his house, or his parents' house, say a quick hello, stroke a child's head, embrace a woman, and return to the column. Perhaps on his return all he would find would be smoking embers of a house and farm; perhaps he would find neither wife nor child. Yet everyone firmly believed that there would be reparation from this war. Tito himself had implanted the knowledge in the nation's heart that even for those who stayed at home there was no escaping the disaster—there was no escape from war. They saw with their own eyes that it was impossible to remain neutral, and that they had to choose one of two ways: either surrender or fight for freedom. But anyone who chose to serve the invader was in danger from the partisans. Most of the peasants thoroughly understood the matter and knew who the real enemy was. There were also traitors who chose to work for Nazi espionage. However, everyone knew that if the shadow of suspicion fell on a person, he would be sentenced to death. The reasoning was simple: better that one man should die, though he be innocent, than endanger the lives of many fighters. The partisans couldn't allow themselves to maintain prisons; a moving army couldn't keep prisoners. There was no choice but to release a suspect or find him guilty. Trials were hurried and public—with the people's participation. Sentences were immediately carried out, with a shot—to the temple, in order to spare the clothing of the executed person. The clothes were removed before the body had time to cool, and someone else acquired them. Prisoners of war were given the choice to serve with the partisans or be executed. Only recently, as the partisans gained strength and many Germans were captured, had prisoner exchanges begun. The German condition was three partisans for one German. The partisans were proud of this agreement, since it showed that one "wild beast" weighed as much as three partisans, but instances of exchange were actually rare. Prisoners on both sides were usually executed. Tito's influence was felt in this, too—he had trained his army for war without compromise, war with the aim of striking the enemy until it was destroyed. The partisans weren't in favor of confrontation. Their doctrine was to hit the weak and run from the strong. With these tactics, which weren't exactly noble, a handful managed to harass and sometimes even destroy large and well-equipped military units.

In one town, where parks and remains of a church bore witness to a once-thriving settlement, only the half-gutted or totally razed houses remained to stare at us through gaping windows. The enemy had apparently found them empty of their inhabitants, who had taken to the forest. We found a family—a man, wife, and daughter—in only one of the houses. They had fled from Dalmatia and like most Dalmatians, spoke several languages.

"What are you doing in this deserted town?" I asked.

"Enough! Enough! I can't anymore!" the woman sobbed. Apparently she was out of her mind.

We walked up yet another mountainside. The partisans promised that this was the last mountain. And indeed, that day we came to the Papuk Mountains.

In the afternoon we went down into a narrow valley. A path ran beside a stream. On either bank mountains rose in a "V"—for Victory—to a tremendous height. We encountered groups of partisans working to construct huts out of beams and boards. A pleasant fragrance was emitted by the trees as the saw cut into their soft flesh. The enemy had left only recently, and they were already setting up camps in place of the ones that had been burned to the ground. Life was returning to normal.

We reached a clearing at the heart of the valley. A few huts were already standing and others were in stages of construction. We were shown to the commander's room. There was a stove with a fire and it was comfortably warm. After the endless walk in the drizzle, it was good to warm ourselves and dry our clothes.

The commander arrived, a young officer with a pleasant bearing. He saluted in the partisan manner, didn't give us his name, and told us that he was among the first partisans to go into the forest in 1941, since which time he had been fighting his people's war. Many partisans crowded into the room to get a look at us and listen in wonder—for perhaps the thousandth time—to their commander's stories. Soon, he said, one of his men with a good command of English was due to arrive and we could talk to him to our heart's content.

After a few minutes a man of about forty-five came in. He spoke fluent English. It was obvious that he hadn't been born in any mountain village. He was a city man, a Viennese Jew who had once been a successful merchant. The Germans had murdered his wife; he escaped to Yugoslavia and was caught and sent to Jasnovac. He saw them kill thousands. Together with tens of thousands of refugees hoping to find sanctuary in this country, the Jews of Yugoslavia were herded together near the river. The place became a prison and slaughterhouse for them. Mercilessly and systematically they were annihilated: with hammer blows to the skull, by hanging, by shooting. There was a brick factory where the corpses were burned in the furnace. He escaped by jumping into the river and swimming underwater. And now he was here, with the partisans, waiting for the day he could leave. He was an educated man with a sense of humor, this Jew, and he was rich—he had a lot of money in an English bank. The partisans seemed to like him, but they also teased him. Joking, the captain asked why he loitered without going into battle.

"Because you need me to work the generator," the Jew answered bitingly.

"Not so, you've found a soft job," the commander threw at him. "All Jews run away from danger. Jews are afraid of death, that's why death comes to all of them. Of tens of thousands of Jews in Serbia, only a few were found who had escaped the Germans and joined us. A nation that doesn't know how to fight for its life hasn't the right to exist."

I was disturbed. A sharp pain pierced me. I knew that if there was some truth in what he said, it was twisted. Yet what could I say without revealing myself? I told them I had been in Palestine and saw Jewish fighters there and had even been in command of a Palestinian platoon whose men had fought well on the desert front. The captain mumbled something, but the Viennese recovered and mounted an unexpected attack. In a bitter voice, he declared: "It's easy to slander the Jews, but there's one thing you can't accuse them of: that they've ever shed innocent blood. But you, the strong ones, even the rebels, you can't ever wash your hands of spilt Jewish blood!" He left in a fury.

The next day we continued our march in bone-chilling rain. From earliest morning until night we climbed mountains whose peaks were wreathed in clouds, until we eventually went down into a valley. Not a bite of food passed our lips all that day.

We arrived at the Papuk headquarters very late at night. The regional commander, a lawyer from Zagreb, received us with Western courtesy, expressed his admiration at our having broken through the German ring, and paid deep attention as we related our plans. He knew of our arrival, he said, and had also received suitable instructions and, of course, would do all he could for us. In two or three days one of his officers was due to arrive, and together with him we would organize future operations. For the time being, we were to go up to the quarters of the British detachment in the area under his jurisdiction, where we could rest from our difficult journey.

And once again we climbed a steep mountain. I stumbled and fell scores of times on this ascent. My machine gun became filled with mud; it was lucky I didn't need it. Much later, we came to the temporary camp set up by the detachment—the permanent camp had been burned down by the Germans and one of the sergeants had fallen in the battle. We went into a hut: a small room with plank cots along the walls. The officer escorting us woke the commander, Captain Owen.

"Who the hell are you?" he asked. His voice was hoarse and his eyes were open in surprise above his long mustache.

"Let us get some sleep and we'll talk tomorrow," I answered.

Without further ado he suggested a place for us to lie down, and we sank down in our rumpled clothes. Drowsily, I was aware of someone pulling off my boots, and then I fell asleep.

In the morning we had a long conversation with Captain Owen. This Englishman seemed to be a decent person who was ready to help us as best as he could. Our appearance had caused a sensation. The three Englishmen in the delegation, who had been in that forest for over a year, were eager to hear from us what was going on in the world. They hadn't managed to establish bonds of friendship with the partisans, and dreamed of the day they would get out. They were bored stiff and longed for close contact with a woman. The belief was prevalent here, too, that should a stranger lay a hand on a woman he had no choice but—death. Each of them had his own craze and three had grown mighty mustaches. The captain asked if we had come across the Russian woman parachutist, who was, rumor had it, in the Casma region. I understood that he was referring to Hannah. Great was his amazement when I informed him that she was from Palestine, an officer in the RAF. "Wonderful, unbelievable!" he said with pride. From now on he would be able to boast to the partisans that the British team also had its female heroic fighters. That night another group parachuted in. This time they were Americans. The hut was too constricted to hold all of us. The three Englishmen and ourselves settled into another hut. The English were our age, merry fellows, who regarded their mission in partisan country as an interesting adventure. One of them, Fred, a commando officer, never stopped talking about his adventures in every country in the world. He had a rich imagination and a gift for expression and appeared to believe his own suspenseful tales. We laughed and thoroughly enjoyed his stories. We had a good time and almost became friends. The English knew nothing about events in Palestine. They shared our pain at the fate of European Jews, which they heard about from us for the first time. Peretz burst out with the story of the expulsion of the refugees trying illegally to enter Palestine on the "*Atlantic*": "British policemen beat our women and children who had been rescued from the Gestapo," he said.

"That's a lie!" yelled Fred. "You're a fifth columnist. No Britisher would ever do such a thing. You're a liar. I don't want to have anything to do with you!"

From that night on, the relationship between us became worse until we barely spoke to one another. We waited impatiently to be able to leave the place.

At long last, Colonel Ilia's man arrived. Our departure depended on him. Short, plump, unshaven, he wore dirty civilian clothes. He stretched out his hand: Major Stipa. He had come from a tour of the border zone. He drew a long "mauser" from his belt—it reached to his knees. I couldn't understand how he had managed to carry such a large weapon all that way. We spoke in French. He told us that he was commander of the local saboteur brigade, had been in the Spanish Civil War and in concentration camps in France and Germany, and had escaped and joined the ranks of the fighters. When it emerged that he knew Hungarian, the conversation became much livelier. He told us he had good connections with the Hungarian underground movement and had been working together with them for about six months. There were many people in the movement and they had bunkers and plenty of weapons. They were led by a lawyer. My heart pounded: maybe I had found the end of the thread leading to the Jewish underground! Before we left Palestine we had been informed that Moshe Schweiger (a Yugoslavian Jew, a lawyer by profession) had been appointed by the establishment in Palestine to head the Jewish defense movement in Hungary, and had constant contact with Tito. Stipa took upon himself the task of getting us over the border into Hungary. We arranged that in a few days we would set out. I was happy: the idle months hadn't gone by in vain.

That night Peretz arrived. We immediately tried to establish radio contact with Hannah, Reuven, and Yonah in order to suggest that they join us if they hadn't yet found a way to cross the border, but we weren't able to make contact. That same night Yonah turned up, glowing with enthusiasm: a group of Jews and Christians had arrived from Budapest. With them was a man who claimed he was a member of British Intelligence Services in Budapest and said he had a communiqué from the Hungarian prime minister to Churchill. It said that Hungary wanted to surrender to the Allied forces, and the man wanted to pass the exciting message through us. In the group, there were two Jews headed for Palestine and two Frenchmen, ex-prisoners of war. Two of the Jews and one Frenchman were prepared to go back with us and act as guides. They had excellent connections with seasoned smugglers. There was no end to our happiness: everything was turning out fine. Not only one way, but two opened before us.

Stipa told of plans to set up a partisan movement in southern Hungary. He assumed we had contact with Jewish organizations over the border and wanted to know what our strength was and how many people we could muster.

In the beginning I was enthusiastic and promised to recruit many Jews into the Hungarian partisan forces.

The next day I spoke to the area commander of the partisans about the recruitment of Jews into the partisan movement they wanted to set up in Hungary. I said that if there were many Jews in partisan brigades, they would be likely to lose the support of local people, since anti-Semitism was widespread in Hungary. The partisans couldn't operate without a civilian front, or without civilian support. On the other hand, it was possible to recruit thousands of Jewish fighters who could be a great force, since they would be fighting courageously, with a desire for revenge. This force should be given the opportunity. Therefore, I suggested moving all Jews wanting to fight against the Nazis into Yugoslavia, which was relatively free of anti-Semitism; here, a Jewish Brigade could operate. The commander admitted the logic of my suggestion, but he hadn't the authority to respond. He had to consider the matter.

Two days later, a messenger arrived to summon me to the commander. He welcomed me and said that the suggestion for the establishment of a Jewish Brigade was feasible and would be implemented if enough Jews were willing to go into battle.

I pressed his hand in heartfelt gratitude. I presumed that agreement had come from the High Command. There was no doubt that the form in which he had presented the question and his positive attitude had considerably influenced Marshal Tito's decision.

When I came to take leave of Fred and his group—the friends who had turned hostile—I asked them for a pack of ammunition. My supply was low. They refused. Not to give ammunition in partisan country was like refusing to share water in the desert.

On May 25 we departed. Our direction was northward—to

the border. Abba left us; his way led to the east, to Romania. That refined human being with the sensitive face, who loved to philosophize, ended up in Slovakia, where he died.

The three of us, Peretz, Yonah, and I, went by cart on the highway. Dense forest rose on both sides of the road. Signs of the recent battle were everywhere. It was possible to see how the partisans had blown up trees on both sides of the winding road, so that the giant trunks had fallen on the columns of the enemy as they passed. All crossings over the river had been blown up. Many tanks had been hit by well-laid mines. The husks of vehicles and tanks and the anonymous graves marked the invasion and retreat route of the enemy.

We came to Vocin. This had once been a real city. The people would flow from all corners of the land and even beyond to the church, in the belief that here barren women would become fruitful and the sick would find a cure for their disease. The city of Vocin was destroyed by a new system: a truck with a pump went through the streets spraying petrol on the wooden, thatch-roofed houses, and then they set fire to the entire city, at one strike. The inhabitants who didn't manage to flee, or who believed that the Germans wouldn't harm them, were shut in the holy church and went up in flames with the building. Those that tried to escape the flames were shot by machine guns in the attempt. Occupied Zagreb's radio version was different: it was the partisans who had destroyed Vocin and razed their thousand-year-old church to the ground.

We stood silent in front of the ruined church. A banner had been raised over the ruins: "Fascist Culture!" How many of our synagogues could tell a similar tale of destruction and killing with nobody to protest, even by raising a banner like this one. A trace of envy stole into my heart—this nation, settled on its own soil and fighting its war, could believe in tomorrow despite its many sacrifices. How great the difference between these freedom fighters, filled with belief in their victory, and the fighters in the ghettos and towns who fought like hunted animals, without any choice and without a chance of victory.

We traveled for two days to the partisan border village, Djakovac. There Major Stipa awaited us. He told us to muster our patience—it was impossible to move at the moment. We were forced to wait a few days. There was a large partisan force in the little village. In the meantime, we made ourselves at home in the office of the brigade. It was a good arrangement for one night. But early in the morning a girl, Marika, arrived, and began typing. She knew German and she and Peretz soon established friendly relations. She was educated, blonde, and lovely. Peretz discovered that she sang well, and we sang Dalmatian songs together.

The days passed and Stipa would relate all sorts of nonexistent difficulties that had arisen. It gradually became obvious to us that he had no intention of keeping his promise. We suspected he was acting this way on orders from above. Even when he said he was going to the border himself to prepare our crossing, he made no move. We were impatient and Stipa held on. We pushed him every day, arguments became frequent, and relations between us worsened. We were close to despair. Slowly we came to the decision to leave and join the second group, believing that the partisans were deliberately stymieing us. On June 6 we packed; as we stood waiting for the partisan and pack horse that were to accompany us, joyful shouts arose on all sides. We were soon surrounded by scores of partisans, all trying to shake our hands, dancing around us, and firing into the air. Finally we found out: the Allies had invaded France! All bitterness was forgotten. We knew that the commencement of a second front was decisive in bringing the war to an end. Stipa beamed with happiness. I took the opportunity to say to him, "Soon the Russian offensive will begin and our job is to help the Russians by marking targets for the bombers. If we don't stop the flow of German supplies to the Hungarian front, there will be many more Russian casualties and the whole offensive is likely to be endangered."

Stipa sank into thought for a moment. This reasoning was conclusive. "Good. Put on civilian clothes," he said. "We leave in half an hour."

I arranged with Peretz that I would leave with Stipa to check the situation on the border and examine the possibilities for our crossing. Perhaps I would also try to clarify the chances of smuggling Jews into the ranks of the Yugoslavian partisans.

We passed the guard posts on the edge of the partisan-held district. They were on the mountain peaks overlooking the Drava Plain. My heart jumped when my escort pointed to the churchspires in the distance: Hungary lay there!

At nightfall we went down to the plain. Beacon fires had been lit on the mountain peaks—it was a great day. We wanted to let everyone under the Nazi boot know that the British and American armies had invaded European soil. We saw a train explode in the distance and heard shots. Stipa smiled broadly: "That's the way to celebrate! Not like those fools this morning, wasting ammunition. I told them: You want to shoot? Shoot at the Germans tonight."

The night hummed with detachments of guards who had been confused by attacks on all sides. We crossed fields, taking care to remain in the shadows at all times. We checked every path, and by the way the crops had been flattened we knew which direction the guards had taken. At times we turned into a peasant's house. By knocking lightly, almost inaudibly, Stipa announced his arrival. His signals were recognized and the door would open and we would be received with drink, fat, bread, meat, and whatever else came to hand. We stayed at each house for only a few minutes. When we had received the required information, we would be on our way again. Toward morning we arrived at a very small village huddled on the shoulder of a large, splendid one. The big village had been inhabited by rich German landowners, who had lived there in safety until the partisans overran the plain. The Germans had then fled, and the German army had cleared Serbian villages in safe areas, settling the landowners there. The method of clearing the villages was simple: they had killed the Serbian villagers and replaced them with the "Volks-Deutsch." But the partisans had informed them: "Whoever dares enter a Serbian house or use Serbian property will have one end— death!" The Germans understood the message and settled in the yards of the houses, under the open sky, protected by the Nazis. In the little village, however, all the farmers were partisan supporters.

We went into one of the poorest houses. In a narrow room that also served as a kitchen and workroom lived Ferro the shoemaker, his wife, three daughters, and son. Ferro roused his family and they immediately made two of the family's three beds available to us. The family took on themselves the task of keeping guard over the house and its surroundings while we rested.

They woke us at noon. An enemy platoon was approaching. We leaped from our beds, dressed in a flash, and left the village. Stipa cursed: he didn't like the area. "There's no forest here, no mountain. They'll trap us like mice."

Under cover of the corn, we ran doubled over until we came to a wood. As we ran I saw how the partisan intelligence system worked. People came running from all sides. These were local people who didn't want to encounter a Ustaše or German platoon. We could see those who were running away from a distance of kilometers. They had seen our escape from the village behind us, and the news of the German approach spread like lightning. At first I thought that it might have been a false alarm. I expressed this possibility to Stipa, but he replied: "The partisans don't run without a reason." When we reached the woods we hid ourselves well and followed what was happening. Shots could already be heard. The enemy had arrived. Suddenly we discerned in the distance a force of some fifty men making its way directly to our village and surrounding it. "The bastards," fumed Stipa. "They got information about us. It's us they're looking for."

That was a hard day. We made our way through swamps, among piercing reeds, with water up to our necks. Suddenly there were shots right in front of us, and the barking of dogs testified that the Ustaše had determined to get the famous Major Stipa this time. They probably never dreamed that another good catch was hiding with him.

Standing in a swamp with water up to one's neck is not one of life's pleasures. Swarms of mosquitoes plagued us. Every movement caused panic among the birds and was likely to give away our hiding place. We had no choice but to be prey to the mosquitoes. When dusk fell and everything became silent, we emerged from the swamp devoid of strength. Stipa decided we must return to the mountain. We would certainly be caught if we didn't get away from there.

At a forced pace, we walked in the direction of the mountain. Close to our destination I was terrified by a shout. "Halt!" We stood frozen. I was certain the last minute of my life was at hand.

"Who are you?" the voice asked.

Stipa mumbled something.

"Documents and hands up!" came the command.

Like Stipa, I raised my hands. Then I saw the black figure of a Ustaše soldier pounce out of the darkness with his bayoneted rifle pointed at us. He drew closer and again called: "Documents!" Stipa lowered one hand and put it into his pocket. In a lightning movement I barely caught, he drew his revolver and fired. As the soldier was swaying and collapsing at the knees, Stipa cried, "There's your document!" We immediately began to run for our lives. We heard shots, shouts, and men swearing as they scrambled in the dark. We ran like madmen. I don't know how long we ran or how much ground we covered. I thought my heart would burst out of my chest. I was suffocating. I fell and got up, got up and fell, leaped ahead and carried on running behind Stipa's plump shadow until we reached dense forest. We lay for a few hours, exhausted, like dead men. When our strength returned, we rose and carried on until, at dawn, we arrived at the same guard post we had left thirty-six hours earlier.

After a short rest we set out in the direction of Djakovac. Yonah and Peretz were waiting for us impatiently, and dejectedly listened as we told of our failure. Stipa consoled us: "We'll wait for two days or so until they give up, and then we'll go out again and succeed."

I rose in the partisans' estimation when they heard Stipa's stories about our journey. Generally, the three members of Kibbutz Maagan were popular in northeastern Slovenia: while I was roaming around with Stipa in the border zone, Peretz and Yonah had been busy on an important project. They had actively participated in national celebrations over the opening of the second front. The nation was happy, since they saw the second front as a sure indication that the war would soon end. The peak of these celebrations had been the appearance of the two from Maagan. Peretz had stirred the people with a speech promising that the invading British army and air force would strike a victorious blow at the enemy, and he exhorted them to greater effort.

The day after my return, we were at a celebration in one of the villages. There had been a conference on "The Fighting Woman" and we were invited to the closing ceremony.

The party took place in the ruins of the school. On a decorated platform sat the celebrities, and the hall was filled from wall to wall. The speakers talked enthusiastically, encouraged by the cheers of the audience. They cheered for Soviet Russia, America, and England. We stood on the stage receiving their cheers with a salute. After the speeches, it was time for dancing. To the strains of a flute and an accordion, the crowd began to dance the "Kolo," the national dance that resembles our "Hora." There was an impressive circle. The girls wore red and gold embroidered blouses, and bright, tastefully embroidered scarves bound their hair. Only the women fighters of the brigades wore uniform. The men swayed and spun in a stormy circle, their weapons on their shoulders and the hand grenades in their belts swaying to the rhythm of the dance. When we, too, joined the dancers, the villagers' enthusiasm reached its peak. It is no mean thing to dance the Kolo with British officers. We knew stories of this event would be repeated in all the villages the following day.

The partisans would embellish them with their usual imaginativeness and would tell tales of wonder about our heroic deeds at the front.

The British officers working with the partisans weren't accustomed to fraternizing with them. They never came to sing or dance with the people and tell tales of war. Their attitude was usually cool and superior. I came to the conclusion that the partisans' warm reception of the British was largely because of our group.

On June 12 I left with Stipa. We followed the same road, but this time we didn't stop at any houses.

"God help the traitor!" Stipa cried. "I'll kill him with my own hands. One of those whose house we were in last time, gave us away, but I don't know yet who it was!"

Stipa trusted only Ferro, and we went to his house this time as well. Stipa began to tell us why.

"There are two kinds of people," he said, "those who help with all their hearts, and those who care only about themselves. Ferro is an innocent, good-hearted man. He, poorest of the poor, isn't afraid the Ustaše will rob him of his only pig. His small possessions aren't the center of his world. He is not like those who are coldly calculating. They'll serve you a meal if you stop at their houses, whether you're in partisan or Gestapo uniform. They'll also offer you a bed, but they'll never warn you if the enemy's approaching. Those serve both sides, serving the one and betraying the other by turn, because they don't know who will finally gain control. They are very dangerous and it's hard to expose them, unless by chance. And why do I trust Ferro? Let me tell you.

"After the Spanish war was over I escaped with many others to France, where we hoped to find refuge. But the French, who were afraid of their German neighbors, betrayed us: they imprisoned us in a camp as dangerous criminals. That was our reward. Even though we had fought there, in Spain, for France's future as well. The Fascists convinced us that the world had sold us out. When the Nazis invaded, the Vichy government offered us to the Germans on a platter. We were sent to the interior of Germany, where we worked in factories for the Nazi army. It was fate's joke that we, who had been the first to fight against the Fascists, were forced to produce cannons and tanks for fascism. The SS would stand behind us egging us on with their bayonets. Our food was a dry crust and some watery soup. My strength was failing. I saw no point in life. I've been a fighting soldier for ten years now. I've been face-to-face with death for ten years, and I'm not afraid of it. But there, in the hands of the Germans, I didn't want to die. I swore an oath that I would pay them back in full. I decided to get back here whatever happened.

"I didn't have the strength to run away, and I had no papers either. There was one way: to appear to be faithful to the fascist regime, and in that way to win the Nazis' confidence. All informers were freed from the camp. Those who were outstanding in service to the Nazis were even given permission to visit home.

"I didn't confide my intentions to a soul. My friends of Spanish days felt the change in me and thought: Stipa was a traitor too! But I didn't care. I had recognized the fact that it was no crime to cause the death of people who had surrendered to the Nazis and were waiting for miraculous rescue, meanwhile producing tanks for the Germans. Anyway, they would be killed, or die of hunger, sooner or later. They would contribute nothing to the war against the Nazis. Whereas I would get home, go into the mountains, and become a guerrilla fighter—we didn't know then that we would be called partisans. I began to inform against my comrades. I revealed petty crimes which by SS law were punishable by death. One had hidden a pencil. I informed on him, and he was executed after being cruelly tortured. I had no regrets. He had been a good man, that Guillermo, but his fighting spirit had left him. He was no good for anything anymore. I got a prize—I was appointed works manager, that is, a slave driver. After a month I was given leave to go home and see my family, whom I hadn't seen for several years. When I was given my papers, the SS sergeant parted from me with the injunction to have a good time and get back in good shape, because there was great need of men like me.

"I went home. I didn't confide in anyone in my village, not even my brother. They had forgotten me anyhow. I had aged in the ten years since they had seen me. There had even been rumors that I had been killed in Spain. I came to Ferro. In our youth, he had been a swineherd and I would go out to pasture our two cows, together with him. It wasn't pleasant to be a swineherd's friend, but I never took that into account. He would give me the beautiful stones he found without expecting anything in return. He was a good lad and we became friends. Meanwhile, he had also aged, set up a home, and become a shoemaker. To this day he's the poorest man in the village. Miracles don't happen to Croatian villagers: the poor man stays poor all his life and only the rich man sometimes gets richer. But Ferro was satisfied with his lot: he had three beautiful daughters and the apple of his eye—his young son.

"Ferro was the only one I told of what I planned. He opened his eyes wide and wondered: 'Do you plan to be a bandit in the forest?' I explained to him what fascism was, and the meaning of the Nazi conquest. I told him what they had done to the Spanish peasants and what they were likely to do to us as well.

"'I'm going into the forest and from there I'll fight against fascism!' I said to him.

"'And what will you eat?'

"'The peasants will support me; it's their war I'm fighting.'

"'And if they won't give?'

"'I'll take by force!'

"'Not good, not good.' He shook his head. 'People will see you as a forest bandit, an enemy.' I won't go into detail about those first days of the movement; how I attacked a German soldier in the middle of the village, knocking the life out of him with a stick to get his rifle; how I crouched in a cave during the winter, until my legs froze and haven't healed to this day; how Germans and fascists chased me with hounds. Nor will I tell you about the hardships of hunger. As the days passed, people gathered. Those came whose families had been murdered for resisting the confiscation of a cow or pig, or because they had been informed against. The bitter-hearted came. The peasants refused to support us at first, and we had to rob them to stay alive. We never took more than we needed, and we gave them notes they could cash after the liberation, but who believed in the value of such notes? Who believed we would be an army one day, and that we would chase the Germans out of the country? And we—did we ourselves believe in victory? Maybe all that beat within us was the spirit of vengeance. That's when Ferro appeared. In his village he said he was going to Hungary to make a living, but he came and joined us. I accepted him happily. Indeed, he wasn't young any more, and he had no war experience, but I knew he had heart and that he was committed to a war of liberation.

"We learned that a group of some thirty Germans had set up a camp in the forest, not far from our place. Apparently they didn't suspect that there were partisans in the vicinity. We decided to attack. When night came we surrounded the camp and opened fire. We didn't spare ammunition, being sure that plenty of booty would fall into our hands. The Germans defended themselves courageously, but were exposed to our fire. There were only seven of us, but they thought there were many more. After I had thrown a grenade into the middle of their camp they surrendered. We found eight dead, fourteen wounded, and six surrendering. One of ours was killed and one was wounded in the arm. We had to extract the bullet. My comrades got rid of the wounded and captured, while I operated on our wounded man. While I was still busy, I heard the sounds of a quarrel. I went over and saw four of our people standing facing Ferro, threatening him, and preparing to end the argument in the shortest way. They had fallen upon the dead and found money, rings, watches—a gold one on the officer—and gold teeth. The men craved these treasures, but Ferro was trying to prevent the desecration of the corpses.

"'We're freedom fighters, not robbers,' he asserted. 'Let the Germans come and find their casualties without uniforms and weapons, but with their gold rings and watches. Then even those swine will respect us.'

"I knew his family was near starvation and that one gold ring could break their hunger. But the partisans' good name was more important to Ferro. He showed the way to create a great, honorable movement.

"Ferro isn't in the forest anymore. He returned to his shoemakers' hammer and last. He's sick and the winter wreaked havoc on his body. He can't fight anymore, but he's a good man and he helps us more than anyone else. He acts as a contact for us. Since that day I've had perfect faith in him."

As the story ended we drew near Ferro's house. I looked at this village shoemaker, whose life story I had just been told. He had a simple, crude, unshaven face, appearing to be slightly backward; yet how much there was to be learned from him.

On July 13—again the 13th!—we crossed the Drava in a rowboat and, at long last, I stood on Hungarian soil. The owner of the boat said that our friends were already waiting for us. I tensely anticipated a meeting with Moshe Schweiger, whom I had known before immigrating to Palestine. We entered the village inn. Three people were sitting in the room. Not one of them was Moshe.

I listened to Stipa's conversation with the Hungarian partisans. There was something I didn't like about these people: they were too cultured. How could a man with lacquered nails be a par-

*Mission companion Hannah Szenes, who was executed
in prison in 1944.*

tisan leader? Yet this same polished man understood things. He presented us with a plan for blowing up the main bridge over the Drava.
The information he gave us about the guard roster and the bridge's
vulnerable points was relevant. The Hungarians had other sabotage
plans, too, and all seemed to be practical and of value. I found it necessary to take part in the discussion in order to justify my presence
and cover up the purpose I had come for, and together we planned
the operations in detail.

I asked them about travel conditions inside Hungary. It emerged
that, according to a new order, travel by train was allowed only with
a permit. One of them, a government clerk in the district comman-
dant's office, could easily obtain the required permits, and he would
pass them on to us within a few days.

When we left them, I expressed my fear to Stipa that something wasn't as it should be here. After our tremendous efforts to get this far, everything was suddenly going too smoothly! He calmed me: they were friends, his connection with them went a long way back. Had they been traitors, they could have turned him over to the Hungarian police a thousand times already. There was nothing to fear. What's more, they had agreed to bring four railway workers to the next meeting. These would undergo training in Yugoslavia, as saboteurs, and would be hostages to ensure our safety.

When I got back, I found Peretz alone. Yonah had lost patience and returned to join Hannah in Koprivnica. At the arranged time, when we were ready to set out to cross the border and begin operations in Hungary, John Eden turned up. He had made a special trip, coming from headquarters in the Papuk Mountains, to deliver important news.

"I know what the Jews of Hungary are going through," he said. "This suffering will come to an end with victory over the Nazis. We have to do everything we can to bring about a swift victory—that's our task. But if we do something which on the face of things will help the Jews, yet which will harm the war effort, it would be no service to the Jewish people."

"Rescuing the Jews most certainly can't be seen as harming the war effort," I replied.

"Understand," he explained, "that the political commissar of the high command of the sixth camp is afraid you're planning to encourage Jews to wander from Hungary to the partisan-held areas. The partisans are unable to support or protect them. When you get to Hungary you will be obliged to prevent this. You have to spread the rumor that the partisans kill Jews, and that's that."

The blood rushed to my head. I jumped up and shouted: "Bastards! Both you and the Commissar! It's a disgrace to the British army that a swine like you wears its uniform!"

"You'll stay behind," John shouted back at me, "and you'll take your words back at a court-martial!"

"I'll go," I answered, "and when I return I'll present myself for trial. But I'll repeat your words for the whole world to hear."

With restrained anger we loaded our belongings, the transmitter, and the ammunition onto a cart and left. We reached Ferro at midnight. We ate our fill and continued toward the river. The owner of the boat was there, but he advised us not to take our belongings. We climbed onto the opposite bank far from the village.

We entrusted our gear—the transmitter, the uniforms, and the weapons—to Ferro's keeping till further instructions, and got into the boat.

That was on June 19.

At that time, the Jews of Hungary were being expelled to death camps. But when we set foot on Hungarian soil we knew nothing of this.

Chapter 4

On the Rack

THREE FLOUR MILLS mounted on the decks of boats in the middle of the Drava drowned out the sound of our oars with the sound of their motors. It was a dark night and the riverbanks were indiscernible from mid-river. We were between two countries, two worlds. We were going toward a blind destiny, into darkness concealing and promising things unknown. I took out my miniature compass to check our direction. In doing so I also quieted my pounding heart: there was only one road, only one direction. Both compass and conscience indicated this. When the bow of the boat struck the reeds on the Hungarian bank, I whispered to Peretz: "*Alia iacta est!* The die is cast!"

We penetrated the forest of reeds, with sheepskin bundles on our shoulders to make us look like smugglers should we be caught. We moved along tortuous paths over the difficult terrain, sinking into the bog from time to time. Our guide, a smuggler and sailor who was the landlord of the tavern in which I had met the Hungarians, knew his way around. A local, he had been born here and here he would end his days. Nevertheless, he occasionally lost his way and led us along a confusion of paths and, despite the night chill, we worked up a sweat and took off our jackets. We walked like that in silence, four shadows in the blackness of the reeds. Suddenly a sharp voice sliced the silence: "Halt! Who goes there?" The three of us, Peretz, Stipa, and I, dropped to the ground, drawing our automatics as we did so. It wouldn't have been difficult to wipe out the Hungarian sentry, but we restrained ourselves. A shot would alert the guards all along the border and we would have no chance of crossing for weeks. We were also likely to endanger our Hungarian partisan comrades who were waiting for us at the tavern. Stipa whispered to the smuggler: "Arrange things with a bribe!" The smuggler slowly paced toward the guard and began talking. He came back at once and asked us for money. We breathed a sigh of relief. We went on our way encouraged.

With catlike tread, we passed through the gardens until we came to the tavern. The strips of light that came from inside showed that they were waiting for us. We whispered the password and went into a room lit by a Lux petrol lamp. The light dazzled me for a moment. When my eyes adjusted, I saw the three Hungarians but immediately noticed that the four who were to have come to take the saboteurs' course according to the agreement weren't there.

We introduced Peretz and sat at the table. We were given a hot meal and good wine. Stipa made a practical suggestion: we should finalize plans for blowing up the bridge at Barcs. This bridge was the key to German control over both banks of the Sava. The German division was now in southern Hungary as an occupation army. Should the partisans start any sort of action, the Germans would be able to transfer large forces across the heavy iron bridge and strike at them. The partisans were indeed planning an extensive operation: to take control of the plain and hold it for the harvest season. The year before, the partisans had prevented the transfer of wheat to the Germans by means of a simple stratagem: they had sabotaged all threshers in the area and the Germans hadn't the means of transport to move the wheat unthreshed. This year, the Germans had brought new threshing machines, which were being kept under strong military guard. To prevent famine and to ensure that the partisans in the mountains and the peasants in the villages had enough to eat, the partisans had to control the plain, even if only for the harvesting and threshing. By blowing up the bridge, the partisans would be opening the attack, and Tito's National Liberation Army would then have time to become entrenched in its positions.

The blowing up of the bridge was vital to us as well. In the first place, I believed such an operation would evoke a response among the population. Second, it was very important that partisan control should extend to the Hungarian border. We had had our own direct experience of the difficulty in traversing areas in German hands. The transfer of many Jews over the area between river and mountains while the border was in the hands of the Ustaše was an impossible mission.

A plan was presented: with the help of an officer of the guards at the bridge, who was a partisan supporter, partisans in Hungarian army uniforms would replace the guards on duty; the bridge would then be wired for immediate explosion, and the men could get away in time. My question regarding the absence of the men who were to join the saboteurs' course was left without an adequate answer. I made a sign to Peretz, who stepped outside with me for a second, and I told him the whole thing bothered me; after all, they were supposed to have been hostages for our safety.

"We've been waiting for this moment for three months," said Peretz. "If we don't go this time, who knows how many more months we'll have to wait. I'm impatient with all this waiting. One or the other: either we go on to Budapest, or we go home." He shook his head. "Who knows if we'll even find any Jews in Hungary."

He was right. We had to go. We couldn't be put off by unfounded suspicions.

We went back to the room and asked for documents. They were ready. We took them and parted from Stipa. We agreed on a secret code by means of which we would notify him when to transfer our transmitter, the uniforms, and weapons we had left with Ferro, and we went to the railway station. For a while we walked with the three Hungarians, talking about the state of the world. One of them, apparently impressed by what we said, asked: "If Stipa is a major, what are you? You must be generals!" We laughed, but again I had a twinge of suspicion. He had earlier complained bitterly that he couldn't live on his salary. Maybe he thought that there's a fair price to be had for people like us. When we arrived at the railway station, the lawyer offered to accompany us as far as the next town because here, in the border zone, strangers were suspect. If we were in his company we wouldn't arouse suspicion. I liked the idea: it was best that he be with us while we were taking our first steps in Hungary. We said good-bye to the other two and went into the station.

It was a strange feeling. The people waiting for the train, traveling as they pleased, were dreamlike to me. Women in colorful dresses, men in suits and coats. It was as if the partisan country, so nearby, did not exist. Peace and calm reigned here at the little station and, had it not been for the Hungarian sergeant with his medals proudly displayed on his chest, one could have thought they knew nothing of the war raging in the world.

I was very tired. On this of all days, when I had to be alert, I felt that my strength was running out. I knew, as I mounted the train, that if anything happened now, I would be unable to respond as I should. I sat on the bench listening to a festively dressed man complain bitterly to his neighbor about having been called up to the army at his age—fifty—but soon I fell fast asleep.

They woke me when we came to Pecs, the town where we were to wait a whole day. The train to Budapest left at midnight.

As we left the station, a man in a gray suit approached us. He had an unpleasant face and gray hair. He examined us closely. I knew he was a detective, apparently on the Pecs police force. He had certainly noticed that we were foreigners, but didn't find it necessary to follow us.

We took leave of our comrade. We didn't want him to know where we were headed. We arranged to meet him at a certain place in a week's time. He was to bring our suitcases there. We told him there were powerful and sensitive explosives in the suitcases, intended for an important act of sabotage. He must not dare to open the cases since they were booby-trapped and everything would blow up if the lid was raised. Should we find that we had no need of the stuff, we would send a telegram to the landlord of the inn saying that "Aunty is sick"—the signal that he was to come without the suitcases. We found a hotel in which to rest during the day. We didn't want to wander around the city to no purpose. We rested for a while and then went down to eat breakfast and read a newspaper.

Since leaving Italy we had received virtually no information about the status of the Jews in Hungary, regarding either changes in their legal status or even their survival. I opened the newspaper and saw that three of the four pages dealt with matters concerning the Jews. Articles reported how the Jews had been imprisoned in ghettos and what valuables had been found on them. The journalists referred to the Jews as the "yellow stars." It seemed they were forced to wear such a badge. If so, there were no Jews in this town—we hadn't seen anyone in the street wearing a yellow star. How could we find out where the ghetto was? How could we ask without arousing suspicion?

I looked through the window and saw a sign on a shop: "A. Rosenkranz, Grocer." The shop was closed. There was no doubt in my mind that this Rosenkranz was a Jew. I turned and addressed the proprietress of the cafe, a woman as round as a barrel, who read a newspaper through rimless spectacles as she munched on a roll.

"Do you know where that filthy Jew, Rosenkranz, is? He owes me a thousand pfenning. I want my money back before they hang him."

"Too late, sir, they've taken him already!" the fat woman replied, continuing to chew.

"I know, but where's their ghetto? Where have they been taken to?"

"I don't know, sir. They imprisoned them here in town, then they took them on trains. They say there's nothing to worry about—they won't be coming back."

"Terrible!" I shouted and Peretz gave me a startled look.

"I understand you, sir. A thousand pfenning is a lot of money. Maybe at the municipality you can claim it from the confiscated property, if you have proof," the woman consoled me, adding with a wicked flash from over the top of her half-spectacles: "You don't have much hope of getting Rosenkranz to testify."

I tried to put a smile on my lips.

So the Hungarian Jewish affair was finished and done with. There were no more Jews here. We were too late. It seemed unimaginable. Where were the one million Jews? There were no parents, brothers, friends—nothing. On trains, the woman had said. We knew very well where the trains took Jews. Was it feasible that only those who had been herded onto the death trains had no idea of Auschwitz-Birkenau? Didn't know, or didn't want to know? For had they known, it didn't seem possible that they would go to their deaths like that. Had a million Jews really stretched out their necks for the noose without resisting? And we had been so close, so long on the road trying to reach them! I lay on my bed and wept aloud. That day I would have been able to murder, to annihilate—but my anger was not directed at those who had led my people, my family, to their deaths. Those bastards I knew. I had expected nothing else from them. Rather, hatred swelled in my heart for those who had had it in their power to rescue them and had not done so, for those who had held us back from rescuing our people.

We lay unmoving without a sound for hours. Evening came. Night would soon fall. "What now?" asked Peretz finally.

"We'll go to Budapest! We must see with our own eyes. Maybe someone is left alive after all!"

Upon arrival we encountered crowds rushing about, porters' cries, packed carriages, and suitcases being carried back and forth under the glazed roof of the huge station. Facing the train that had just brought us to Budapest stood the Berlin-Bucharest express, ready to leave. Beautifully dressed people sat in the restaurant car having their evening meal.

With our heads spinning we alighted from our carriage and were swallowed into the crowd. After months of living in the silence of the forest we were not used to the turmoil of the city. We stepped along slowly, making a way for ourselves through the crowd streaming in the direction of the departing train. Police stood inspecting the people leaving the station. We saw them stop a man with a big suitcase to check him. For safety's sake, we handed our bag to the luggage depot and walked along empty handed. We passed through the gates without being stopped.

The big square in front of the station was filled with people, cars, and trams. Budapest received us with the clamor of a big city. It was morning and shops were beginning to open.

"It's still early to go in and ask after people," Peretz said. "We had better walk around a bit and have a look around."

I noticed that he was pale despite the healthy color we had acquired in the Yugoslavian forests. No doubt I was too. We were a little shabby in spite of the efforts we had made to appear like orderly citizens. We were also both in need of a shave.

We began to walk in the direction of one of the main streets. We didn't want to ask our way. I was beginning to find my own bearings in the city. With every step it seemed that a hatch opened onto a cell of memory. The human brain is a strange thing. Many years before, I had spent a few days in Budapest but had been unable to recall a single memory of how the city looked. At once everything I had seen and done during those five long-ago days was revived, as though I had left it only yesterday.

I took the lead: "We'll go and have breakfast at the restaurant next to the national theater. I remember the wonderful coffee I drank there!"

We walked confidently, as though familiar with every street. Suddenly I felt as if I had been struck with a powerful blow. A girl was coming toward me. She had black eyes, hair like charcoal, and she wore a blue coat. She walked along with hurried steps, her eyes darting from side to side in her pale face. On her chest was a fist-sized Star of David made of yellow cloth.

I gripped Peretz by the arm and restrained myself with all my strength from revealing my emotional reaction. Peretz also looked at her, but immediately glanced away. So there were still some Jews here. Not all had been expelled from Hungary. We were not too late.

It began to rain. We were confused. If we stayed outdoors without raincoats we would arouse suspicion. We decided to buy coats, shopping separately as a precaution. I went into the first store I found and chose a coat. I said my coat had been stolen on the train the night before. When I started to pay, they asked for my ration book. I was startled: I had never heard of any such thing. I recovered at once and said: "Listen, sir, I had no intention of buying anything, but then my coat was stolen and it's raining here. What can I do?"

"I can't sell you anything without the book—the fine's too high."

"Very well, I'll bring the book when I'm in town again next week and I'll leave you a deposit for the amount of the fine."

He accepted my suggestion and I went happily out, wearing my new coat. I walked around on my own. It was best not to be together. If anything happened only one of us would be in trouble. I saw many German officers and soldiers, and also SS men wearing the death's head on their caps—men whose function was the destruction of the Jews. I went to a restaurant and sat down. An SS officer entered. There were no vacant tables, so he came over to mine. He stood at attention and asked permission to share my table while giving the "Heil, Hitler" salute. I answered: "Heil, Hitler. Certainly!" He politely seated himself and began an innocuous conversation.

It was time to telephone Erzsebet Kurcz, whose name, address, and telephone number I had committed to memory. She was my contact with the Zionist underground. I went into the restaurant's telephone booth, dialed her number, and identified myself by the password: "This is the labor union speaking." This identification code had been arranged before we left Palestine through the illegal immigration institution in Istanbul, which had contact with the Zionist pioneer movement in Hungary. One of the diplomatic couriers was our go-between; for money and the promise of protection when the war ended, he carried money, letters, and information between our delegation in Istanbul and the rescue committee in Budapest. By the same method, the underground contact was extended also from Budapest to Czechoslovakia, Poland, and even as far as the camps. In this roundabout way we obtained the addresses and telephone numbers of people in the movement and passed the identification code on to the comrades in Hungary.

I asked about Moshe Schweiger. A few seconds passed in silence. I repeated my question. She answered in a choked voice: "I don't know what you want, sir. I don't know anyone by that name."

"That's impossible. You do know. Moshe, a lawyer, a Yugoslavian."

She did not respond.

"And Dr. Rezső Kasztner, don't you know him either?"

"No!" she answered and slammed down the receiver. Her "No" sounded like a cry of terror. She didn't trust me, apparently. Or maybe there was another reason for the denial?

I was confused. What would happen? Three contact points had been fixed at the time: one was Shmuel Springman, but when we were in Bari, in Italy, we learned that he had since arrived in Palestine. The second was Yoel Brand. However, when we were in the Papuk Mountains we received a message from Cairo: "Don't make any contact with Yoel Brand." And now the remaining one was denying us contact. I didn't despair, but I was worried. We have to get in touch with our people, I thought, but we'll take it slowly and think carefully because haste will only mislead us.

I continued to walk around the streets that were most certainly full of Hungarian and German detectives. I saw houses marked with the yellow Star of David—Jewish houses! This was a sprawling ghetto, which was hardly better than a concentrated one. It wouldn't be possible here to organize a defense and resistance movement along the lines of Warsaw; we would have to find other ways. It was difficult as yet to establish what these would be. Conditions had to be studied. Earlier, I had seen Jews in the street, but now, at noon, there was no trace of a Jew outside. Apparently the Jews were forbidden to be seen outside at certain hours, and there were most likely searches in the evening to catch those who might attempt to slip out of the special Jewish houses.

I knew Dr. Kasztner's address. I knew of his activities and it certainly would not be wise to go to his house, but there was no choice. I had to meet him urgently. Perhaps I would find him at home toward evening. And perhaps a detective whose suspicion I had aroused—a young man who should be at the front, now wandering around aimlessly, wearing civilian clothes—already was lying in wait for me. Suddenly I had an uneasy feeling that I was being followed. "One setback and already your nerves are on edge!" I said to myself, trying to overcome the suspicion. I started looking at the people passing by and couldn't find a single face that aroused suspicion. Something, however, was unsettling me but I couldn't discover what it was. I felt that the battle had begun.

I had to think with a clear head. I would visit Kasztner at four o'clock. If I was being followed, I must not go to Kasztner and, by doing so, reveal the connection between us. Yet I had to see him. Therefore, I had to make sure nobody was following me. If someone was behind me in this rain, then he was a detective and I would have to mislead him. He would certainly be happy to feel sure he could find me in a few hours and so could go into a bar and have a glass of wine.

I went to the ticket office of a cinema and bought a ticket for the three o'clock performance. A tall man came behind me and bought a ticket at the same price. Not surprisingly, he was given the seat next to mine. I went to the café adjoining the cinema and sat down for a cup of coffee. Was it only chance or was this proof that he was following me? I went out and continued strolling around until a taxi drew up. I jumped inside and gave the driver an address at random. Shortly after I halted the taxi, I got out, hopped on a tram, and then took a subway, returning finally to the cinema. When the lights went out I left, and after a few more rides I went to a restaurant for a meal. To the best of my knowledge nobody was following me.

At four o'clock I arrived at the elegant pension where Dr. Kasztner lived. I climbed the stairs and there was his wife coming toward me. I recognized her from my childhood when I used to visit her father's house, and I saw her several times after she had married Kasztner. My heart pounded. Would she recognize me? Many years had passed since last we met. I had a mustache now and was wearing a Hungarian hat with a feather in the band, in the manner of the nationalist-fascist students. I saw this meeting as a test to find out whether I could stand in front of my friends and acquaintances and pretend not to know them.

She looked at me without recognition. My confidence rose. The spacious waiting room was crowded with people—most wore the yellow Star of David on their chests—waiting for Dr. Kasztner. They stole glances at me. My appearance was arousing tension, even fear. Apparently I gave the impression of being a detective. So be it, I thought. Better they be afraid of me than suspicious.

After a quarter of an hour, Peretz turned up as planned. We ignored each other. His arrival heightened the tension in the room. A few people left, preferring to do without their consultation with Kasztner, though they had waited so long. One stood up and asked my name. I gave him the name listed on my documents, a common Hungarian name. The man entered Dr. Kasztner's room. I understood: he wanted me to go in and then get out of there. My presence there was a source of discomfort. As two people came out, Kasztner put his head around the door and called: "Mr. Varga, please!"

His face was furrowed with deep wrinkles; in his thinning hair there was a glint of gray. He was tired and harassed, but my heart rejoiced to see him alive and active.

I had known him for many years. I was four when my parents came to live in the same apartment house he lived in. He was eleven years older than I and that, maybe, is why he was so engraved in my memory. He was the symbol of maturity for me. When I reached high school, he had already finished his studies and was working as a cub reporter on the sports section of a newspaper. Years later he became known as a talented political correspondent. Leadership, talent, audacity, Jewish warmth, and Zionist enthusiasm were all combined in this man. He was head of a militant Zionist movement of intellectuals and students—"Barissia"—and I had been one of the leaders of the pioneer youth movement that had an ideological and organizational connection with the group. In him I found a man who could be relied on when in trouble. He had good connections in government circles and with his help we had managed to evade the heavy hand of the regime that so often plagued the members of youth movements. More than once we had been arrested and expelled from schools for illegal activities—the government didn't differentiate between revolutionaries and Jews wanting to emigrate as pioneers to Palestine. We had worked together for some years. I had thought we weren't only partners in action, but friends too.[7]

I stood, looked straight into his eyes, and with a strong handshake said: "Varga."

"Dr. Rajo Kasztner," he replied. "What can I do for you, sir?"

I had been needlessly apprehensive. If he didn't recognize me, my own mother probably wouldn't have either.

"I would like to speak to you in private," I answered.

"As you wish." He waved me into his room. When he had led me inside and closed the door, I asked: "Israel, don't you recognize me?"—purposely using his Hebrew name.

"You!" His face became pale and his eyes widened. "Yoel! Yoel! Are you mad? How did you get here?"

"It's a long story. In the meantime, invite in the fellow who calls himself Pinter, out there in the waiting room. That's Peretz Goldstein. You must remember him."

Kasztner was confused and shocked at our appearance. It would seem, therefore, that Hannah hadn't come before we did.

It wasn't a good time for a lengthy conversation. We spoke briefly. Kasztner told us that Jews from all over Hungary had been sent to the death camps. The fate of my parents and my sister was unknown. The fate of the Jews of Bucharest would be determined very soon. There was some large and daring plan by the rescue committee. Peretz's parents were imprisoned here, in a German camp, but they weren't in danger. He would elaborate on everything the next day. Now we would have to go and make our arrangements for the night.

We found rooms in a hotel and went out to scout the city. There were no signs that the nation was negatively disposed toward the Nazi invader. A noisy group of Gestapo officers was having a good time in the restaurant where we ate that night. The possibility of disapproval or even attack from the local population did not perturb them. I was so agitated that I was afraid to hold my glass in case it shattered between my fingers. I thought how easy it would be to strike the Gestapo, here, inside the city. Plans filled my head: if the partisan movement Ilia and Stipa spoke of were established, it would be possible to carry out espionage and sabotage operations of great importance. Even our dream didn't seem to be unrealistic: we would transfer Jews to Yugoslavia. We would organize small units, strike forces that would train with the partisans. They would come back here to carry out actions. We would obtain explosives by air. As I sat in the company of these Gestapo officers who came and went, drank and made merry, my reflections were cut short by the sudden awareness that these were mere daydreams without any basis in reality. After all, the days of all Hungarian Jewry were numbered. We had come to save, but the sands had run out; there was no time left to organize, to train, to prepare them, no time to arrange supplies, no time for anything. It seemed we were destined to be eyewitnesses to the annihilation of the remaining few. What was my duty now? Was I not meant to go with the transports in the death trains, to tell them while on the threshold of the gas chambers about Palestine, about Eretz Israel? Was I not needed by those who were made to dig their own graves, by those who did not run wild with spades, attacking the murderers, dying with honor as they took revenge? Perhaps that was the task today: to join the diggers, to turn the spades into swords, to set an example for the Jews who would come after me. Or maybe, if there were no more Jews in Hungary, the task was to fight the Germans, to hasten the end of the war for the sake of those still living in the death camps, for those still living in Romania, Sweden, France, Switzerland, England, America, and Palestine, those whose turn was yet to come if we didn't finish off the Nazis.

I drank another brandy and stood up to leave. I was tired and bewildered. Early next morning we would meet Kasztner and hear the details of what he had to tell us. Then we would know what our situation was and what we could expect.

I went to Kasztner as arranged. In a dark room, over a cup of strong coffee, the story unwound before me of the struggle waged by the few young and old comrades, the best of the people, against the Nazi might that had set out to destroy the remnants of Jewry. The movement activists, some known to me personally, knew that there was no relying on miracles, knew what lay in store for the Jewish population under Nazi conquest. They had gained much bitter experience from their work rescuing Jews from Poland. They were fully acquainted with the procedures for destruction: first, the yellow patch, then the ghetto, and finally the loading of the Jews into carriages intended for the transportation of cattle before the journey to the gas chambers. There were some who had escaped the executioner and had seen with their own eyes, felt on their own flesh, the reality of the extermination camps. Those who had managed to escape to Hungary had infected the movement activists with their sense of the danger that loomed. And they worked together, as one body, endangering their freedom and their lives, to extend a rescuing hand in the direction of Slovakia and Poland. Now that the murderers had reached Hungary as well, they vowed that this time it would not happen! Even before the Nazi invasion, they began massproducing false certificates of the kind issued to Aryans. These certificates testified that the special bureau in charge of racial purity confirmed that the holder was a pure Aryan and that his family was free of all trace of Jewish blood as far back as four generations. The movement's members urged Jews to equip themselves with such certificates and flooded the ghettos with them. But most of the Jews didn't believe the tales of atrocities and extermination camps and were unable to perceive that such things could happen to them. They were afraid to use false documents, Gentile documents.

When Hungary fell to the Germans and the annihilation of Hungarian Jewry became a concrete threat, the underground intensified its efforts to produce and distribute the forged documents, but the Jewish establishment, the Jewish Supreme Committee that was appointed by the Nazis, did everything to allay Jewish panic. They published bulletins fostering the illusion that no harm would befall the Jews. They believed that the Hungarian dictator, Admiral Horthy, would never allow "his Jews" to be hurt; they were loyal to Hungary and all they had to do was to obey instructions. They were to gather in the ghettos or the special houses as requested—and, for heaven's sake, to refrain from annoying the Germans and their partners. If Jews were being shoved into cattle trucks, hadn't it been promised to the Jewish Supreme Committee that they were only being transported to work and would not be sent beyond the borders of Hungary? The Jews believed this because they wanted to, and heard what they wanted to hear. But they did not believe what our comrades were shouting: "Run, escape, because death carriages, furnaces, gas chambers are waiting for you! Save your children, because they'll strip their skins to heal Nazis burned at the front! Save your daughters, because the Nazi hand is stretched out to assign some for death and some for prostitution to serve the army at the front!" This they did not believe. These were difficult things to listen to. A courageous girl—her name was Hannah Ganz—stole into the ghetto on the night of the expulsion, at risk to her life, with a suitcase full of forged certificates, saying: "Take these, save your lives!" And some shouted: "Get out, or we'll hand you over to the police!" They were afraid they would be sent to prison for forgery. They were afraid of prison—and they went to Majdanek. Hannah Ganz was one of many. She remained alive to tell her tale, to tell of her rescue. But many of the rescuers paid with their lives in their attempt to save those who didn't believe them. Once a rumor was spread, apparently from an official source, that there weren't enough huts where the Jews were going and anyone who came too late would be left without a roof over his head. And some pushed and shoved to be the first to be expelled, saying: "There can't be anything worse than the ghetto anywhere on earth."

The youth movement and rescue committee tried to smuggle Jews to Slovakia, which had already been "cleansed" of Jews and was not relatively safer than Hungary, or to Romania, where the Jews were as yet untouched and from where there were even hopes of going to Palestine. The code name for this operation was "Tour." I met comrades who had dedicated themselves to this operation— Kasztner, Rafi Friedl, Peretz Révész, Hansi Brand, and others. I saw these people endangering their own lives a dozen times a day. I saw them in their joy when a group managed to get across, and in their despair when Jews were caught and sent to death camps. Despite their awareness of what happened to Jews in the camps, they weren't sure that they had the right to take upon themselves the responsibility for another person's life. After each defeat, they were conscience-stricken: "Who knows, perhaps if we hadn't sent him, he might still be alive. . . ."

The extent of the rescue operation compared to the Holocaust that struck the Hungarian Jews was slight and success was meager. But the valor, self-sacrifice, resourcefulness, and dedication invested in it were stupendous. It was hopeless, apparently purposeless work to smuggle Jews from Poland to Slovakia, from Slovakia to Hungary, and from Hungary back to Slovakia or Romania, and for how long? And would the Nazis reach Romania or attack Slovakia a second time? Was there any point in carrying on? Even when an operation succeeded, there were sacrifices, and the most daring of the activists often paid with their lives. Nevertheless, they said: "We have to carry on. There's no other way!" However, another way had to be sought, and they wore themselves out until they found one. The ones who, in their innocence, thought they had found the way were Yoel Brand, Otto Komoly, Dr. Kasztner, Hansi Brand, Shmuel Springman, and Endre Biss. If it worked, they would be able to save Hungarian Jewry.

Kasztner's eyes burned with a flame of faith when he spoke of it. They made their suggestion to the Germans. It was simple: it wasn't worthwhile for the Germans to destroy the Hungarian Jews as well. It would merely be adding to their crimes in the eyes of other countries, and the Germans would have to bear the consequences. World Jewry and the Western powers would be prepared to sacrifice much in order to rescue the Jews, and Germany would profit from it. The suggestion was accepted in principle by the beasts of prey. The murderer of millions of Jews, Eichmann, expressed his opinion thus: "Valuable merchandise for valueless Jews"—a fitting style for the crazed Nazi.

At Eichmann's command, Yoel Brand was flown to Istanbul by the Germans in order to conduct negotiations with international bodies. The Germans wanted a ransom in the style of ancient days—gold for blood. Both the Nazis and Kasztner were waiting impatiently for Brand's return. Eichmann promised that for the time being they wouldn't destroy any Jews, but keep them "on ice," as he put it. The Germans were taking the matter seriously. As an indication of goodwill or a payment on account of the deal, 1,686 Jews had already been put aside in a special camp, ready for dispatch to Spain. Peretz's parents and some friends from the movement were among them. Actually, the Germans were permitting these Jews to emigrate to Palestine. Spain was designated as the country of destination of the transport because of a promise to the Grand Mufti, Haj Amin Al-Husseini, that the Germans would annihilate the Jews and give Palestine to the Arabs. Therefore, they were not able to send the Jews to Turkey or directly to Palestine, but to Spain, thus getting out of their obligation to the Mufti.

"We'll save hundreds of thousands!" Kasztner cried, with shining eyes.

I was shocked. I thought that in their great despair, these dear friends believed Churchill and Roosevelt when they declared that if the Germans harmed the Jews of Hungary, they would pay dearly for it. They were deluding themselves that the Allies were really ready to do everything they could to save them. Did they really believe that anyone, to save Jews, would impose sacrifices on themselves, would make efforts to rescue them? Did they believe that anyone would give one truck for the sake of a hundred Jewish lives? Did they really believe the Allies would supply equipment to the Germans to use against them? This was naïveté or, God forbid, unbalanced behavior. And the Germans, did they believe it? They spread the slander that the Jews were a great international power and that Stalin, Churchill, and Roosevelt were agents of international Jewry. Had they, in fact, begun to believe this themselves? Did they believe that American and Russian Jews had the power to force the Allied governments to enter into negotiations with the Germans in order to save their brethren from the Nazis, even to supply the Germans with weapons to use against them? If the Germans really believed this madness, something immense was happening: a quarter of a million Jews had not yet been expelled from Budapest, their fate hanging on the outcome of the negotiations. Tens, perhaps hundreds of thousands of Jews were in death camps. Perhaps there was truth in Eichmann's words to Kasztner that he was keeping these Jews alive for the exchange. If this was true, there was time to gain, and he who gained time gained life. Today, June 22, was the sixteenth day of the Allies' invasion of France and the first day of the great attack on the eastern front. Who knew what the coming days would bring? If it was at all possible to strengthen the Germans' belief that Jews could be traded, perhaps we would save a great many. It wasn't likely that the war would continue for more than a month. Germany would collapse with the fall of Paris. Nevertheless, it was best to be cautious. Those at the top should see the situation clearly; if they didn't, they were likely to fall victim to their own naïveté.

Kasztner looked at me as if he didn't understand my words. In fact, how could he understand that the Great Powers would not raise a finger to save many human lives? Would they really tell Brand, "What do we care? Let all the Hungarian Jews die"? After all, the Allies, in all their might, were able to destroy with one hand what they gave with the other.

I continued without mercy: "Even if the powers wanted to make the deal with Eichmann, they would be forced to drop it because of negative public opinion at home and on the battle front. The soldier at the front would rebel against providing military equipment to the enemy; mothers would raise a cry that their sons were likely to fall in battle as a result of it; factory workers wouldn't agree to produce equipment for the enemy; all of this 'only' for the sake of rescuing Jews. Furthermore, the supply of military equipment to the Germans is likely to cause a split between England and America on the one hand, and with Russia on the other. The Soviets would regard such a deed as a betrayal since, to this day, the Russians are carrying most of the load, and most of their losses are in the war against the Germans."

Kasztner deigned not to listen. He looked at me with the smile of an adult to a child, the smile I had known ever since I first showed him my efforts at writing when I was a boy. He rose and took a bundle of telegrams from a drawer.

"Negotiations proceeding. Signed Yoel Brand." "Chances good. Yoel Brand." "They're interested. Yoel Brand."

"Then why is he delaying his return?" I asked.

"A three-week delay," he mused aloud, "is no cause for worry. You can see for yourself that everything's going fine." He pointed at the telegrams.

"Don't you understand?" I flung at him. "Brand is not back because he's not able to come back! He's caught on to the real meaning of the situation: if he returns empty-handed, they'll begin the expulsion immediately. Had he come back three weeks ago, there wouldn't be a single Jew left in Budapest, and the gas chambers would be working to capacity by now. No, your friend Yoel Brand won't be coming back, and that's just as well. It's not a betrayal, but an act of wisdom. He'll keep sending telegrams until it becomes clear to him that there's nobody left to send them to, nobody left to receive them. We have to prepare ourselves for that moment. But till then, we must do whatever we can to keep alive the Germans' belief in this crazy mission of Brand's. We have to gain time!"

Kasztner suddenly gripped my hand and asked in a choked voice: "Tell me, will the Allies win this war?" His voice betrayed the doubt that was torturing him.

I looked at him. Now I understood. He thought it possible that the Germans might win and therefore had placed his hopes entirely on the Allies' agreement to send whatever Eichmann demanded— otherwise all was lost and the end was near. Whereas I, who believed the Allies would soon be victorious, knew they would send nothing in order to rescue Jews. Rather, I saw the point of negotiations continuing because this gained time and allowed us to hold on until victory.

"Without any doubt, and soon!" I answered. I hoped that if his belief in an Allied victory could be strengthened, he would understand things my way.

After that conversation, I met Peretz alone. He agreed with my assessment of the value of prolonged negotiations with the Germans. We concluded that we had to go along with them, though chances were slim that Eichmann and his cohorts would remain patient, or that they would not realize they were being misled from Istanbul. For the time being, it would be best not to let Kasztner and his comrades know about our dual mission. We wouldn't tell them we were officers in the British army. They weren't able to help us, and having that knowledge could complicate their situation. We decided to send a telegram to the innkeeper: "Aunty is sick." It would be dangerous for us to have the suitcases with the transmitter in our possession now.

We arranged a meeting with a few of the rescue activists. We chose to meet at the Jewish community building in the morning. Thousands of bewildered Jews crowded the building in search of advice and guidance.

We arrived on time and were shown into a side room. It emerged that Peretz Révész, whom we were to meet, would be a little late. One of the comrades had been arrested on the street with a case full of forged certificates; Peretz was following him to see where they were taking him and what could be done to rescue him.

I went out of the room for a moment and looked at the crowd. I wanted to eavesdrop and discover what was in their hearts. Suddenly I again had the feeling I was being followed. I saw two men clearing a path through the mass of people in the corridor. One was tall and muscular, the other short and fat with a small nose that didn't suit his build or face. Both wore the Yellow Star, but it seemed at odds with their confident bearing and composure. They wore no expression of despair or bewilderment that was characteristic of the Jews, and there was something cruel in their gaze. It was patently obvious that they were not Jewish.

I went back to the room and told Peretz we had better leave—and separately. We arranged to meet in an hour at a certain bar and, as usual, also made an alternative arrangement at another place and time. We went downstairs as if all were normal. I saw Hansi coming toward me and, without stopping, told her that I was being followed. I went into the street.

And I was not mistaken. The stocky one was behind me. I walked in the direction of the main street and saw him go over to an old man dressed in black, in the style of 1914, with a furled umbrella in his hand. The two walked a few paces together, after which the stocky one parted from the man with the umbrella, who now followed me. It was quite clear: they were following me in relays. Was I merely a suspect, or did they know about me? In any case, they wanted to keep track of my movements and find out whom I met. Troubling thoughts flitted through my mind. I was now being watched only by the old man. I decided to get rid of him. I went toward a tram stop. When the tram moved, I ran after it and jumped in. I thought that the old man certainly wouldn't be spry enough, but I was mistaken. He also jumped in and found a seat near the steps at the other end of the carriage, ready to jump off.

I rode for two stops and then alighted. I was opposite a subway station. I went down the steps and bought a ticket to the last stop. The train arrived and both of us, the old man and I, went in. I got out at the first stop. I took one step and halted. I stopped as though to tie my shoelace and saw that the old man had also left the train and was passing me. He lit a cigarette and climbed the stairs slowly in the direction of the only exit. In an instant I took a step backward and managed to get back into the train just before the door closed. The train moved. I saw the old man running toward the train, but the railway attendant forcibly stopped him. I almost burst out laughing.

At the next stop I left the train and, despite the danger, crossed the tracks and climbed onto the opposite platform to go back in the same direction I had come from. A railway attendant saw me and, with an admonishing finger, shouted: "Hey, that's forbidden!" But the train had pulled up and I was inside it, returning to the same stop where I had left the old man. I was certain he had alerted all the stations to come to his help, but he wouldn't think of standing and waiting for me right there of all places, just where I had evaded him.

I went up the street. I felt as free as a bird. For safety's sake I rode aimlessly around the outskirts of the city alternating trams and taxis, leaping onto trams that had already started and jumping out before they came to a halt. After an hour of such traveling, I went into a modest restaurant and sat down to eat. I reflected on this first engagement which, apparently, I had won. But who knows what had happened to Peretz.

A probing thought arose: how had they spotted us? It was certainly not by chance that I had drawn the detectives' attention. It was clear by now that they knew something. But from where? There could be only one possibility—betrayal. But who was the traitor? Stipa? Ferro? Or those "Hungarian" partisans? Did the enemy counterespionage in Zagreb know of our wish to cross into Hungary? How had they found out? The generals had known about it; Ilia knew. It was possible that one of them had let something slip—and walls have ears. It was possible that one of our Englishmen had spoken to an untrustworthy person. Perhaps it was John who had talked and tripped us up. But none of this explained the detectives' presence in the community building, dressed as Jews. One way or another, the police were after us. But what did they know? If Stipa was the traitor maybe he had handed the transmitter to the police. But if the traitor was one of the "Hungarian" partisans, perhaps they didn't know we were soldiers and thought we were partisans. And another question: for how long had they been on our heels?

I knew I should not return to Kasztner's house, but perhaps I would manage to meet him on his way home. As I drew near to his house I met Shalom Offenbach, one of Kasztner's people who had been sent by him to intercept and warn me. A search had been conducted in the pension where Kasztner lived. They were looking for two spies. The ring was tightening! I was to meet Kasztner the next morning at Elisheva (Erzsebet) Kurcz's apartment. She was the person who had denied contact with me on the telephone. Apart from us, two or three of the activists were to attend the meeting where we would weigh matters and put our heads together to work out what lay behind the new developments. I couldn't return to my hotel but it was dangerous now to wander around the city in search of a new place. I decided to spend the night on the train. I traveled to the city I had left to come here, a journey of a few hours. There I waited for the train that would take me back to Budapest. I rode back and forth all night, and the next day I arrived, tired and worn out, at the meeting place.

Elisheva received me warmly and apologized for the strange telephone conversation. Moshe Schweiger had been arrested as

Four volunteers from Kibbutz Maagan for missions in Europe (standing, left to right): Tibi Kedar, Palgi, Peretz Goldstein; (seated) Yonah Rosen.

soon as the Germans had entered Hungary. He was accused of planning an attempt on Hitler's life. She wasn't aware that the password was known to agents from Palestine, and hadn't understood how anybody that knew it could be ignorant of Moshe's arrest. She had great respect for Moshe, but thought that they had perhaps managed to get something out of him by torture. She never imagined that we had been given the password before Germany had invaded Hungary.

A few comrades were there already. Peretz Révész of the Young Maccabis, a gaunt young man who was meticulously dressed and combed, apologized with a pleasant laugh for knowing no Hebrew and little Hungarian, and requested that we speak German. Rafi Friedl—who introduced himself as Rafi Ish-Yaari, his Hebrew name—was a member of *Hashomer Hazair* (the Young Watchman).[8] Pil, today known as Moshe Alpen, was also a member of *Hashomer Hazair*. All three were from Slovakia. Zvi Goldfarb of Dror, and Eli S. of the Zionist Youth, were from Poland.

As we spoke there unfolded a marvelous web of daring, effective operations carried out by the pioneer youth movements, who worked together in complete cooperation and in a spirit of brotherhood, as underground fighters. They operated in three spheres: first, border crossings to smuggle Jews from countries where they were in immediate danger to countries where the danger was less at that particular time; second, the forging and distribution of documents, which required expertise, up-to-date information, and contact with the holder of the document, because the authorities constantly changed the document formats and the underground was obliged to track down their clients and issue new documents each time; third, the preparation of bunkers and weapons for the day when cunning would be of no use anymore and it would be necessary to fight and die with honor. The leaders of the pioneer and rescue activists were refugees, members of the movement who had escaped or been rescued from their countries of origin and had taken refuge in Hungary. There, they pledged themselves to prevent the Nazis from destroying the Jews of Hungary as well. Transylvanian and Hungarian members held secondary positions in the underground movement.

"We know the job," explained the leaders. "We're also more aware of the need for the operation. The Hungarian comrades know what has happened to Jews in other countries, but they haven't seen it for themselves. They still don't comprehend that it's possible to annihilate people, just like that! We didn't understand either till we saw it with our own eyes. Nobody can understand; it must be seen to be understood. It's impossible to grasp what the systematic annihilation of a people is."

They told of their method of operation, about their struggle, their bitter attempts to cross the Yugoslavian border. In their opinion, it was impossible to cross without encountering Nazi agents.

As we spoke, a young man and a tiny girl who looked about fifteen came in. Her hair was golden and she had blue eyes that beamed with innocence. The young man, dressed in railway worker's clothes, was skinny and gloomy, with unkempt hair and a beaked nose. His sharp features and the hat he wore lent him an un-Jewish look. They burst into the room crowing with joy. "Success!" cried the girl, Zippora, as she sank into an armchair, bursting into tears. Her story tumbled out.

"They arrested Yehudit and Mimish when they crossed the border. They took them to the Gestapo at Szeged. They tortured them for four days. Three days ago, when they were being moved from the lock-up to the Gestapo prison, they managed to escape. Mimish got away, but they caught Yehudit and vented their rage on her. She was black all over from the force of their blows. Her body was an open wound. They rubbed salt into her back, threw water on the floor and, with whips, they made her wipe the floor with her naked body, and when the floor dried they threw more water on it, and so on, endlessly.

"Poor Mimish! He ran around like a madman, beating his chest: 'Egoist!' he wailed. 'I looked after myself. If I had helped her, maybe she also would have been saved.' I knew that unless there was a miracle and Yehudit was rescued, Mimish was finished too. His nerves were completely shaken. And then, two days ago, Ivan Lida—a Serbian who had joined the Gestapo in Szeged—turned up. He whispered to her, 'Give me the address of your husband or friends. I'll rescue you. I have a plan. I'm a Tito partisan and I was sent to work in the Gestapo.' Yehudit believed him. They would get nothing out of her with their blows and their threats of death, but she told Ivan. She seized her last hope and gave him our address.

"His appearance placed us in a difficult situation. There was only one possibility—to trust him. The balance was in his favor—he hadn't turned Mimish in. But perhaps this was part of a satanic plan. Perhaps he was trying to uncover our whole operation. It was certain that we had to be careful, but we were convinced we had to try to save Yehudit. We couldn't leave her to her fate.

"Ivan wanted a girl to accompany him. I went with him. This was the plan: I was his young sister-in-law, and I was to come to tell him that his wife was sick and needed a maid. Perhaps someone would suggest that he take one of the prisoners, whereupon I would go to the cells with him to choose a girl and the one I would choose would be Yehudit.

"We separated when we reached Szeged. Ivan went to the Gestapo. When I arrived there, Ivan and his friends were eating supper. Ivan introduced me as his sister-in-law. They invited me to join them at their meal. I told Ivan about the trouble at home and said he had to find a maid to help his wife, my sister, while she was sick. One of the Gestapo men said to Ivan: 'Take one of those damn Jewesses; let her do some work before they turn her into sausages!' and he laughed delightedly.

"I laughed too, and said: 'Don't you worry, we'll know how to take care of her.' I sat down to eat and drink with them. Some of them came over and, pinching my cheek, said to Ivan: 'I wouldn't mind being your brother-in-law. Pity she's still so young,' and things like that.

"I lowered my eyes like a shy girl embarrassed by the compliments. Slightly tipsy, the men rose from the table. I told Ivan I would leave on the train that went in an hour's time. I was uneasy because my sister was very sick.

"We went to the cell accompanied by several of the Gestapo. The staff-sergeant yelled in a blood-curdling voice: 'Any filthy Jewess who wants to be a servant—stand up!'

"When my eyes became accustomed to the darkness in the cell, I was shocked. Women who seemed devoid of human form crouched on the floor. All bore fresh signs of beating on their faces. They tried to cover their nakedness with their hands and their tattered clothing. Their hair was wild and, in some cases, had been torn out by the roots, leaving raw patches. And their eyes . . . those eyes . . . they had a crazed flicker . . . green, blue, brown eyes, but without a glint of life. Dim eyes, following every move of those who entered, full of terror. . . . Jewish women who had reached the end of their lives, but they still breathed, the blood still flowed in their veins, for their hour hadn't come yet. They still were objects for the Nazis' sadistic abuse.

"Suddenly a light flashed on a pair of brown eyes. I almost cried out: 'Yehudit!' But Ivan, standing next to me, gripped my arm.

"Yehudit, of erect carriage, the high and confident forehead. Yehudit, beside whom I always felt small and weak, who had been the Student Union's delegate to the anti-fascist congress in Moscow, now huddled like a beaten puppy, her face unrecognizable under encrusted blood, wrapped in rags, her feet bare and swollen.

"She saw me, disbelieving her own eyes. She tried to stand up, but her strength failed. The sergeant asked: 'Is that one any good?'

"'Yes!' I answered in a strangled voice.

"'Perhaps we should look for another in better condition?'

"'Leave it.' Ivan intervened. 'They're all the same. That one looks pretty strong.' Then, kicking her: 'Up, pig, up!'

"I received a certificate from the Gestapo authorizing me to transfer the Jewess to a place of work. The trip went off without trouble."

"Where's she now?" Rafi asked.

"She's with Mimish, in good hands! When he saw her, he couldn't utter a sound. Then he suddenly said, 'Yehudit, I want us to have a child!'"

Kasztner came. He was depressed. The Germans were questioning the truth of the telegrams Yoel Brand was sending. He was also very worried about the search for us in his house and the hunt for us in the community building and the streets of the city.

We sat down to assess the situation. There were two possible assumptions: one, the Germans' faith in the negotiations was undermined. Their intelligence sources in Istanbul had informed them that Yoel Brand was getting nowhere. The other was that the Germans thought our coming to Budapest was connected to the negotiations being conducted in Istanbul. They were thinking: instead of trucks and military equipment, they've sent us spies and saboteurs.

Meanwhile, the train that was to take 1,686 Jews to Spain had been stopped;[9] anxiety over their fate was increasing. We knew that high officials in the Gestapo were opposed to the deal with the train and refused to free its passengers. Perhaps our presence had contributed to the stopping of the train? Perhaps its passengers would be sent to the death camps because of us? The Gestapo already had the ransom in hand—$200,000. They could now divide the loot and send the Jews to the furnace.

Kasztner suddenly made a shocking suggestion: Peretz and I were to present ourselves to Eichmann as emissaries of the Jewish Agency who had come to examine the truth of what Yoel Brand was saying. The proposal Brand had brought to Istanbul in the matter of "merchandise for blood" was arousing doubt in the West, and we had been sent to clarify Brand's story that he spoke for Eichmann and his superiors. Were the Germans, in fact, prepared to free Jews for trucks?

It would be superfluous to explain my amazement at these words.

"The Gestapo know of your presence here, after all. The damage has already been done," Kasztner continued, convincing us, or himself.

"Brand's mission in Istanbul has apparently run aground—you said so and perhaps you are right. But your appearance before Eichmann could give the matter new impetus. We'll gain time! Look," Kasztner continued with growing enthusiasm, "you could tell Eichmann that the first condition for convincing those who sent you that his intentions are serious and that he really intends to free Jews for trucks is that the rescue train must reach Spain! Later, if negotiations don't proceed, if the British aren't prepared to supply the goods, we'll offer them money! A lot of money! To the Gestapo! The Reich! To individuals in the Gestapo! We'll drag out discussions. We'll gain time and delay the expulsion, and until these tricks run out of steam, maybe, with God's mercy, Germany will be on the threshold of destruction. Perhaps Eichmann and partners will stop believing in Hitler's ability to hand them the Nazi Reich for a thousand years. If they start worrying about their personal future and that of their families, we'll have plenty to offer! We'll be able to buy many Jewish lives, very many, for the promise that when they are brought to judgment we'll defend them by virtue of their efforts to rescue Jews."

His own eloquence convinced him and his suggestion became a plan of operation in his mind. In growing agitation I listened to him. This was madness, if not worse. Perhaps there was some logic in this lunacy, but there were two things he didn't know: that we were soldiers, and that our appearance before Eichmann was as good as treachery. And also that another parachutist, Hannah, was due in Hungary any day. What would happen if she came and they picked up her tracks? How would her arrival tally with this crazy plan?

My face must have clearly expressed my doubts and speculations. Suddenly, Kasztner quietly said, "I informed them that you were coming."

Peretz and I leaped from our places as though stung, and our shouts came simultaneously. "What have you done?"

"Understand," he tried to explain, "all we knew, over the last day, was that you had been seen running down the street with detectives after you, and since then there was no trace of you. Hours went by without a sign from you, and I was sure you had been caught. It was the only thing I could do to save you. I thought if you had been caught by the Germans my request to Eichmann would be opportune, as your arrival would be explained and you wouldn't be treated as spies. And also, if you had been caught by the Hungarians—I knew the Germans would get you away from them."

It is difficult to describe what went on in my mind during those moments. Conflicting thoughts raced through my brain: the man had betrayed us! He was saving his skin at the price of our lives! But if he had wanted to save himself, he need not have been here, but in Istanbul or Jerusalem! Was there no way out but to play it according to his script? Had all these months of effort and risk been for nothing? This man had ruined all our plans and sealed our fate.

I felt like a hunted animal and saw no escape. What could be done? Should we kill him and run? Was the house surrounded already? Had he, knowingly or otherwise, led the Gestapo here? What would I gain by running? All possible harm had already been done to us. What was I to do? Save my own life? Was that what I had been sent for? Was it for this that I had parachuted into Yugoslavia and fought in its forests? No, obviously not. Nothing remained but to carry out the task Kasztner had set for me, whatever the reason for our being here. And I had to try and succeed at the assignment, even if the chances were one in a hundred.

So I would go to Eichmann and present myself as the Jewish Agency's emissary to the Third Reich, sent to further negotiations begun in Istanbul. But I would go alone. I had to release Peretz from this dreadful mission, apart from which it was hard to believe that the Gestapo would swallow the tale without thorough investigation. I had no way of knowing how I would withstand such an interrogation until I was actually interrogated. If both of us went and were both interrogated, we could not possibly achieve complete collaboration of our stories. A practiced interrogator would crack our testimony, which would likely seal our fate and that of the negotiations.

It was, therefore, best that Peretz should leave Hungary, either on the train to Spain or by stealing across the border into Romania. I would not know his whereabouts and even if they tortured me I could not reveal what I did not know. This was what we had been endlessly taught during training: act independently whenever possible and restrict contact with each other.

Peretz rebelled against my plan.

"How long, in your opinion, will it be possible for you to sell that tall story?" he asked.

"And what do you think? Do you imagine I'll go home and let you face the Germans? And if you don't come back? How will I live with myself?" I felt for him, but I spoke harshly. "There's no commander here, I know, and each of us is his own commander, but this is a situation we couldn't foresee. Therefore, today I'm taking over and I'm ordering you to go back and report. I take responsibility for that order—for life or death."

Peretz looked at me, not knowing how to react. His right eye twitched as it always did when he was about to say something biting, then he changed his mind, stood up, gripped my hand, and turned to the other Peretz, the Slovakian: "We'll go!"

It was arranged that I would live in Yoel Brand's apartment. Now that I would be his partner in the negotiations with the Germans, there was no need to obey the orders to avoid contact with him. On the contrary, it was in keeping with the new role to establish the connection with him.

I went with Hansi, Brand's wife, to their apartment at 40 Buyovsky Street, and we decided that she would pick me up the next day and take me to the Fountainhead Mountain's Majestic Hotel, headquarters of the Gestapo's special unit for the "Final Solution" under Eichmann's command.

I was very comfortable in the apartment. There was an excellent library and I was hungry for a good book to divert my mind for at least that night. After a hot bath, I opened the bar, chose a fine French cognac, and lay on the bed with a book by Steinbeck in my hand until sleep overcame me.

I was awakened by air raid sirens. The night was filled with their wails. The tenants of the building were in a panic. The crying of children and hysterical voices were heard. Instinctively, I jumped out of bed and began dressing, but at once changed my mind. I removed my shoes and burst out laughing: would I run from our own bombers? None of our bombs could possibly hit me. Fate wouldn't be that cruel. Apart from which, where would I run? It wasn't a good idea to go down to the shelter. The appearance of a stranger would arouse unwelcome attention. I wouldn't go down. I would lie quietly and watch the performance.

The wail of the sirens had barely subsided when the thunder of anti-aircraft guns was heard. The sky was lit from top to bottom—the searchlights of the city's defenders blended with the lights on small parachutes dropped by the bombers. We had called them Chanukah lights in the Western Desert, and we were very much afraid of them because they revealed us to the German pilots. Now I was happy. With mounting tension, I watched the planes; wave upon wave they came, but they withheld their bombs. Anxiously I waited. Would they stand up to the anti-aircraft fire? The sky was like a vast network of exploding lights. I had a feeling for an instant that I was witnessing a surrealistic competition. Or was I dreaming? But this was a game of life and death. I restrained myself from yelling into this satanic symphony: "Drop them! Bomb away! Hit the target!" I no longer felt alone. It was as if an unseen bond stretched between the pilots and myself. What did they know about me, up there? They didn't know that I, together with another quarter of a million Jews, awaited them and even if we were harmed, we would be happy and bless them with our last breath.

Suddenly I heard a piercing scream which I recognized from the Western Desert. The dance was on and I rejoiced to my innermost depths. The air filled with the shriek of bombs followed by explosions that went on endlessly. Thunder rolled against thunder and a sea of flame engulfed the city. This was carpet bombing. Meter by meter, the southern sector of the city was systematically being bombed.

Despite the raid, I fell asleep. I was awakened by the shock wave that flung me out of bed and I saw the shutters ripped, the windows shattered, the furniture and the bed in which I had been sleeping hurled from their places. The walls were cracked. It had been a close hit!

"Never mind," I said to myself. "Sleep anyhow."

Now it was difficult to fall asleep. Toward morning the raid came to an end and people came out of the shelters, pensive and silent.

* * * * *

Hansi came to fetch me at ten o'clock. We hurried to the Fountainhead Mountain, which for some reason the Gestapo command had fixed on for their headquarters. Perhaps it was because of the name of the mountain, an ancient name that bore witness to the fact that the Germans weren't newcomers to Hungary, but had settled there long ago, the word being a nickname for a German. Or maybe it was because it was far from the town, or because of the fabulous villas and grand hotels there—a resort for the world's wealthy. The higher we climbed, the more the mountain revealed itself to us in all its grandeur. We heard air raid sirens again in the distance. American bombers were now finishing off what their British comrades had begun the night before.

We came to the Majestic Hotel. The sirens were still wailing when, glinting in the sunlight, the "Liberators," the "Flying Fortresses," appeared with their escort of fighter planes. The car came to a halt outside the building and we went inside, to the sound of an orchestra of anti-aircraft guns and explosions.

It turned out that Eichmann wasn't in Budapest. We asked for the efficient Colonel Klages. We found his deputy, Sievert by name, a tall, thin man with a serious expression, like a diplomat, and very elegantly dressed. He received us politely. He gave me a manly handshake and said, "Pleased to meet you." Klages had phoned to say he would be ten minutes late, but because of the air raid it was possible that he wouldn't come at all, and therefore he was substituting. First he asked the purpose of my coming to Budapest.

I was very quiet, as though I weren't party to what was going on around me, as though I were here as an observer, invisible.

"I'll be brief," I began. "You sent a man by the name of Yoel Brand to Istanbul with a certain proposal. I heard of your demands and promises from him. Pardon me for being so outspoken—we don't have much faith in you. They want to know what guarantee we have that after we meet your demands, you'll keep your part of the bargain. What guarantee do we have that after we send you the vast amounts of equipment, which we find so hard to acquire and to give up, you'll free the Jews? It's in order to clarify and ascertain this that I've been sent."

"Fine," he said, "and what do you wish?"

"You have to do something to prove that you plan to stand by your undertaking. That's the only way the road will remain open for negotiations."

"That's clear," he answered, "and what is it we must do?"

"Send the convoy to Spain."

"Where is your friend?" he asked suddenly. "Why hasn't he come here as well?"

"I don't know. He disappeared. It can be assumed that he's been arrested by one of the German or Hungarian security branches. I would like to request that you inquire into the matter."

A slight smile appeared on his face.

"You have to tell us how you came."

"As you wish," I answered.

"I'll pass on what you said to my superiors. In the meantime, kindly tell one of my officers all the details of your journey. I'll arrange a time for a meeting with the Colonel and let you know, via Mrs. Brand, and till then, look around and you'll verify that we do everything seriously."

He lifted the telephone receiver and asked for Mr. Krauss, and I reflected on how I should interpret his last words—as an encouragement or as a threat?

"Krauss!" He introduced himself on entering the room, extending his hand to me with a forced smile. "May I ask you, sir, to be so kind as to come into my office for a few minutes?"

"Of course, most willingly," I said, extending my hand to Sievert.

We went into the corridor, which was thronged with SS and Gestapo men. Everything was so strange, so unreal. I was strolling around the Gestapo building like a guest, nodding my head in response to the salutes of the SS who, apparently, thought I was one of them.

From the distant city, the sounds of explosions could still be heard.

A gray-haired man came out of one of the offices supported by two soldiers. Red weals across his face showed that he had been whipped with a thin cane. On his chest he wore the yellow Jewish patch—a fist-sized Star of David. The man, who was weeping bitterly, stumbled, and the soldiers dragged him like a sack.

I passed him without blinking an eye. Krauss regarded me with a sidelong look. It was possible that he had ordered the man beaten and then brought out in order to prepare me for the conversation with him.

We came to Krauss's room. He opened the door, inviting me to enter. I sank into a deep easy chair. He offered me a cigarette, apologizing that he was unable to give me a "Camel." I smiled at his joke and lit the cigarette, then waited tensely for his questions. This was the man to be wary of. If I can allay his suspicions, I thought, I will have won.

He asked me to tell him how I had arrived in Budapest.

I was ready to answer with a combination of lies and truth. They certainly had a good enough intelligence service, and there was nothing to be gained by piling on words without any basis.

"A week ago," I began, "I left Tel Aviv by car for Cairo. Everything was ready for me there—a uniform, British army papers, and Hungarian papers too. The British Intelligence officer who was to go with me to Yugoslavia"—I gave a fictitious name—"was paid two thousand pounds for his services by the Hagana contact man. He helped us dress in army uniforms at his own apartment, and explained elementary things that should be known to anyone in uniform. That same night we took off in a plane carrying supplies to Yugoslavia. In the plane they strapped parachutes onto us and told us we didn't have to do a thing except go through the hatch—the chute would open on its own. The main thing was not to get into a panic, not to make any frantic movements, and we would get to the ground safely. When the sign to jump was given, I didn't have the courage. An officer standing behind me gave me a push and I jumped. The chute opened and after a while my feet touched ground. Not far away I saw my friend and Bill [the imaginary British officer] descending as I had. Many partisans gathered around us and fell upon the bundles that had also fallen when the plane circled a second time. Threatening them with his submachine gun, Bill prevented them from opening the containers that had fallen from the sky. We stayed where we were to guard our property until a partisan commander arrived"—here I again used a fictitious name—"and we began to negotiate with him to take us over the border into Hungary. At first he refused, saying that the border was well guarded, but when we offered him twenty bottles of genuine Scotch whiskey and a gold watch, he agreed. But we had to wait two days for one of his men, who took us into Hungary. We also had to change our papers, because it turned out that the ones we had received in Cairo weren't in order any more."

"What's the job of that British officer who received the money?"

"I don't know."

"Could he have done it all on his own? His superiors in Cairo must have received part of the payment. Who are they?"

Could he have believed the story? If so—he wanted the names of the British officers open to bribery. Therefore he had to be given food for thought.

"I don't know. I only remember that one brigadier came out of the Semiramis Hotel, the British High Command's residence in Cairo, and he came over to our car, shook hands, and wished us luck."

"What did he look like?"

I gave him a detailed description. I said that his right thumb had had one joint amputated.

Officer Krauss was very satisfied, and so was I. I imagined Nazi agents searching for the brigadier with the amputated thumb. I hoped they wouldn't find anyone like that. Krauss never doubted for a moment that brigadiers could be bribed. Was this a sign that such deeds weren't rare in the German army?

"And finally, one question," he said with a broad smile. "I fully appreciate your courage in coming to Budapest and finding us. But didn't you stop to consider that we can send you to a place you'll never return from?" The last few words were said very sharply and his face took on a new expression that suited him far better than his smile.

"I know, but why should you do that? I've come to you on business. What would you gain by imprisoning me? Are you short of Jews to exterminate? However, if you harm me, the deal is off."

I looked straight into his eyes. It was best to make things clear. He, apparently, sensed he had gone too far and his smile immediately returned. He said: "Of course! I merely wanted to see how you would react."

"Now I have a request," I said. "Provide me with a document stating that I'm in the Gestapo service. It wouldn't be very pleasant if I was arrested, even by mistake!"

"Come here next Monday and you'll get a document. Meanwhile, note the number 59187, which is our bureau's secret telephone number. If you get into any trouble, don't answer any questions; just demand that they ask about you at this number."

He accompanied me to the door and asked if my car was waiting. If not, he would put his car at my disposal.

"The air raid's still going on," I said. "I can't go back to the city now. I'll get my fill of the mountain air."

"I understand. It's beautiful up here! In spring there's nothing nicer than to hike around this area."

I went down the steps and left through the gate. The guard gave the "Heil, Hitler" salute, to which I responded with a wave of the hand, stunned at the ease with which I had been able to get out of that building.

I began walking along the slope of the mountain. Suddenly I stopped. Where was Hansi Brand? In my elation at having come away from the Gestapo and at having apparently succeeded in deceiving them, I had forgotten that she had brought me. Why hadn't she waited for me? Had she believed that I wouldn't come out of there? God forbid! There must be a logical explanation. When we would meet it would all be made clear, I was sure.

Far from the mountain, the ground fire was continuing and thousands of shells were being fired in order to drive the bombers away from their target—the industrial zone. And here on the mountain, a warm, serene, and smiling sun. It was Saturday and lovers filled the grand promenades. I continued walking and came down from the mountain on foot. People were going about their business in the city. The streets were quiet. Of fourteen million inhabitants, one million had been uprooted. A million human beings had been torn from their homes and had vanished, and nobody asked where or why, as if something just and correct had been done. By accepting it, this nation made itself a partner to the crime.

On Sunday, Shalom Offenbach and his family came to the apartment. He was the man in charge of finance on the committee conducting the negotiations with the Germans, and for this reason he had been permitted to remove the yellow badge and was also promised a license allowing him not to live in a Jewish house. However, he hadn't received his license yet. No, he hadn't seen Hansi for two days. Nor Kasztner. They had begun asking too many questions in the house where he had been hiding with his family, so he had escaped to this apartment. I got some Hungarian money from Offenbach and handed the gold over to him; it had been weighing me down all the time.

A consultation had been arranged at the flat that afternoon, among the "Comrades"—the leaders of the Pioneer-Zionist underground. But the Jews were suddenly forbidden to leave their houses. At the same time the Gestapo had demanded that preparations for the convoy to Spain be completed since it was due to leave at any moment.

One announcement followed the other. Offenbach came in a panic with the news: detectives had again raided the pension where Kasztner lived. This time they stated clearly what they were seeking—two young spies.

From the confusion it began to emerge that the ones searching for us were Hungarian detectives, unaccompanied by German Gestapo. According to Kasztner, the Hungarians didn't know anything about the cooperation between the Gestapo and the Jewish Rescue Committee. They had once arrested and severely tortured Hansi in an attempt to get her to say, without success, what her husband was doing in Istanbul and what their connection was with the Germans. It was Colonel Klages who had taken Hansi out of the hands of the Hungarian detectives. The Hungarians sensed that the Germans were about to make some profit out of the Jews. All of a sudden the Hungarians discovered that the Jews belonged to them. For extermination, they had no problem handing them over to the Germans, but business was another matter—here they felt it was their due, for these were their own Hungarian Jews.

The meeting never took place. Most of those who were to attend disappeared as if the earth had swallowed them. It was reported to me that there was a bustle of activity around the camp holding the Jews who were due to go to Spain. The members of the movement were sneaking more and more of their comrades onto the convoy, especially those who looked particularly Jewish, or whose fluent Hungarian had a Yiddish inflection. The rumor that the convoy was really about to set out had apparently spread far and wide. Not merely a few Jews bribed the Gestapo soldiers guarding the camp to let them inside. The number of Jews in the camp grew. Was there a connection between my visit to the Majestic Hotel and the train's impending departure? I hoped there was. At least there would be some point to what I had done. The main thing was that the train should be on its way!

Peretz appeared in the evening. I was astonished to see him. We both knew we must not meet. They were searching for both of us, and if one was caught he would bring disaster upon the other. He was in despair. The fellow in whose house he was staying had disappeared; it seemed he had either been arrested or had left Hungary. He was afraid to stay on in that apartment and hadn't been in contact with any of the comrades. He didn't dare go to a hotel, either, because they were searching all the hotels for us. He had been left without a roof over his head.

It was obvious that he couldn't stay with me. I asked Shalom to help him. Just then a young woman named Margit came in. Margit was a Christian who, being divorced, lived alone in a small apartment. She was in a position to have a handsome lad like Peretz in her house. At worst, her neighbors would talk about her, but they would never suspect her of harboring a Jew.

Margit agreed. I didn't want to know what her surname was, nor where she lived. I had a feeling I would yet be interrogated in connection with Peretz and, as the saying goes, you can't reveal what you don't know.

On Monday I was about to go up to Gestapo headquarters when the city was again bombed. The industrial centers were once more the main target, and many leaflets were dropped warning the citizens of Budapest not to assist in the murder of the Jews. It was explicitly stated that the Hungarian nation was responsible for Jewish lives and would pay for innocent blood spilled.

The sirens had caught me in the street and I had no choice but to go down to a shelter where I saw how the people reacted to the leaflets. All agreed that the Americans and the British were working for the good of international Jewry. "It's because of the Jews that we're suffering! If it weren't for the Jews they wouldn't be bombing us." "The Jews should be concentrated in the industrial centers; let them bomb the Jews and not us!" If there were some who thought it would be better to leave the Jews alone to avoid being bombed at all, I didn't hear them. The man in the street had tasted Jewish blood and wanted more. They had been promised there would be no more Jews, and they rejoiced to see, with their own eyes, that the promise was being kept.

The air raid continued until the afternoon, and there was no point in going up to the mountain. I bought myself a new suit and went back to the apartment. I had decided to alter my face and manner of walking. I shaved off my mustache and rearranged my hairstyle. I had been wearing worn, dark, modest clothes. Now I bought an elegant blue suit. I practiced walking with movements that were foreign to me and that were likely to change the way I looked on the street.

The doorbell rang at four o'clock. The same tall man I had seen in the community building was standing at the door. With him was another man—young and blond, with a bandaged hand. They begged my pardon and showed me their Hungarian secret police identification papers.

I licked my dry lips and asked in a hoarse voice: "What can I do for you, gentlemen?" It was dark in the long narrow passageway. They didn't recognize me.

"Could you give us some information, please? We're looking for a young man who, we believe, came into this building."

"I'm sorry, no young man lives here apart from myself. There must be some mistake."

"The young man's tracks led straight to this building actually. We assume he's hiding somewhere and we're searching the building. If you object, we can get a warrant in a quarter of an hour."

"On the contrary, search if you wish," I answered.

I was amazed—would I get out of this mess by such childish means? He was talking to me and he didn't even recognize me. One of them went inside the room, with me following. The other remained beside the door, now closed. Just then the bell rang again. I wanted to open the door, but the other man quickly said: "Halt! I'll open!"

When the door opened I was stunned. All was lost! Margit stood smiling on the doorstep.

"Please come in, madame," my "visitor" said, playing the host.

"Please sit down," I said. "I'll be free in a moment."

She caught on at once that these were detectives and looked at me in shocked confusion. I cursed her silently—she had chosen a fine time to visit. If they got me now, she would also be arrested for interrogation and they would find Peretz at her house. The whole lot at once.

The tall man carried on with his tour of the rooms, with me behind him. I tried to get to my jacket with the revolver in it. I begged his pardon for not being properly dressed and put on the jacket. The revolver was there in the pocket, now under my hand.

When he completed his search, he apologized for disturbing me, but at that moment I must have made some revealing movement.

"Hell!" he shouted. "It's you!"

I pulled out the revolver, but he was more agile and dealt me a blow to the jaw. I collapsed and in a second was handcuffed.

"Where's the mustache? Where's your friend?" I heard him

scream, and with each word another blow landed. "You thought you would get away, you bastard!"

My mouth bloody, I mumbled with difficulty: "Stop! You'll pay for this! Phone the Gestapo immediately! I'm under Gestapo protection!"

"Don't worry, friend," he mocked. "You'll get to the Gestapo in good time."

With blows and threats with the revolver, they got me outside. Three cars stood at the gate and the building was surrounded by men. I was put into one of the cars.

The car dashed through the city, passing the river, and came to a halt in front of a two-story building. One iron gate opened and then another and I was shoved inside. I decided not to answer any questions. First I would try to find out what they knew about me.

Chapter 5

From Prison to Prison

✴ I HAD A WEIRD FEELING when the gate shut. I had often tried to imagine how I would feel if I was ever arrested. What would become of me in a prison? I thought despair and fear would overcome me, that I would be paralyzed, incapable of thought.

But it was not like that. I felt only the tension preceding some fateful turn of events. I had had such a feeling when going by jeep from Mersa-Matruh to Salum, when I had first arrived in the Western Desert. A German fighter plane had dived over the road, spraying us with machine gun fire. We had jumped from the jeep and scattered. I was without panic and all I felt was the sensation of an electric current through my body; a slow, light current that was trying to break out through my fingertips.

There was a sort of anticipation, almost curiosity as to what would happen, but it was as though it had nothing to do with me. Of course, I knew I would have to draw on all my strength and alertness to withstand the experience. I had to discover whether they had explicit information or were groping in the dark, and not fall into any trap when interrogated.

They pushed me into a basement. I passed along a dimly lit corridor. On either side of me were iron doors, each with a bolted hatch. At the end of the corridor was an open door, which I was made to enter. This was the guard room. A table with a cheap radio on it stood in the corner, and facing it was a big closet. Soldiers were stretched out on some beds, snoring lustily.

A sergeant seated at the table jumped to attention: "At your command, lieutenant, sir!"

"Take this man, search him properly, and give him a nice room! Look after him like the apple of your eye. This is a bird that's likely to spread his wings!"

"What's he, a Jew?"

"The devil knows!" He screamed. "Dog, are you a Jew?"

"A Jew!" I replied.

"Say, 'A Jew, sir,' and if you don't—I'll smash your skull! And where's your star?"

I did not answer.

"Are you dumb?" he raged, flushed with anger.

The snoring soldiers stirred, sat up on their beds, and watched the show.

"I'll teach you how to speak! You'll hang by your tongue!"

"What's he done?" the sergeant inquired.

"Keep a sharp eye on him. A British paratrooper! He came with a transmitter. Double the guard. These bastards have friends outside—they'll try to free him."

One of the soldiers jumped up from the bed, shouting: "Swine! You direct the bombers! You killed my daughter!" He raised his hand, but the officer stopped him.

"You can leave that job to us. And as for your friends," he said to me, "you won't miss them for long. You'll all be together before the night's over."

A shot in the dark doesn't hurt, I thought. I have no friends. But the jump and the radio—where had they found out about the radio? We had been betrayed! By whom? Kasztner? Never. It was unthinkable. Anyway, Kasztner knew nothing of the transmitter. Stipa? Possibly. He knew about the transmitter. Ferro? Had he dared to open the suitcase? He had been warned, though, that there was a bomb set to go off at a touch. Perhaps he had been arrested and the transmitter found. No, no, it couldn't be. They would not have found us then, nor would they have discovered the connection between us and the transmitter. The Hungarians at the border could have turned us in. They knew of two suitcases, but they did not know they contained a transmitter. The only person all the threads led to was Stipa.

That sort of villainy suited his personality; if betrayal furthered his ends, he would not hesitate. He had himself told me, on our way to the Hungarian border, how he had betrayed his comrades in France as the price for returning to his homeland, to the forest.

The partisan major, fighter of Spain, was therefore a Nazi agent!

But another explanation was possible: they knew something—that I was in the British army, and a parachutist. And who had ever seen a spy without a transmitter? Perhaps it was a blind shot, a guess. Could be. I would deny emphatically that I possessed a transmitter.

"Finish up with him quickly. I'm coming back immediately to take him to have a friendly chat!" said the officer as he turned to leave.

The sergeant ordered me to strip; they gave my clothes a thorough search. They were experienced at it and did their job energetically. Nevertheless, they missed the tiny compass I had hidden under a button. They took all my valuables, my belt, and my shoelaces and then allowed me to dress.

They put me into cell number 3. The door immediately shut behind me. I was a prisoner.

The cell was more pleasant and more spacious than I had expected. Two cots stood below the hatchway. They each had a straw mattress, clean sheets, and two blankets. I sat on the edge of one of the beds.

So that was that. We had been betrayed. Shamefully. After the immense strain of the past few days and the last hour or two, silence and loneliness descended on me with their full weight.

What next? If they had really found the transmitter, the situation was serious. Not only our lives, but the lives of all those with whom we had been in contact, were in danger. They, their friends, and their acquaintances . . . and they were the leaders of the movement. The movement that stirred the Jews to resist Eichmann's plans for extermination was now involved in espionage and sabotage. The entire movement was in danger. And the rescue project? Instead of rescue—total failure. And the convoy? The convoy would leave, not for Spain, but for the death camps. And Kasztner would be arrested for espionage.

I had to get Kasztner out of this affair. I would deny everything. I would declare that he knew nothing. I would deny it all, whatever happened!

And what would the Germans say when they got to know about the transmitter?

The door opened suddenly and the sergeant yelled: "Move!"

I was startled by the force of this unexpected voice. I stood up and walked forward, holding my head high. I would show them, the swine, that a Jew could be proud. They could beat me, torture me— no doubt they would—but they would not be able to break me. They would not humble me.

Holding my head high, I marched between two soldiers with bayoneted rifles.

We went up to the third floor, where they took me to a well-furnished office. Sitting at the desk was a thin man with a high forehead and a long face. He indicated a chair with his long finger. There was something elongated about his whole figure. I was sure he topped two meters in height.

A plump man sat at a typewriter. He had a piercing gaze and short hair brushed upward in the Prussian manner.

"Smoke?" the long one asked, standing to offer me a cigarette. He was indeed very tall.

"Thanks," I said, taking a cigarette, instinctively searching my pockets for matches.

He chuckled. "We don't usually let our prisoners have matches," he said, giving me a light from his own lighter.

"I see that you are an educated man," he began. "You will have no trouble understanding that you have lost the game. There's no point in hiding anything. We can get anyone to talk, even the Sphinx. I advise you to answer all our questions. If you don't tell any lies, we'll remain good friends. If you do . . . "

The whole speech was accompanied by an encouraging, friendly smile. This is method number one, I mused: softening up the victim.

"I have nothing to hide and I have no reason at all to lie. But I am under Gestapo orders not to discuss my business with you. Contact Commissar Sievert. If he gives his permission, I'll gladly answer."

"If you're yearning for the Gestapo, I'll hand you to them,

don't worry, but first I'd like to hear from you, understand? What's your name?"

I gave the name by which I had introduced myself to the Gestapo.

I was rewarded with a mighty slap. My head spun and I almost fell from my chair. I felt neither pain nor shame. I was ready for anything from now on.

"Filthy Jew! Traitor! Is that how you repay kindness? I invited you to sit, gave you a cigarette! Where are your friends?"

"I don't know what you're talking about!"

"I'll remind you right away!" he screamed, fuming. He pressed a button on the table, and two ponderous men with grim faces came in.

"Open his mouth!"

The two fell on me with rubber truncheons, raining blows on every part of my body. I decided to be silent, not to shout, but I soon felt the blood flowing down my face and could not control myself. The pain cut through me and my mouth opened in a wail. They continued to beat me.

I do not know whether hours or minutes elapsed until there was quiet. I felt my whole body was swollen. I wiped my eyelids and the blood and tears that covered my face. My head was spinning and there was thunder in my ears. I looked around and found that I was on my back on the floor. I rose with difficulty and stood erect, seeing the two who had whipped me wiping the perspiration from their faces. The long one sat comfortably smoking. My legs betrayed me and I leaned against the table to prevent myself from falling.

"So, my friend, where are your comrades?" he again asked in a gentle, almost fatherly voice. I had no strength to answer. I merely shook my head in denial.

"Carry on!" he bellowed.

The two kicked me and I fell to the floor again. They tied me with a rope. They put a pole between my arms and knees, lifted me, and set the ends of the pole on two tables so that my bare feet faced upward and my head knocked against the floor. Again they beat me. I stopped feeling. Apparently the connection between body and mind had ended. I fainted.

When I opened my eyes I again found myself on the floor with my hands and legs free. I tried to lift myself, but without success.

"Have you anything to tell me?" asked the long one, crouching over me with a satanic smile.

No. My mind was still clear. If they carried on beating me I would die. Death would be preferable to any more of this. They would kill me anyhow, even if I told them what they wanted to hear. No. No. No!

I mumbled with difficulty: "You can carry on!"

He kicked me and punched me in the face. I fainted again.

When I opened my eyes for the third time I was soaking wet. They had apparently thrown water on me. The long one decided I had had enough for today. Maybe he was scared I would die. His face again adopted a friendly expression and he said, "You're made of good stuff. We'll be friends yet!" He gestured and the two men grabbed me under the arms. A terrible pain pierced through me at their touch. I screamed horribly.

"Gently, hey, gently does it with the lieutenant!" the long one laughed. His laughter followed me down the deserted corridor.

The thought that I had heard something significant passed through my fevered brain, but it flitted by and I was unable to grasp it. I fainted again.

The two men dragged me along the corridor, legs trailing behind me and knees banging against the steps, to my cell where they dropped me.

I was alone once more. Swollen all over, the slightest movement aroused terrible pain. The congealed blood stuck to my flesh. I lacked the strength to get up from the floor and onto the bed. I think I fainted again.

A pleasant chill cooled my forehead. I opened my eyes. The face of an old man in an army uniform was looking at me. His gray hair glinted in the weak light, sticking out from under a small cap, much like a British army hat. When he noticed that I had opened my eyes, he began whispering: "Easy! Easy! Come, I'll help you. Lie on the bed."

I mustered all my remaining strength to get up and he helped me. I noticed then that a wet handkerchief covered my forehead.

"Did you put it there?" I asked him.

"Yes. You'd fainted. Lie down. You need rest and strength."

"Why are you doing this?"

"Because you are beaten and suffering."

"You've heard what I'm accused of, haven't you?"

"That doesn't interest me."

I lay on the bed wondering who this man might be. I had the glimmer of an idea: perhaps I could use him to communicate with our people on the outside. And again, as he covered me with a sheet and a blanket, I asked him why he was doing this for me.

"I'll tell you. I am a Hungarian citizen, but I've spent most of my life in Paris. I have a daughter and a son, more or less the same age as you. My son is also a soldier, at the front. I'm an old soldier now, guarding this purgatory. My brother is a fascist leader and I'm afraid of God's vengeance. I want to do penance for my brother's sins. Perhaps you've heard of him; his name's Páger."

I had certainly heard of him. Antal Páger. He was a talented actor and had volunteered to serve as a propagandist for evil and murder. And his brother—how humane he was. Humane? Perhaps he was part of this interrogation. Perhaps he was playing at being good in order to win my trust, so that I'd divulge my secrets?

"Calm down. Pull yourself together. They're cruel, but it doesn't go on for long. The main thing is for you to have enough strength to hold out."

"Hold out? What for? They'll hang me anyway in the end."

"Don't be a child. Everyone knows you're a British paratrooper, an officer. They don't hang British officers here."

They know I'm a British paratrooper? An officer? Then the hint about the transmitter was genuine. I remembered: "Gently does it with the lieutenant!" the long one had said. Who had known my rank? Stipa was the only one who had seen me in uniform. Had they found the uniform with the transmitter? One way or another, it was clear that the transmitter was in their hands. Perhaps it was in this very building.

"Listen," the old man continued, "there was a girl here, also a paratrooper, the daughter of a Hungarian writer. I've forgotten her name. She got only five years' imprisonment, and she also had a transmitter."

Hannah had been here! Hannah had been arrested! I thought the five-year-long punishment was a figment of the old man's imagination, a ruse to revive me and give me faith. But he could not have invented a girl, daughter of a writer, who had come with a transmitter!

That was why she had not turned up anywhere. She had, apparently, arrived in Budapest under arrest, or she had been caught on arrival.

Hannah was in prison. Was she still alive? What was left? Peretz would be caught, without a doubt! Margit would not be able to stand up to interrogation. Everything was ruined. The operation for the rescue of Hungarian Jewry with which we had been entrusted had failed at the outset. And what fate was in store for us? We would die under torture or by execution.

After how long was a person executed? Would they hang me? Or did they execute by firing squad? I had the right to claim that I was a soldier. I would claim my rights! I had to persevere and choose a good death for myself. It was very important to die with dignity.

I was feverish with awful pains. My gaze wandered over the walls. I saw names and dates. "Paul Metzini, 2.6.1944." This was apparently the previous tenant of my cell. Why had he been arrested? Was he still alive? The fascists did not dwell on such things. They executed people without a second thought. Squares had been scratched into the plaster; they bore the numbers five to twenty-six—a calendar—and there was also a name. Danziger of Szeged had sat for twenty-one days in cell number 3 in the counterespionage section of the War Office. In what month? Which year? Danziger of Szeged had not bothered to note the year. One day he had certainly been executed, and nobody knew about it. All he had left behind was his name. A Jew from Szeged who had wanted, perhaps, to change in some way the fate of the Jews, or the course of the war—and now was no more.

I rose to my knees and scratched at the plaster with my finger-nails. I had to leave greetings for those coming after me. Thus we would keep the chain going until there would be no room on the wall, until the earth was sated with blood.

What more awaited me in life? Was it worth going on living, bearing these tortures, only to warrant the dramatic moment facing the firing squad? Who knew whether I would be able to hold out under torture? How long would I have the strength to remain silent? I had already been persuaded that they had the ability to force even the Sphinx to talk.

The Sphinx? . . . Egypt? Suddenly I remembered being in a round room overlooking Suleiman Square, where we were sitting in deep leather armchairs. There were three of us: Hannah, Enzo, and

I. Enzo was in high spirits, as usual, and every so often he interrupted Hannah and me as we pored over our maps by reading us amusing bits from the English humorist P. G. Wodehouse. Suddenly Hannah said, as though associating two thoughts: "And what if we're caught as spies? With a transmitter?"

Both of us looked at her. She had expressed the question we had all been asking in our hearts. Enzo stopped reading and his face became serious. He raised a finger—as he always did before saying something important—and said: "Take poison with you!"

"Poison?" I asked, partly aloud, partly to myself.

He fixed a piercing gaze on us, through his glasses, and his deep voice seemed to echo from the depths of a well: "They'll torture you. And take note: there's no hero who can withstand torture. You'll become traitors. And afterward they'll kill you anyway. They'll have neither pity nor mercy. Don't delude yourselves. They'll have no mercy, even for you, Hannah."

A heavy silence fell on the room. It seemed as though cold, steel fingers were squeezing my throat. I jumped up and shouted angrily: "You have no right to talk like that!" And I left the room.

That conversation was never mentioned again. Poor Enzo—I had hurt him unjustly. He was the only one who knew what we were getting into. And we had not listened to him. Hannah must also have remembered Enzo's words in this prison, and she must have remembered that I was not prepared to discuss it seriously.

To die! I had to die! And what was death? The end of life. An end with no new beginning, no continuation! They say that deeds and thoughts live on in the world, in the memory of mankind, for coming generations. I had finished the task I was apparently born to do. My life was over, though I still breathed. All spiritual motives for continuing to live had vanished. Everything of value in life was lost. Why need I continue breathing and suffering for a few more days?

What would my friends say when they learned that I had committed suicide? "He was too weak to stand up to the ordeal." But Enzo would understand. He would know why I had done it. He would testify that it was better to sacrifice one's life before being forced into betrayal.

I would die! Now, at once!

How? Perhaps I would manage to smash my skull against the iron leg of the bed. This was hard to imagine; after all, I was devoid of strength. Perhaps for this last effort of my life I would find the required strength. I got off the bed and raised the frame in order to wrench the leg free. Something fell to the floor with a metallic sound. I picked up the small object. It was a little aluminum square. One side was engraved with a number and the name Robert Johnson. It was the identification tag of an American soldier! Robert Johnson, what were you doing here? Did you bequeath your tag to me? Thank you, Robert Johnson!

The sound of the guards' footsteps was approaching. I lay on my bed and covered myself with the blanket. I heard a light rustle at the hatch. The guard observed the prisoner. I closed my eyes. He moved on.

I held the tag in both my hands, bending and straightening it by turns, until it broke. The break was blunt. No matter—I would still be able to tear the skin and arteries. I started on my loathsome task.

At first I felt pain. I recoiled a few times. I began to experience some doubts: perhaps, after all, it was worth staying alive? There could be a miracle. Germany could fall the next day. Wasn't the end of the war near? Perhaps they would bomb the city an hour after I died, and the building would be hit. I would be able to escape then. I became strong again. I dispelled my illusions. My blood had begun to flow in a thin stream already. I had not reached the artery yet; the wound was not deep enough. I took the aluminum tag between three fingers and continued to cut into my flesh. Suddenly a sharp pain shot through my hand, sending a shock from my palm to my heart like a powerful blow. Ah, I had reached the artery. Now for one strong courageous movement—good-bye to you, my country, my home, my kibbutz. Good-bye to you, girl. I will never return, no.

A warm stream of blood burst from my arm. I was shivering with cold, and the blood warmed my body. I rested my arm on my chest so as to feel the caressing warmth and to ensure that the blood was really flowing, flowing. They would not torture me tomorrow! You long bastard, come and see! How are you going to force me to speak? How will you open a mouth about to close forever?

Then the flow stopped. I lifted my arm and felt the blood gush out again. The congealed blood had formed a shield on my chest, which was why I had thought the flow had ceased.

What do people think about in their last moments? It seems that at the end, a person is inclined to return to the source of his or her life. I suddenly saw scenes from my childhood. Father, mother, where are you, father, mother, sister? I came too late. Had I only come earlier, had I not been arrested, I would have saved you. If only . . . if . . . if . . . if . . . If there were no Hitler; if the Jews had known how to defend themselves; if only I had told her I love her, truly love her. Could she sense what was happening to me at this moment? Was she still waiting for me? Was she still sitting there, on the shores of Lake Kinneret . . . no, not the shores of Kinneret, the banks of the Nile. Apparently the end was near. I was confused. I was with her on the Qarun, in Egypt. In the land of Joseph and his brothers, not the shores of the Kinneret. In Egypt, Qarun was a sea, too. A sea with boats on it, boats full of Jews. Jews traveling to the Land of Israel. Our Jews; I had rescued them. The sea was red. All red. A sea of blood. And I was on the surface of it, drowning in warm blood, swimming in the wake of the boats. And Jews were rejoicing on the decks. The meeting is adjourned, said the Captain. And I got up to leave. But Stipa stood in the yard threatening me with a submachine gun. Hey, that's mine. How did you get it? And he shouted at me: Don't come near! One more step and I shoot! I was afraid to move and sat on a bench. It was the bench in our garden. How had I come home? Kasztner had said that mother and father were no more! The train had taken them, yet here they were, hugging me and weeping with happiness. They were saying something, but it was impossible to hear because of the dreadful rumbling. What was rumbling like that? The engines, the engines! Of course, because the red light was on and the Australian was standing behind me with his right hand raised. . . . Prepare to jump! . . . The green light goes on. GO! The Australian roars in my ear and I jump, falling . . . falling . . . What's wrong with this parachute? . . . It isn't opening. . . .

I opened my eyes. A pleasant chill enfolded me and I felt wonderful. I lay limply as though hovering in space. I wanted to lift a hand, but my hand did not move. I closed my eyes again. It was so good, so quiet, so clear all around me. But something was buzzing in my ears. The sound grew louder. The sound of water. Human voices. Where am I? Yes, we're bathing in the cool stream next to our hut. Yonah! I shouted, and was shocked not to hear my voice. I opened my eyes again and saw strange faces. I gazed in bewilderment as the reality slowly penetrated my consciousness: here was the sergeant who had conducted the search, and there was the old guard. He was shaking his white head—apparently dissatisfied with something. Then I noticed that I was lying on the floor of a shower and a stream of water was spraying down on me.

I remembered. I had cut my artery and the warm blood had spurted out—and I had died. No, it seemed, I had not died. I lifted my head with difficulty and saw that my arm was bandaged with my shirt. They had saved me. Saved! What had they saved me for? You save a person for life. But they had saved me in order to abuse me. They were guarding my life so that they could kill me when they wished.

The sergeant crouched over me, and when he saw that my eyes were open he let loose a rain of curses.

"What do you think you're doing? I have a wife and child. If you die here I'll be responsible for it. I'll kill you like a filthy dog."

He pulled out his revolver and pressed the barrel to my temple:

"Swear you won't try that again! Swear! If not—I'll shoot you. . . . "

He was threatening me with death if I did not swear that I would not commit suicide. I felt an urge to laugh. I whispered hoarsely: "Shoot!"

Apparently he felt he had not found the right way to stimulate my desire to live. He ordered his soldiers to take me back to my cell. There they laid me on the second cot. The first was soiled with my blood. He appointed a guard to sit beside my bed, watching constantly to see that I did not rip off the bandage. He promised me that a doctor and my interrogator would come soon. He had already telephoned them. Meanwhile, he was prepared to send to the nearby bar for anything I cared to order. On my own account, of course, out of the money they had confiscated. I asked for some cognac.

It was good to lie down like that, between consciousness and passing out. I felt as if I were lying behind a glass wall. I saw everything in living form, sharply, but only a muted whisper reached my ears.

A doctor came and bandaged my wrist. I saw him, but felt nothing. The tall interrogator arrived. I saw his hand movements, his long finger pointing at me, his threatening fist. He was most ridiculous, with his dumb-show gestures. Then they all left and I remained there with the guard.

I did not care that I had remained alive, as I would not have cared had I died. I was indifferent to everything, caressed only by the warmth of the blanket when a fit of shivering took me.

* * * * *

I don't know how much time passed before they led me to the torture chamber again. Once more a shower of questions swamped me, but I seemed to hear them in a dream. It was good to be weak. One blow was enough and I fainted. I heard the long one whisper: "Careful! We need him!"

They tortured me again. Asked me my name. The long one adopted a new stratagem.

"Fool," he said, "I know who you are, but I want you to admit it. Why should you take all this? If you tell me of your own accord, I'll let you see your father. He's in the next room."

My father? My father *was* in another room: in the gas chamber. But perhaps not yet? Perhaps he was still alive? Eichmann had promised not to destroy any more Jews until the end of the negotiations in Istanbul. Really, why deny my name? Perhaps they would give me back my father, my mother, my sister, in order to use them as tools to pressure me. In that way I could rescue them, even if only for a while. I started talking. I revealed my name, my parents' names, where they lived, as well as my sister's name, and I gave them signs by which they could prove the truth of my words.

Why weren't they asking about Peretz? Apparently he had also been arrested.

The interrogator was delighted with his victory. He said, "Now we're friends again, so I'll show you my cards too."

He took two suitcases from under the desk. I was horrified. They were ours. There was no point in denying any more. The betrayal was complete. They opened the suitcases in front of me. Everything was there: the uniforms, the transmitter, the submachine gun, the maps. He read out the contents of our conversation about blowing up the bridge. He gave a sign and they brought in a man dressed in a Hungarian uniform, a young officer. He looked terrible, his face blackened by blows.

"Do you know this person?"

"No. I've never seen him before."

Another blow to my head.

"You still deny it? This is the officer you spoke to about blowing up the bridge."

"I have never seen him in my life. But your agent, Stipa, the provocateur, handed him over."

He was surprised to hear the name Stipa.

"Do you think Stipa turned you in?"

"Only he could have done so."

He thought for a moment and said: "If you've come to that conclusion by yourself . . ."

I began to have doubts again about Stipa's betrayal. What had really taken place? I tortured my brain.

"You should know that we've been on your track the whole time. We know who you've met and where. There's no point at all in denial. Start talking."

I concentrated my thoughts. I knew I couldn't hold out any longer. A few more blows and I would break. It was better to talk, but I had to choose what to tell and what to deny. I had to tell only what they already knew, no more.

I began with the story of my life. I told about my emigration to Palestine and my work as a farmer. I didn't mention the kibbutz; to them this would have sounded like Communist propaganda. I told them about how we were alarmed by what we heard about the destruction of the Jews, and that we had decided to send emissaries to the conquered countries in order to influence the governments not to sell their souls to the devil. I had come with concrete suggestions for bringing the Jews to Palestine via Turkey. I had brought the transmitter in order to communicate with official Jewish bodies in Palestine regarding technical arrangements. We thought the Hungarian government would be clever enough to take this path: it would be rid of the Jews, yet it could keep its hands and the hands of the Hungarian people from being soiled with Jewish blood.

The plump one with the German haircut, who had been silent throughout the interrogation, began typing as soon as I started to speak. From time to time he would stop me with a raised finger to indicate that he had not managed to get it all down. I waited for him to finish typing and then continued.

"When I came to Budapest, it turned out that the Hungarian government had already taken the decisive step. It had handed the Jews over to the Germans. I had no choice but to get in touch with

Yoel Palgi, 1943.

the Gestapo to try my luck with them. The Germans are smarter than you. They would surely be prepared, for good money, to sell the Jews they had acquired for nothing from the Hungarians. And it's still not too late. The Hungarians could redeem their honor yet. The end of the war is not far off, and vengeance will follow. War criminals will be punished. There are still some Jews in Hungarian hands. And if you, the Hungarians, would take the initiative, I am the man to tie up the threads for negotiations. I am authorized to promise all those who help save lives that they will not be brought to trial for past deeds."

They were stunned. There was a moment's silence. But at once an evil glint flashed in the interrogator's eyes: "You're lying again. Why did you want to blow up the bridge at Barcs? Why the ammunition? What was the target?"

"I came with the help of partisans. They weren't in on my secret plans. I pretended I had come for sabotage."

"You can go back to your cell!" Apparently he had decided to report on my testimony to his superiors.

The next day I was again brought in for interrogation.

"I have considered your testimony," the interrogator began. "You can prove whether your words are true or not—hand me the transmission code."

This was the secret they wanted to discover. They believed they would succeed in transmitting false information in our name, in order to cause air force casualties. I knew that I would tell everything if they continued to torture me, except for this last item—that I would not reveal! I must withhold the fact that I was not the radio operator and could not help them anyway. I would not hand Peretz over to them!

"The code is in the suitcase," I said.

"Don't lie! It isn't here," he screamed.

I stuck to my story. "It was in the suitcase. If it's lost—you lost it."

The torturing resumed. They stopped me and tied my hands behind me, to my ankles. They beat and squeezed my testicles. I broke completely. I had no more control. I began to confess. I told them I was a soldier, that I had come to fight against them, but the main purpose was to organize the rescue of Jews. I gave them correct dates. I knew that if Peretz was caught they would torture him as I was being tortured. They would not leave us alone until we told them the same things. However, I did not reveal the code.

Once again I was face-to-face with a new quandary: the Kasztner episode. I insisted that he knew nothing about me, and that only after I had met him for the first time in Budapest had I revealed the purpose of my mission. It was then that he had helped me get in touch with the Gestapo. They renewed the beating with a truncheon. They promised to beat me until I lost my mind. I felt that when they saw that I had come to the end of my tether and still held to my story, it would be a sign that I was telling the truth.

From interrogation to interrogation, my human pride dissolved until it was almost entirely gone. I was sunk in an abyss of instincts. I would tremble at every rustle, every slight clatter made by the guard. I wanted to escape into a dream world, but my sleep was troubled and I would awake at any movement, my heart pounding.

Despite my total isolation, scraps of information filtered through. I learned of the prisoner in cell 11; how after they had broken both his legs, they tortured him to death. The prisoner in cell 8 jumped from the window of the third floor and his dying groans were heard the length of the corridor. Hatred for this country grew powerful within me. During every air raid I was overcome with wild happiness and shouted with the thunder of the cannons: "Destroy it! Wipe out this cursed country!"

Once, when I happened to be in the toilet, I encountered a tall man dressed in a British uniform with two stars on his shoulders. Feverishly, I said to him: "If you manage to stay alive, report that three Palestinian Jews were buried here, one of them a girl. Parachutists!" The guards came between us with blows.

"Tell them, and demand that they pay for our blood!" I shouted after him, and he answered, "I understand. And you tell them about me, too!"

According to the lines I had marked on the wall, I had spent four days in prison.

They called me to be interrogated again. I went submissively; there was no longer any trace of my earlier bearing when I thought they would not break me.

Two in Gestapo uniform awaited me in the corridor.

"You're coming with us!" said one of them. I walked between them as we left that dreadful place. Where were they taking me? I had no illusions at all. If only the torture did not start again. How much more could I possibly endure? It was a wonder that my mind was still intact.

"Why haven't you shaved?" the Gestapo man asked.

I gazed at him in amazement and began instinctively to rub my face. It was the fifth day I had not shaved, nor combed my hair. My face was full of scars and my clothes were soaked in blood—I looked miserable.

The gate opened for us and the German said: "If you try to escape I'll shoot you!"

Not a bad solution, I thought, but they gripped my arm with steel fingers and I had no strength to move. They virtually carried me.

At the sight of the street I became dizzy; the noon light dazzled me. Only four days in prison and I had reached this! Passersby stopped and stared mutely at me. For this reason, perhaps, it was unpleasant for the Gestapo man that I had not shaved. Apparently I was ruining their impression. If so, I'd ruin it even more! I knelt, like someone whose strength has run out. The two of them pulled me toward the car, muttering curses between their teeth. We drove through the bustling city until we reached a huge, gloomy building.

We climbed stairs and passed through doorways. Now and then we came to a barred gate, which the guard opened and shut behind us. It was a modern prison, the likes of which I had seen only in American films. Around a central wall as high as the building itself were circular galleries onto which the cell doors opened. One guard standing in the center could scan all seven floors of cells. The cells were crowded with prisoners. Only the solitary confinement cells were in a side passage. This was the Gestapo prison, on FA Street in Buda.

I was put into number 217, a high and spacious cell. There was an iron bed with a blanket on it. A lavatory was in the corner. I was feeling weak and lay on the bed. The door opened suddenly and an SS sergeant poked his square head around it, shouting: "It is forbidden to lie down during the day!"

"I'm tired," I answered.

"You have to stand up when I come in!" he screamed. "Who are you—a Jew?"

"That's the parachutist," an SS soldier standing behind him interjected.

"Is that so?" said the sergeant and closed the door.

What was this? Did they have a special attitude toward army people here? If so, I would try to take advantage of it and insist on respect.

I lay down again. The sound of English conversation filtered through the window. I stood up on the bed in order to reach the opening near the ceiling and looked around. A man of about forty was standing at the window of the cell facing me, one floor up, conducting a loud conversation in English with someone, apparently the prisoner in the cell next to mine.

"Who speaks English here?" I shouted.

Heads appeared at the hatches, looking at me.

"Who are you?" asked the prisoner opposite.

"A Palestine British officer. Are there other English here?"

All the heads disappeared at the same time. The man I was talking to also disappeared. After a moment he reappeared, making signs that I should lower my head. They were veterans of this prison and understood the approach of danger.

Silence prevailed. I lay down, but I couldn't fall asleep. I had pain in my swollen armpits. Fever and chills alternated. Several hours passed like that.

As evening fell, I heard the sound of people and the clatter of footsteps. I heard names being called out. Suddenly: "Hannah Szenes!" I heard it clearly, and Hannah's voice answering, "Ja." Hannah was here! She was alive! I fell upon the door, hammering at it with my fists and feet.

The door opened. "What's up?" barked the guard. I pushed him aside and peered into the corridor. It was completely empty. I went into my cell. Had Hannah really been there a moment ago, or was I hearing imaginary voices in my fever?

Several days passed. A severe infection developed in the wounds on my arms and hands, and they became running sores. Boils developed in my armpits. I was unable to move my arms. All food made me nauseous. I asked the guards to take me to a doctor. They promised to call one, but no doctor arrived.

I became apathetic. I did not even speculate about my future anymore. I barely had the spirit to stand.

On what was perhaps the tenth day of my imprisonment, a barber came to my cell to shave me. "Colonel's orders," he said.

The Colonel! Klages was a colonel. What was going on? Maybe Kasztner had managed to do something for me? The Russians were going from strength to strength, and there was movement on the western front as well. I received this information from the prisoner opposite, who had, it seemed, sources of information. At noon every day he would "broadcast" news in English.

When the barber had completed his task, they took me to the office. Two Germans in civilian clothes awaited me there.

"Where's the other one?" one of them asked.

"He's here already," came the answer.

The other one? Who was the other one? Peretz? The faint hope that stirred in me became stronger. And Peretz appeared. Tall as ever, thinner, but not broken, as I was. He walked confidently to stand beside me. I clasped his hand. I didn't want to reveal my happiness in front of the Germans. Peretz answered with an encouraging smile.

One of the Germans tied my right hand to Peretz's left with an iron chain. I indulged in hope for no more than a minute. If we were about to be freed, why the chain?

"Forward!" came the command.

We went down; a car was waiting at the gate. We drove to the railway station.

"We're going to Pecs!" the German explained.

They placed us in a special compartment. During the whole of the long journey they guarded us—one seated at the door and the other at the window. The rumor of the two captured parachutists spread through the train. Passengers were constantly passing the compartment, looking in at us. Old women expressed their sadness: "So young!" Others threatened us with their fists. A railway worker cursed us because we had bombed his house. All his life he had worked to build himself a house and we had destroyed it. We sat, handcuffed, indifferent, as though we did not understand their language.

We had no chance to talk during the entire journey. When I tried to tell Peretz about Hannah, one of the Germans darted toward us, pointing his revolver. We began conversing in Morse code. Short finger pressure indicated a dot, and long pressure, a dash. We told one another what we had said under interrogation, coordinating our stories for future sessions.

We were driven from one place to another in Pecs. The Germans had no prison in this country town and the Hungarians' prisons were full to capacity. In the end we were "accommodated" in the police jail. We were put into separate cells with an SS soldier guarding each. They took our shoes away and handcuffed our hands and feet at night. The night was endless. My wounds troubled me greatly, and the handcuffs cut into my flesh. I was unable to lie or sit. All my illusions were shattered, replaced by bitter despair.

But during that difficult night I underwent a change. The shock I was experiencing aroused my will to live. I overcame my apathy. I resolved to fight with all my remaining strength. They were listening to the radio in the guard room and sounds came through to me. I listened and managed to decipher the truth behind the flood of propaganda. It was good to hear the German announcer talking about victories while "disengaging from the enemy," a sign that the Russians were advancing and, maybe, planning to conquer Hungary in one sweep. I had to shake myself up and prepare to hold out! Another day, a week, a month—victory would come!

Early in the morning a plump man with gray hair came into my cell. The Hungarian guard humbly addressed him as "Colonel, Sir." He greeted me with "Good morning" and ordered the handcuffs removed. After he had gone the guard informed me, "From today on, you're a Hungarian prisoner!"

I shrugged. What did it matter? I had already been a Hungarian prisoner, and they had handed me to the Germans. But I immediately understood that there was some importance attached to this change. A German officer came to take us for interrogation, and it emerged, from the discussion at the door, that the Hungarian soldiers were preventing the Germans from taking us. We were triply guarded: the Hungarian police watched the jail, the Germans watched the police, and the Hungarian soldiers watched the Germans.

As my desire to live returned, I began to feel hunger. I had barely eaten for twelve days. Now I was assailed by real hunger. We were given breakfast—bitter black coffee and bread. The bread had to last all day, but I ate the whole portion. Lunch was a meager bowl of soup. Supper—nothing. Because of the unrelenting hunger, my longing for a cigarette grew.

The three-way guarding continued for two days. We were locked away, but I grew stronger and felt encouraged. It was a good sign that the Hungarian colonel dared open a confrontation with the Germans.

And then the German guard disappeared. I was very sorry not to have overheard the German-Hungarian altercation concerning us. It would have been illuminating.

I was taken for interrogation at noon to a Hungarian barracks where I was cross-examined by a young officer who spoke fluent English. He asked mainly about Stipa. I understood from the questions that Stipa was in prison. That meant that it had not been Stipa who had betrayed us. The traitors had been the Hungarian partisans, apparently. I did not understand how the transmitter had come into Hungarian hands because I had sent the telegram in good time, warning against sending the transmitter.

During the interrogation, the colonel came in and said he wanted to be left alone with me. The young officer and the stenographer left the room.

"I've received an account of what you said in Budapest and I want to know what you really have to say."

"Too late—you have no more Jews to sell!"

"Why take that tone? I have no intention of selling Jews. You're wrong. The Jews of Budapest and tens of thousands of Jews recruited for forced labor are alive."

"I have only one suggestion: Don't allow the Germans to annihilate the Jews of Hungary. You will pay for that crime. The Hungarian nation will never be able to wash its hands of the crime with the excuse of the German invasion. The Germans conquered Yugoslavia, too, but a partisan movement arose there and the people are fighting. You were willingly induced, without any resistance. You were willing partners to the Germans' deeds and you'll share their fate."

"What could Hungary do? We found ourselves in the middle of a sea of Germans. Neutrality? Only countries like Turkey, Sweden, and Spain, on the edges of the continent, could allow themselves to do that, not those in the heart of Europe!"

"And what if British forces invade Yugoslavia or Austria tomorrow?"

"The moment the first British tank reaches the Hungarian border, we'll turn our weapons on the Germans."

"Give me a chance to get out of here to tell that to my headquarters."

"I can't. Even the little I've done for you has almost cost me my head. British tanks are a long way from here, to my regret. But I promise you I'll keep the two of you here as long as possible; afterward I'll return you to Budapest—to the Hungarians, not the Germans. You can rest assured—you'll tell your grandchildren your life story yet."

We parted with a handshake. When he reached the door, he turned his head and said, "My name is Colonel Török. Don't forget!"

He called the officer and turned me over to him. He warned me that we were to be interrogated by the Germans again.

"But they'll interrogate you here, in my presence. We won't hand you over to them."

I shrugged and told him that, actually, up to now it was the Hungarians who had tortured me, not the Germans.

"What is past is past, and you'd best forget it," he replied.

That ended our conversation.

The regime in jail was fairly easy. The prisoners were petty criminals, such as pickpockets and prostitutes. I remember one, the wife of a sugar factory owner. She was tall, blonde, and as charming as a girl of twenty. Her crime: she had insulted the German army. She claimed that she had had a difference of opinion with her friend, a German officer, and her insults had been meant for him personally, not for the whole army.

Prisoners were allowed food from the outside. Our lives were made even easier. We received blankets. They took me to a doctor who took good care of me and healed my wounds. The pain grew less, but hunger troubled me. It was beneath my dignity to beg the Hungarian officers for food. The prostitutes who cleaned our cells would secretly leave us food and cigarettes. I will always remember with kindness the whores of Pecs, by whose grace I lived for twenty-one days. They cared for us with a simple warmth, and without them we would never have recuperated to face the struggles ahead of us. They were the only ones among those who helped us who did not remind us that we owed them something.

* * * * *

We had two weeks of peace, until the day we heard astounding news: there had been an attempt on Hitler's life! Everyone wondered if Hitler was alive, or if his death was being concealed. While we were still wondering what this turn of events would mean for us, they came and took us for interrogation.

Two Germans in magnificent dress opened the questioning, which hinged on one subject only: the transmitter and the key to the code.

Peretz admitted that he was the radio operator and said I understood nothing about it. This was correct, but the interrogators were certain he was lying and that I, too, knew about the code.

One of the interrogators, a young man of about twenty-four, was a communications expert. This was obvious from his questions. He asked me which book served as the key to the code, what it looked like, whether it was in English. I maintained that Peretz had kept this a secret, and that I had only seen the book once as he put it in the suitcase. I was afraid we might contradict each other and left it to Peretz to describe the false key. The young interrogator was satisfied.

"Your friend claims," he said, "that it was a handwritten notebook, and not a book! What emerges is that there was neither book nor notebook, but that the key is in Peretz's head!"

I was frightened. This was so. Now I knew what to expect: they would torture Peretz, and he would not be able to resist telling them the code. There were, indeed, agreed combinations of signals that Peretz had to use in transmissions, and if a transmission was received without these combinations, the receiver in Cairo would know that the transmitter was in enemy hands. But I knew that the day they got the secret of the code from Peretz, they would have no further need of us and the danger of execution would increase. We had to guard against that possibility at all costs.

I thought it would be better for both of us if I stuck to my original version. Therefore, I repeated that I had seen him putting some book into the suitcase.

"You also know the code," said the second one, the one they called, with great deference, "Mr. Stock." He said, "I'll get it out of you, if I have to kill you!" He spoke quietly, and his coldness frightened me more than the others' ranting.

"I don't know a thing about the code. I only know that even if you do discover the key, it won't help you because Peretz's opposite number, who is waiting for the transmission at our base, knows Peretz's style like his handwriting. If a strange hand touches that transmitter, they'll know immediately that it isn't Peretz transmitting, and they'll understand that you've done away with him."

The two Germans exchanged glances. They got up and went to a corner of the room where they spoke for a few minutes. It was clear from their expressions that they had agreed to the sense of what I was saying.

They came back and told the Hungarians who had been present during the interrogation that they had finished for the time being. I returned to my cell with a sense of victory. I knew we were not out of danger yet, but for now we were saved.

* * * * *

At the end of July, a month after we had been arrested, they sent us back to Budapest. When we came to the railway station, I saw another two prisoners standing with their backs to us. One of them was our friend Stipa. The four of us were put into a special compartment.

One of the many guards assigned to us was a sergeant I knew from before. I learned a few things during the thirty days I was imprisoned. I already knew how to get by. I approached the sergeant with an offer to sell him my gold ring, which had just been returned to me with my watch. The sergeant jumped at the opportunity to buy it at a fraction of its value, but for me this was a fortune. I sent him to buy fruit, bread, and cigarettes. We turned our unexpected outing into a holiday.

The fourth person traveling with us was a Hungarian-born Canadian who had come on a military mission similar to ours. He had been caught in Pecs. I learned that when they caught Stipa they had found letters to us from Yonah and Abba.

The mystery of our suitcases was also solved. Stipa had believed the landlord of the tavern on the border, who said he had received a telegram from us asking him to forward the suitcases. He was a Hungarian agent. Stipa had simply forgotten that we had fixed a password and that he was not supposed to transfer the cases to Hungary without reading the cable for himself and looking for the password.

When we came to Budapest, I found myself in the same prison where the Hungarians had held me the first time I was arrested.

I was put into a cell with a stove that was also shared by the next cell. Some days later, a young Jew by the name of László was put into the second cell. We made contact through gaps in the stove, carrying on long conversations. We soon became friends and he told me his life story. When the guard approached, we kept silent so he wouldn't know we were able to communicate. The story László told was the essence of the hardship and suffering of the Jews who were rotting away in forced labor on the Russian front. It was a hair-raising saga: sixteen Jews were harnessed to a cart with a back-breaking load, which they had to pull for thousands of kilometers, through mud and snow, along bad roads, while Hungarian soldiers whipped them on. The sick were shot, the rebels were killed, and in the end they locked the few who survived into a hut, which they burned. He had managed to escape, feeble and suffering from typhus. He had not had the strength to hold out in the forest until the Russians would come, and he had decided to return home.

He wandered around for months. When he reached his home-town—it was during the time they were concentrating Jews into special houses—he found there was no longer a home awaiting him. He decided to hide. He knew from his own bitter experience what fate the Jews could expect. He forged documents of a Hungarian officer and lived with a Jewish friend, himself a "Hungarian officer." Everything was fine, but to his misfortune he met the man who had burned down the hut with the Jews in it, who recognized him. He had been arrested with his friend and now awaited trial.

"What punishment will you get?" I asked.

"Life imprisonment or death."

"Aren't you afraid of death?"

"No, not anymore. A man reaches a breaking point in his life. His will to live just cracks like glass: the glass doesn't break, but it's impossible to make it whole again.

"I've come a long way. Since early childhood I have wanted to contribute something to humanity. I wanted to create something. I was attached to life. I didn't believe in God and paradise. It was here on earth that I looked for my own and my fellow man's happiness. I wanted to study aeronautical engineering, to build planes. I wanted wings with which to embrace the earth. That's when the anti-Jewish laws appeared. So what, I said to myself, so I wouldn't go to university. I became a worker in an aircraft factory. I believed man was basically good, that he wanted to be good. The day would come and the world would recover. . . . and then the war broke out. I volunteered for the front, but I was promptly thrown out of the army with the rest of the Jews and sent to a labor camp. Bit by bit they broke our self-respect. I was ashamed of myself for continuing to live, but I wanted to live. I didn't want to give up on life. I bore all the abuse. I took it all. Try to understand what a man feels when they order him to take off his trousers, which he does, standing like that in front of a hundred people, while two of them whip him with thin branches soaked in brine. They also command you not to scream. And you bite your lips till they bleed, keeping silent. And then they order you to sing a song from *Rigoletto*—and you sing. You sing and they whip you in time to the song, and your whole body bleeds. Afterward I cried like a little boy. I knew I'd lost something forever. I could forget the whipping, but not the aria from *Rigoletto,* never ever. And all that for the sin of a cigarette which they found in my pocket.

"I felt it was beyond my strength to carry on. I decided on one of the two—to choose life and escape, or to die. Only someone who's not afraid to die is capable of escape. Therefore, I wouldn't fear death anymore. I didn't want to die, but I knew I would never again abase myself.

"I sing well, and they pestered me to sing for them. Once the officer ordered me to climb a tree. 'Now you can be a nightingale,' he said, 'and we will listen to the nightingale's song in the tree.' The officer laughed, the soldiers laughed, and even my comrades laughed with them, not daring to ignore the officer's jokes, but I kept quiet. He became angry, drew his revolver, and threatened me. I kept quiet. It was good, that silence before death. I comforted myself, whispering: After all, we all die anyway. What did today or tomorrow matter to me? They were coldly annihilating us, intentionally, systematically, for their own amusement—but they would not be amused at my expense. I would die with dignity; I would not submit. Silence reigned. My friends who had laughed at first knew my end was near. They stood with bated breath and closed eyes. They didn't want to see my death. They were afraid to look death in the face.

"'If the bird won't sing, what use is it? I have no choice but to hunt it.' The soldiers rolled with laughter: the officer was going to hunt a big bird, and they shouted, 'Fly birdie, fly away before he shoots you!' And he fired. But he was drunk and he missed. Only his fifth bullet hit my leg and I fell out of the tree.

"That was good enough for me. My friends carried me into the hut. They cared for me for a few days and I got better. But the bullet remained in my flesh.

"Ever since," he concluded, "I haven't been afraid of death."

Chapter 6

Strange Bedfellows

✷ **A**T THE BEGINNING OF AUGUST, the two Germans who had taken us to Pecs came again. This time they were dressed in Gestapo uniform. I learned their names: Herpolz Heimar and Stock. Stock was in an evil mood. "Since when have you been in Budapest?" he fumed at us.

The sergeant quickly answered for us: "I respectfully inform you that it has been two weeks, sir!"

"And those bastards didn't inform us that they'd brought you back!" He went upstairs to the office. Our lives hung on the scales again. It appeared that in Budapest, too, they did not want to hand us over to the Germans. With a heavy heart and constricted throat, I waited for him to return.

He came back after a few minutes accompanied by a Hungarian officer.

"These are going with the Germans," he instructed the sergeant.

We went back to the prison on FA street. I was put into cell number 318, a floor above my previous cell.

I was now an experienced prisoner. No sooner had I entered my new abode than I began a more thorough search than any jailer ever made. To my delight, in the straw of the mattress I found a treasure: a pencil and two stamped postcards. I sat down to write on the cards. If the opportunity should arise, I would lose them on the street. Perhaps someone would find them and post them.

Then I heard the sounds of conversation in English. The voice was the same one I had heard last time. This time we were facing each other, and conversation was easier. I stuck my head out and he immediately noticed me.

"Who are you?" he asked.

"The Palestinian!" I replied.

"We thought you'd been executed already. It's good you're still alive. I welcome you to our 'aristocrats' floor."

"Who are you?" I asked.

"Janos Makkai," he answered.

"A relation of the bishop?" I asked.

"He's my uncle, and I was a minister in parliament."

"A minister. . . . I knew that name. Oh, hell! Are you the Makkai who proposed the first anti-Jewish legislation in 1938?"

"Yes."

"And how did you end up here? Weren't you privileged as one of the first Jew-haters?"

"I was wrong. I regret to have had a hand in that outrage."

I got down from the bed. It was absurd, I reflected. Who could understand this crazy world we lived in?

A small, blue-eyed fellow with cropped hair came wheeling the soup pot from which they dished out our supper. As he ladled soup into my bowl he muttered, without moving his lips: "Do you know Hannah Szenes?"

I didn't answer.

"My name is Fleischmann," he continued. "I escorted Hannah from Croatia to Hungary. We were caught together. I also know Gary."

"I don't know what you're talking about," I told him, though with some hesitation. Some people said that Reuven Dafni looked like Gary Cooper. Reuven had no objection to this comparison. He even chose the name Gary as his pseudonym in Yugoslavia. Perhaps this fellow is telling the truth, I thought, but it could also be that the name was known to him through intelligence reports, or else from Hannah under torture.

"Never mind. I'll get a note from Hannah to vouch for me," he said, shutting the door.

I tossed and turned all night. Was this another booby trap they were laying for me, or could I trust the fellow?

When I was arrested I had been wearing a light, elegant suit. I had not taken it off since then. I had "laundered" my one and only light blue shirt a few times in cold water in my mug. I hadn't laid eyes on soap for months. My most daring dream was to own a toothbrush. To add to my troubles, I now had lice. I felt nauseous whenever I would squash one while scratching myself. I tried to keep my body and clothes clean. I felt that the more neglected my body became, the less self-confidence I had. So when Fleischmann said, as he poured the soup, that he had not yet managed to contact Hannah, but that he would help me if there was anything I needed, I asked him for soap, a toothbrush, a comb, concentrated food, and newspapers.

To my pleasant surprise, my cell door was opened the next morning by a warder, and Fleischmann, standing beside him, shrieked crudely at me to get out of my cell and wash my filthy body. I found everything I had asked for beside a tap at the end of the passage. Fleischmann, walking around me as I washed, told me he had wormed his way into being a servant on this floor, and that the servants on all the floors—"domestics," as the Germans nicknamed them—were Jews who moved around freely despite being prisoners. I heard from Fleischmann that I was considered "special" since this floor was the "aristocratic quarter" of the prison. Fleischmann had arranged for me to meet with my fellow prisoners, neighbors on the same floor, from time to time. In this way I came to know and be friends with many of them. This took place during the times we used the communal tap, at cell-cleaning time, and when meals were distributed, among others.

On my right, in cell 317, was a young Jewish doctor, Dr. May, who had joined the Gestapo under an assumed identity. He was found out after a few weeks, arrested, and accused of spying. There were two in cell 316, Dr. Negro, a short, dark Italian whose mercurial temperament reminded me of Enzo. He had been secretary of the Italian Legation, but the Germans found out that he had remained loyal to the deposed king. His cellmate, an elderly Pole, was a clever man who had mastered several languages and was eminently rational. I was unable to pronounce his name, nor did I try to re-member it since he admitted that it was a pseudonym. I called him "Colonel," to which he politely responded, "Lieutenant." I learned, in time, that this colonel had been the Polish chief of intelligence when the war broke out.

There was a muscular young Pole in 315. He had served as courier for the Polish underground, between Warsaw and Budapest. He proudly claimed, "I crossed the border 147 times with the mail, until I was caught!"

My "friend" Janos Makkai, the father of the racial discrimina-tion laws in Hungary, was in 314.

In 313 were Aladár Baróthy-Huszár, who had been chairman of the Senate and a close friend of Admiral Horthy—Hungary's dictator—and Ferenc Nagy, representative of the Peasants' Party in Parliament.

Szentmiklossy, who had been deputy minister of foreign affairs in the Hungarian government until the German invasion, was in cell 312. He was a small, thin young man with a clever face. He had been held for nineteen days in a dark cell with nothing but cold water to drink and no food. He was told that he would not be al-lowed out of the cell until he revealed where the secret files of the Foreign Office were being hidden. He refused to talk, saying that he would not violate his oath to protect state secrets. The new foreign minister, Gonczi, appointed by the Germans at bayonet-point, had come himself to the dark cell to give him permission to reveal the secret. Szentmiklossy had then said that seeing that the oath was an-nulled, he now felt free to declare that he had no idea where the files were. He had not hidden them, nor had he given the order to any-body that they should be hidden. He had been on our floor ever since.

On my left, in 319, was the director of a department in the Foreign Office, Szegedi-Maszák, from a highly respected family: his father had been foreign minister in the Austro-Hungarian Empire.

Two old men, whose gray hair lent them an air of nobility, were the occupants of cell 320. Lipót Barayani, erstwhile spokesman of the Royal Bank, was one of them, and the other, Laky Dezso, had been minister of trade. At the beginning of the year they had gone to Switzerland on the initiative and through the agency of Szegedi-Maszák to conduct negotiations with a secret emissary of the Brit-ish government. They had returned to Hungary a few days before the German invasion. They thought they had begun a vital discussion for Hungary's future after the Nazi defeat. They were arrested as soon as the Germans invaded. The German intelligence worked excellently: the "emissary" of the British government with whom they had negotiated in Switzerland had been a German espionage agent working under Admiral Canaris.[10]

In 321 was Antal, a pleasant man who was consultant in the ministry of the interior. His name was familiar to me from the briefing I had received in Palestine. He had helped Polish Jewish refugees to settle in Hungary, and had also helped by hiding rescue activities from the police.

Endre Bajcsy-Zsilinszky was in 322; he was a national hero and a leader of the Hungarian peasants. He was one of Admiral Horthy's disciples in 1919. When he entered Budapest, the Reds had been expelled, the communist revolution was suppressed, and Jews were murdered. In spite of his extreme right-wing past, he would not submit to Hitler and publicly declared that Hungary had to cut itself off from Nazi Germany.

It came as no surprise, then, that on March 19, 1944, when the Germans conquered Hungary without firing a shot, an SS soldier arrived at his house to arrest him. He was on the Most Wanted List of those destined to be arrested as soon as the invasion started. As leader of the opposition, he did not know what was about to happen. He was sleeping innocently when they informed him that armed German soldiers were about to burst into his house. He did not open the door but telephoned the minister of foreign affairs, demanding that a protest be made to the German government.

"Where are they?" asked the minister.

"On the staircase!"

"And they're also inside, here, in my room," sighed the minister.

The Germans were on the point of breaking his door down with the butts of their rifles when Bajcsy-Zsilinszky emptied all the bullets in his revolver, firing at the door. The Germans returned fire with their submachine guns, and Bajcsy-Zsilinszky fell bleeding from three bullets that had hit him. But his wounds were not fatal. That was the only battle to take place with the invasion, and the only incident of armed resistance to the Germans.

Last on "Aristocracy Lane" was a small, refined, and very elegant man with gray hair. The wardens called him "Herr Schmidt." It was possible to see that he was given special treatment, even from a distance. He had a gold watch and his cell was cleaned daily. But he was prevented from having any contact with other prisoners. According to rumors circulating in the prison, he had been one of Himmler's major agents, whose task it was to sow confusion in each of the countries Germany planned to invade. He was once heard to complain that he had been wrongly arrested and was waiting to be released at any moment. Two days later he was sent to Auschwitz. They said he was a Jew and, apparently, a typical traitor. His operations began with the invasion of Vienna and then Prague, Warsaw, Belgrade, and finally Budapest. Germany, it seems, had no further need of him, as he had completed his task.

They left me in peace for a few days and then came again to take me for interrogation by the Gestapo at the Majestic Hotel. The warders were instructed to take great care that Peretz and I did not meet. But those that brought the prison car had not been told of these instructions and we were put into the same car. We took advantage of this opportunity, telling one another what we had each said under interrogation and coordinating our stories for the coming sessions.

We were separated again when we arrived at the hotel. I was brought into a room full of people. The officer who had interrogated me in Pecs was there—Stock—and the communications expert, Herpolz Heimar, as well as Sievert and Krauss, my acquaintances from the first meeting in this hotel to which I had come with such innocence and stupidity, accompanied by Hansi Brand. It looked as if they had decided to unravel the whole episode again, to get to the bottom of it.

Stock offered me a cigarette and a chair and asked a few casual questions. Then he asked how I had been treated in prison, and what living conditions were like there. I had no wish to humble myself and told him I had no requests or complaints.

"Are you aware of what's going to happen to you?"

"Yes. You'll exchange me for a German prisoner, or you'll keep me as a witness in your favor, when the English or the Russians get you."

"Apparently you haven't heard about the V-2.[11] Neither England nor Russia has a hope of winning anymore. The war is about to end in victory for us. But why should we have unnecessary losses? And why should you die? Help us and save yourself and your friends at the same time. I promised that you'd stay alive. We'll transfer you to a nice villa, here on the mountain, and you can live there very pleasantly."

I felt the episode was reaching a breaking point. A suggestion like that had to be answered directly: yes or no.

Nevertheless, I tried to gain time.

"I don't know how I can help you," I replied.

"Say 'Yes,' and the rest will follow."

It was pointless. The game was over, I thought. "All is lost except honor." I recalled the words of a French general.

"The answer is no!" I wanted my voice to sound clear and sharp, but it emerged choked and rather hoarse. "I want to live, but not at the price of betrayal. I won't save myself at the expense of my brother's blood."

"Really. Then your brother is more intelligent than you, because he has agreed!"

I knew he was lying. There was no point in refuting his words and being beaten for my impudence. So I answered: "Everyone can do as he wishes. I hope my friend is also no traitor."

Silence. He gestured to the sentry, who took me out of the room. I didn't know what my fate would be; my sole comfort was that I had kept my dignity.

I was transferred to a small house in the vicinity of the Majestic. It had two rooms and a kitchen, and served as a temporary prison for prisoners being interrogated. One room was for men and the other for women. The guards were in the kitchen. The room was full to capacity. I tried to get information about Hannah. It turned out that most of the prisoners knew her from trips to interrogation points. They spoke with enthusiasm about the way she encouraged everyone and gave them strength to carry on.

"I had reached a state of despair and planned to commit suicide," one old man said, "but she encouraged me, telling about the Jews living in Palestine and preparing a place for us there, too. She turned me into a Zionist!"

I learned that Hannah was being held in cell 512. If I could attract her attention, we would be able to establish eye contact.

An old Jew was sitting in the corner, deep in thought and mumbling constantly. His face expressed despair and his tears flowed. I took pity on him and wanted to start a conversation. I put a hand on his shoulder, but he roared: "No! No!" Someone said, "Let him be, he's out of his mind."

"How did he get here?" I asked.

"Son," one of the prisoners said, "you're new here, and young. No sane person can understand these animals. That's a shoemaker, a simple man; Cohen's his name. I've seen people tortured before, but what they did to him goes beyond all imagination. No part of him was left untouched. They crushed his testicles. He's spitting blood. His right leg and arm are paralyzed. He's already crazy, but they carry on torturing him. You won't believe what they're accusing him of: the Germans claim that this Cohen organized the shoemakers into a partisan movement. They say 20,000 shoemaker partisans stand at his command. He admitted everything. Who knows if he understood what he was signing. But they continue to torture him to reveal where the weapons are stored. In another day or two the old man will certainly die."

"It's hard to believe," I said. "The Germans are capable of any evil, but they are logical and they won't chase after things that don't make sense."

"Logic? I'm a pure Aryan, a clerk, with a wife and two babies. I went to the printer to order some visiting cards. The Gestapo car arrived to arrest one of the workers who was suspected of being a communist. They arrested all the other workers with him, as well as the owner and me. That was three months ago. Since then they've been torturing me, they've completely broken me, my children are starving, and who knows what's going to become of me. I wasn't a member of any party, but I voted for the Fascists. Now I know what they are, what Fascists are!"

The door opened and a man stumbled in, groping his way along the wall. His face was swollen and scarred, and there were red welts on his palms. He was about forty and he sobbed like a child. People gathered around him, trying to encourage him. I thought he was a new prisoner, but then I recognized him; it was the stocky engineer who was "considered Jewish" under the new law. He had been taken from here no more than half an hour earlier for interrogation. His ancestors were Christians—so he had told me—but his parents' parents had made the fatal error of marrying converts, and now he was considered a Jew.

They were looking for his sister, who had disappeared. He told them he didn't know where she was. I tried to comfort him by saying that the day of reckoning was close, but he only repeated: "I couldn't suffer anymore, and I would have told them where she was. I'm happy that I don't know where my sister is now."

The door opened again and a frozen silence fell. The guard officer, the sergeant, came in. We held our breath; who was going to be the next victim? His piercing eyes roved about the room until he pointed at me.

My heart was pounding; the end had come. I tensed my muscles and got a grip on myself. I must keep cool. They must not detect any sense of fear in me.

In the kitchen-cum-guardroom they offered me a cigarette. Four SS soldiers sat at the table, one very young—about seventeen.

"Is it correct that you are an English officer?" the sergeant asked me.

"Yes."

"A parachutist?"

"What's this all about?" I asked instead of replying.

"We'd like to hear from you when you think this war is going to end."

"In two or three months; Germany may even surrender in the next few days. The criminals will be punished. Nothing will happen to the innocent."

"Who's going to believe that I never harmed anyone?" the sergeant protested.

"You've still got a chance; let us escape and I'll be a witness in your favor when the time comes."

The four of them looked at one another in shock. My hands shook with excitement—perhaps I would succeed this time. The sergeant broke the silence.

"Impossible. We would be risking our lives. But if you manage to stay alive, remember us kindly."

I did not meet Peretz on my way back to the prison. We were taken in separate cars. When they brought supper, I received a note from him via Fleischmann.

"They suggested that I work for them. They are apparently scared that if they transmit on my transmitter it will be noticed that I am not the sender. I asked for three days to think it over."

I was shocked; what was there to think over? Had Peretz been broken? He was so young, his life was dear to him, but could he possibly have come to this?

On the reverse of his note I wrote a poem by the Hungarian poet Jozsef Attila, "On the Spanish Soldier's Grave":

> Franco called me to fight against honesty and law
> I was afraid; if I didn't go I'd be hung at dawn
> I went to fight in blood-soaked fields
> against father and brother all day
> and death found me anyway.

The next day at noon I received an answer from Peretz:

"You, too, Yoel? I wanted to gain time, not only for myself, but for you as well. I don't need any lessons. I'll know what to do when the time comes."

✳ ✳ ✳ ✳ ✳

I tried to attract Hannah's attention through the window every so often. It was possible, with difficulty, to see the edge of her window, and I noticed that she was very active. There were letters appearing in her window one after another, and I saw that she was answered from across the way. She was using this improvised technique to "transmit." As time passed I understood that the others in our movement were imprisoned in cells opposite hers. I surmised that Hannah was probably encouraging them and telling them about Palestine. Moshe Schweiger, the Hagana commander in Budapest, had also been imprisoned here before they sent him to the death camp.

After much effort, I finally managed to catch her eye. In the morning the sun came into my cell through the hatch in the door, and in the evening it lit Hannah's window. If I could get a mirror, I would be able to signal her in the morning and she could answer in the evening.

At the same time, we found a new method for passing notes and objects from cell to cell. We would tie the item to a cord that we could swing like a pendulum until it gained enough momentum for the inmate of the next cell to catch it and pass it on the same way. This was how we were able to obtain a variety of items and how I got my precious cracked pocket mirror.

Every morning I signaled in the direction of Hannah's cell. It took days before she noticed.

How happy I was when the bright spot appeared on my floor. It came and went systematically, dot, dash, dot . . . and contact was established. It was difficult because I was not proficient in signaling. But the content of the message was not the main point; what mattered was the daily confirmation that Hannah was alive. Peretz was on our floor, but his window faced the street. Through Fleischmann I knew how he was and could convey messages between him and Hannah.

"My mother is here," Hannah informed me.

"Don't despair," I signaled back.

The prison commander, Scharfuehrer Lammke, was a sadistic murderer. He was square-faced with watery, terrifying eyes. One of his pleasures was to walk along the corridor with catlike stealth and suddenly peer into the cells. He invariably caught prisoners breaking the Nazi prison laws. For the slightest offense, he would beat the "criminal" until he drew blood. He would rub salt into the wounds and kick him in the testicles. More than one of the "accused" met his death at his hands. He tortured prisoners without regard for status or sex. Princess Odescalchi, imprisoned next door to Hannah, also received beatings from him.[12] She was imprisoned after her husband, a pilot, had tried to reach the British in Italy, but he was shot down by the Germans.

Lammke's patrols were a nightmare for all the prisoners. On one of these patrols, he saw Hannah cutting paper. She was apparently preparing her letters. He immediately burst into her cell, his eyes burning with sadistic madness. He was used to his victims being shocked and cringing against the wall, begging for their lives. The fear in the prisoners' eyes and their pleas were the fuel for his unbalanced outbursts. Lammke would brandish his fists for murderous blows, but Hannah remained seated, shot him a glance, nodded as in greeting, and murmured, "Please sit down," and then continued what she was doing.

Lammke was amazed. This had never happened to him before. Faced with her calm he became confused.

"This is the English parachutist," whispered the German wardress.

Lammke nodded and his eyes roved around the cell. He saw two paper dolls on the bed, a boy and a girl embracing.

"What's that?" he asked.

His attendant looked at him in amazement; what had happened to Lammke? This was the first time they had heard him talk in a prisoner's cell, rather than scream.

"Dolls," said Hannah.

"You aren't allowed to make boy dolls," he ordered. "If I ever see you with such dolls again, I'll punish you." He left the cell as if he had had a victory.

From then on his rounds always included a visit to Hannah's cell. He would come in, sit down politely, and listen to her as she explained why Germany would be defeated and what awaited him and his comrades for their crimes.

This story spread throughout the prison. The Gestapo monster, Scharfuehrer Lammke, changed in her presence. She was the first and only one who dared to say to his face what the Gestapo secretly knew, that the day of reckoning was near. He weakened in the face of this truth and her spiritual strength.

Prisoners employed as clerks in the prison offices succeeded in convincing their superiors to have her transferred to the cell next to her mother's. Our contact was broken by this move, but I would be able to see her through my window occasionally. I would see her walking hand in hand with her mother when the female prisoners were allowed into the small exercise yard.

In mid-August 1944, the American air force began its systematic bombardment of Budapest. Every morning, exactly at ten, the air raid siren was heard—a nerve-wracking wail. But how sweet I found that siren song, and how disappointed I was on the days the bombs failed to come.

When the siren sounded, the activity in the prison corridors increased. Prisoners who were outside their cells were hastily put back in. The doctor visiting inmates quickly left the corridors and the prison's nun hurried to her cell to pray.

She was strange, that nun. A baron's daughter, she was a member of one of the most influential families in the country. While still a child, she had vowed to bring the light of faith to those who needed it most—to sufferers in prison. She had spent twenty-six years behind prison walls, living in a cell like a prisoner. It was still possible to see signs of her fading beauty. I respected her for dedicating her whole life to an ideal. She was tall and thin, her voice was soothing, and she was most gentle. The means employed by her and the priest were fairly effective. Anyone who went to Sunday morning prayers in the chapel received two slices of bread and sausage at the end of the service. It was not clear how many believers there were, but there was never a lack of worshipers on Sunday.

With the sound of the sirens could be heard the pleasant voice of Sister Magdalena: "Virgin Mary, Holy Mary, Mother of God, intercede for us!"

She would continue thus until the sounds of explosion drowned out the sounds of prayer.

At first I fumed when I heard Sister Magdalena's prayers. What did she want? What was she pleading for? That they should not bomb? I jumped up and roared: "Virgin devil, holy devil, Satan's wife, plead for us!"

Her voice was silent for a moment, but she immediately continued: "Holy Mary, Mother of God, the Anti-Christ has come. Plead for us!"

I did not know whom she regarded as the Anti-Christ—me, or the pilots dropping their bombs on her believers. It must be said for her that she would also pray when she heard the screams of someone being tortured by Lammke.

Criminal offenders were on the first two floors. During air raids they would be taken to the shelter, while the political prisoners remained in their cells. Sometimes I would fantasize about a bomb hitting the building, tearing my cell door open, and giving me my freedom. I was always disappointed and upset when I heard the all-clear signal; only when I again heard the sirens warning of attack did I feel calm and well.

One day we heard that they were again preparing to send prisoners to the camps, and that about half the inmates were on the list. The lights went on at two in the morning, and the tramp of boots terrified the prisoners. With bated breath, I heard door after door being opened and names being called. The sound of steps approached my cell. The next door opened and they called the colonel's name. I got up and dressed—I was next. The heels clicked closer, stopped a moment, then continued. I slumped onto my bed in a cold sweat.

Then suddenly, unexpectedly, the sirens sounded and directly afterward came tremendous explosions. The Germans ran about the corridors, shoving the prisoners back into their cells. I stood on my bed and watched the bombers through the window, as well as the searchlights tracking them. I yelled: "Bless you, fellows! Just in time. You've saved hundreds of lives!"

But the raid was short and immediately afterward the candidates for the furnaces were again taken from their cells and, even before the all-clear, silence filled the prison. About one thousand people set out on their last march.

The following day I was given a note from Fleischmann, informing me that we would be sent to Auschwitz soon. The sentence had been passed on all prisoners.

There were about one thousand prisoners left in the prison. I began to work out an escape plan. The four Jewish "domestic worker" prisoners had freedom of movement in the corridors. Each floor was closed with a barred gate, but these workers moved freely within the floor. The guards, who were not particularly alert, kept the cell keys. Those on night shift even allowed themselves a nap now and then. I passed a message to Fleischmann, asking him to come and see me. When he came I detailed the plan for him. The four "domestics" on our floor would overcome the guard and finish him off. The workers on all the other floors would do the same, and in this way we would gain control of the whole prison within minutes without anyone on the outside finding out. The domestic workers would quickly free us together with four other English prisoners. We would then be seven trained men in possession of the guards' weapons. We would put the telephone exchange out of commission, cutting contact with the outside. Even if we had to get into a skirmish with the SS in the guardroom at the gate, they would not be able to get reinforcements and we would overcome them. We would then free all the one thousand prisoners. In the chaos it would be easy to escape.

When he first heard the plan, Fleischmann was stunned, but he was persuaded that it could be put into operation. But would the rest of the "domestics" help? Despite everything they had seen in prison, they still hoped, as Fleischmann put it, that a miracle would befall them and that they would be saved because of their status.

"Explain to them, convince them that there's no other way out. We'll all be destroyed, including them. Their only chance of staying alive is if our plan works."

We clasped hands: We would try!

A new vigor filled me. I was ready for the night to come.

Fleischmann came back toward evening, downcast. They did not agree. They also threatened that if we did not abandon the plan, they would inform on us. They knew what they could expect, but were more afraid of torture than of death. Further, if we did manage to escape, the Germans would adopt their usual method: they would arrest their parents and relatives and harass them.

We found out that the guards were preparing another transport early the next morning. This time the "aristocrats" were on the list— our whole floor. Makkai, the politician and anti-Semite, assured us that it would not happen. they had sent a letter to Horthy, the admiral without a fleet, the dictator with no power.

"He would never agree to the annihilation of his good friends," he added.

I had no belief in a miracle. Perhaps Horthy would rescue Baróthy-Huszár, Barayani, and Makkai, but us?

Night came and Fleischmann whispered through my closed door: "We're surrounded by the Hungarian army and tanks, the whole street is humming with activity. The transport won't leave."

It was a night of vigil. Nobody shut an eye. The transport would not leave! We waited tensely for morning, but inside the prison no change was evident. Even the guards were not relieved at the end of their shift. Apparently the new shift was not being allowed to enter. Nobody came and nobody left.

I assumed that the Hungarian takeover of the prison was a direct result of the change that had taken place at the front. The British were advancing at Aachen. The Russians were pressing on the Hungarian borders. Horthy had dared to use his power and defy the Gestapo's will. It was a good sign: Hungary was going the way of the Balkan states and would surrender to the Allies. My informant, Makkai, who was allowed newspapers, announced: "In a week or two we'll be out of here, and we'll surrender to the Russians!"

He was working out his plan for a new political career. After all, he had a testimonial: he was imprisoned by the Gestapo! He kept asking me if I had met any Russians, and what impression they had made on me. He had totally forgotten his inflammatory speeches against the "Reds." All of a sudden he was seeing them as pink.

I knew that they had grounds for hope, but not us. I had no doubt at all that the Germans would kill us before the Hungarians could surrender. Were they in need of living witnesses against them?

I decided to write to Horthy myself. And I did. I asked Barayani to pass on the crumpled note: "Seven British officers are imprisoned in the Gestapo prison, a woman among them. Hurry and do everything to transfer us to the Hungarian authorities. If you do not— our blood is on your head!"

September 9 was a beautiful day, the most beautiful since my arrest. They came to whitewash the cells and they moved the "dangerous" prisoners, who were kept in isolation, into one spacious cell for a whole day. The entire assortment met for the first time, with only Bajcsy-Zsilinszky missing. He had been taken to a concentration camp near Budapest a few days earlier. At last I met my new friends face-to-face. I heard much from them that day: information, guesses, gossip, and secrets. They related how Hungary had been dragged into the war and how it had been conquered by the Germans. They stressed that they, the prisoners being held here, were not guilty. It was the Hungarians of German extraction, the Swabians, who had gained key positions in the government and army and who were the guilty ones. Baróthy-Huszár said that the Royal Council had decided against Hungary's entry into the war, but the chief of staff, Szombathelyi, a Hungarian of German extraction, had taken the offensive against the Russians on his own initiative.

The occupants of that cell were carried away with gaiety that day. Everyone believed that salvation was near and that they would be compensated for their suffering.

"We'll take power! We'll be the only candidates for government because only we are innocent!" declared old Baróthy-Huszár.

Makkai was enthusiastic. "We'll immediately establish a Free Hungarian Government! I want the Information portfolio!" He was the youngest of the group. The rest, older than he was, looked at him with reserved glances: Take it easy! But as veteran politicians they were all caught up in the formation of a government for the new Hungary. Since there were many portfolios and few Hungarian politicians imprisoned by the Germans, they granted Makkai's wish and elected him unanimously. Only two remained without a government portfolio: Ferenc Nagy and me.

"It's a pity I'm a Palestinian Jew," I said. "I'd also like to be a minister."

Barayani, just elected prime minister, was generous. "You can be British ambassador to Budapest, with the approval of the British government, of course."

We joked, but I had no doubt that they took the whole thing seriously. It was a real possibility that some of them could hold office in any regime that would follow the surrender. So I started a conversation with Barayani concerning the fate of the Hungarian Jews and the return of the property stolen from them. I presented a clear demand: any property belonging to Jews who were no longer alive belonged to the Jewish people. He promised to consider the matter—even in this political operetta he preferred to be wary and noncommittal.

Two days later, one of the SS came to my cell and told me to pack my belongings.

"Where to?" I asked him.

"Officially, I don't know, but I'll tell you as a friend— Congratulations! The Hungarians are taking charge of you."

Excitedly I took my toothbrush and soap, and I scratched on the door: "11th September, 1944—I have been released!"

Then I went into the corridor. People I did not know gathered one by one. Suddenly Peretz came. He had lost weight and was pale. With raised thumb, I expressed my happiness. He smiled sadly and made a dismissive gesture, indicating his doubts. His long-fingered hands were like those of a pianist. He did not know where we were being taken. Fleischmann also turned up. There were now four of us, standing in a line with our faces to the wall. Suddenly the barred gate opened with a creak. We all turned our heads— Hannah was coming down the stairs. She had grown thinner, but she had become startlingly more beautiful. She was wearing a blue skirt and a white silk blouse. She had a light raincoat over her arm and carried a small black suitcase. She smiled at us as though she had come from a long journey and was stepping out of a railway carriage. She came and stood beside me, walking lightly I put out my hand, which she clasped warmly. The Gestapo officer burst out, screaming: "This isn't a café. I'll teach you!" He pulled out his revolver and released the catch to let us know there was a bullet in the barrel.

They called Hannah, Peretz, and my name. Antonin Tissandier—to which a small, agile, and muscular man answered, "Oui." His front teeth were missing. Fleischmann. Schwartz— a tall, ginger-haired man with a shortsighted gaze and uncertain movements—answered "Yes." Szecsen, Sipos, Kantorovic—all most likely Croatians.

We were surrounded by an impressive guard and went down to the courtyard. There the familiar vehicle awaited us. There were three like it. They contained three single cubicles, two side-by-side and one facing, as well as a large cubicle. Hannah and I were put into the adjoining cubicles and Peretz was opposite. The others were in the communal one.

We had left the Gestapo jail.

Chapter 7

Fateful Decisions

OUTSIDE—the glory of an autumn day. Free people, women, children, walking about the street. What did they feel when they saw this car? Did any of them sense what was in the prisoners' hearts? Did a feeling of compassion stir in them?

I said "Shalom" to Hannah by lightly tapping on the division between us. She replied. I picked up her question—"What now?"—and answered with the opening bar of Beethoven's Fifth Symphony: V-for-victory. Peretz had his face pressed against the bars of the opposite cubicle, his eyes fixed on us. I didn't dare speak to him, only showing him the victory sign with my raised fingers. A boyish smile lit his face and, with his hand, he inquired, "What?"

We arrived. The guards lined the width of the pavement, closing it off, and took us out in pairs. We had come to the same Hungarian prison where I had been so severely tortured. The officers I knew only too well were at the entrance, though not the long one, Rózsa. They extended their hands one by one and greeted us, gathering around Hannah with affection, inquiring after her well-being and that of her mother. It was as if the evil spirit of the place had passed away. The little rats already sensed that it was worth being friendly. One of those who had arrested me whispered in my ear, "Will you remember that I was good to you?"

They showed us into cells. "Orders are orders," they apologized.

We felt the change in the basement, too. The sergeant and the guards were polite. "In a day or two you'll be taken to a military prison, where you'll be made comfortable. You won't be in prison much longer." They apologized for having to search us. Offering him a cigarette, I told the sergeant that I wanted to talk to Hannah.

"Sit here, by the door. When anyone comes, get up as if you're waiting to be searched."

We were left on our own. I looked into her blue eyes for a long time. It was so good to see her and hold her hand. Her eyes sparkled with a love of life.

"Is this how we arranged to meet?" she asked.

I saw that one of her front teeth was missing. "Hannah, what happened to your tooth?"

"I lost it in Szombathelyi. One of the gendarmes was positively impolite."

"Tell me everything that happened to you after we separated."

This is what Hannah told me.

"The day you and Abba left, Reuven and I left too. Yonah stayed behind to take command of the expected jump.

"I won't tell you all that happened to us on the way. You know what it's like to move with the partisans. We had a taste of more than a few attacks. The Germans adopted a new strategy: they would attack suddenly, without preliminary fire, to take us by surprise. We were saved at the last minute on more than one occasion. Once we sat for hours in a bunker, with the Germans right next to us, and they didn't discover us. General Matačic was with us. He saw himself as responsible for us and he was anxious about our fate.

"We spent days and nights wandering around. I asked the general to help me cross the border. He refused. 'Under present conditions there's no possibility of making the slightest move,' he said. I was almost in despair. We had made contact with some smugglers already, even though the partisans had warned us that they served all masters. Then the group from Hungary arrived. The one you know about. I decided to go the way they had come. We sent Yonah to you, to Papuk, to let you know about this, and to tell you to follow me if you found no other way.

"We had discussions with three of the group that we thought would be ready to join us. Two were Budapest Jews and one was a Frenchman. The two Jews, Kallós and Fleischmann, were friends. Kallós was in *Hashomer Hazair,* and had spent about two years in Palestine. He spoke Hebrew. Fleischmann you know. The Frenchman was a prisoner of war who had escaped from prison seven times, most recently about two years ago. He had been living in Budapest since then. He had come to Yugoslavia in the hope of joining the Free French Army. He suggested that they come back to Budapest with me and join our activities there. The two Jews agreed at once. Maybe they had hopes of saving their families. The Frenchman also agreed. Perhaps he was hoping to smuggle out 800 Frenchman, ex-prisoners of war who had escaped to Budapest, so that they could join the Free French Army.

"I took the papers of a girl who was with them. The photograph was blurred and could have passed for one of me.

"I asked the partisans for a guide to a small village on the Hungarian side of the border, where there was a band of smugglers who had taken Fleischmann's group into Yugoslavia. They trusted the smugglers and thought that if we reached them they'd help us get to Budapest. After an exhausting discussion, the partisans agreed to take us, but only as far as the Drava River. In their opinion, there was no way of crossing the border without being caught. Where we crossed, the river flowed through Croatian territory and the border was twenty kilometers north of it. I equipped myself with a map and compass, and we set out without a guide. Kallós was sure he'd find the way.

"We got to the Drava without a hitch. The partisans had found a boatman whom they had ordered to take us over to the other bank. We crossed safely. We had arranged with the partisans to wait at a certain place at a given time, since we wanted to send the papers back for your group.

"We advanced under darkness when we were on the north bank. Kallós went first, navigating by memory, while I checked the map. We came to a tributary of the Drava. It was a sizeable river. My companions stood there in shock, because on their way here there had only been a stream that they had crossed by jumping from stone to stone. We had taken the wrong route. We decided to follow the river upstream in order to find the crossing they had used. After a two-hour walk, it became obvious that there was no such place.

Palgi (far right), with his parents and his sister, Lucy, in Cluj, 1931.

Apparently it had rained in the mountains since they had crossed and the river had swelled. There was no choice but to swim across. We undressed and began swimming back and forth with the baggage. The current was strong and the water was icy. We swam using one hand while holding our load out of the water with the other. I dismantled the transmitter and we took it over piece by piece. We were very tired when we finished. We sat down for a half-hour's rest to get our strength back in order to continue.

"This sort of adventure happened to us four times that night. We could barely go on. At this point disagreement broke out in our little group: the Frenchman was strongly opposed to continuing that day. He was experienced in escapes and border crossings, and he was afraid it would be daylight before we reached our destination. The transmitter worried him as well. If we came across a patrol it would be hard to get away with some story. I was also sorry we had taken the transmitter. Perhaps it would have been better to leave it and have it sent to me once I was in Hungary. I was also afraid something would go wrong with it from being dragged around. When I had last set it up, I hadn't found the earphones. I thought they were lost. They weren't, but I'll tell you about that later.

"The Frenchman suggested waiting in the bushes all day, and carrying on the next night. Kallós claimed that the border wasn't far away, only a kilometer or two, and there was no certainty we could hide for a whole day so near the border. The border guards were likely to come across us at any moment.

"I agreed with Kallós and we continued walking. We broke up and hid in the bushes. When the sun came up we saw a village ahead of us, some two or three kilometers away. Kallós swore this was the village we were headed for—Mala Subotica. Apparently we had crossed the border without knowing.

"Kallós and Fleischmann set out to check if we really had come to the right village. They were both Hungarian-born and knew the area well. Tony, the Frenchman, and I remained in the bushes.

"We waited for about three hours for them to return. Meanwhile I hid the transmitter and the rest of our things in a wheat field. Our hiding place wasn't a good one; the road rose close by and from it we could be seen through a good pair of binoculars. But it was too late. It was more dangerous now to move around looking for a better place than staying put. Anyway, we couldn't go far, or the other two wouldn't find us.

"Suddenly Tony noticed a squad of soldiers coming from the road, followed by another and yet another. We began to crawl among the bushes in the direction of Yugoslavia. We hoped we weren't far from the border. We saw a wood a few hundred meters away, which we assumed was in Yugoslavia. Perhaps we could proceed under its protection until we came to a forest.

"It was all pointless. When we drew near, we saw that the wood was in enemy hands. We were surrounded. The way they were spread out indicated that they were searching systematically. They were looking under every bush. They were approaching on all sides, and the ring was closing.

"There was no chance of fighting our way through. I counted some two hundred soldiers. We hid our revolvers and anything else that might look suspicious, and began to pretend we were a pair of lovers.

"The soldiers were surprised to find a young man lying in the bushes, with his head in the lap of a girl who was fondling his curls. 'Were these the ones they were chasing?' asked one of them. But the sergeant answered, 'We'll take them, and if it's a mistake, we'll let them go and they can carry on making love.'

"I still didn't know what had become of Fleischmann and Kallós. I heard the story from Fleischmann when they were taking us to Budapest. I'll tell it now, so that you can follow the course of events.

"They reached the village safely. Kallós was right; it was our destination. As their bad luck would have it, the smugglers weren't at home. The woman treated them with suspicion and wouldn't let them into the house. Therefore, and so as not to attract the villager's attention, they had decided to come back to us and wait until dark, as the smugglers were due to return home that night.

"On their way back, they had noticed two Hungarian gendarmes coming toward them. They had considered running, but understood that they would only alert others who would come in search of them. They were on a plain of corn fields. The standing corn was treacherous. It would give away anyone hiding in it. So they decided to carry on walking with an innocent air.

"At the gendarme's request, they presented their papers, which were apparently in order. Nevertheless, they were taken to the guard post for a more thorough examination of their papers. This was a common trick used by the Hungarian gendarmes. The suspect was put to the test by being asked to come along for further investigation; if he showed signs of nervousness, he was taken for interrogation, but if his responses were calm, they let him go.

"Fleischmann and Kallós walked side by side, their revolvers in their pockets. Kallós had a Colt and Fleischmann had two Barrettas. The two gendarmes walked a few paces behind them, rifles slung on their shoulders. The surrounding countryside was completely deserted, except for a few peasants working a field in the distance.

"Fleischmann hinted his intentions by miming pressure on the trigger with his finger. He put his hand in his pocket and released the safety catch on his revolver. Kallós plunged his hand into his pocket and at that moment one of the gendarmes whispered to the other—'Let's take them a little further and then let them go.'

"Fleischmann breathed a sigh of relief. Slowly, so as not to arouse suspicion, he removed his hand from his pocket, when suddenly there was a shot. Before he knew what had happened, he was gripped by steely fingers and his hands and feet were quickly handcuffed. Only then did he realize the magnitude of the tragedy.

"Kallós had shot himself in the temple. His body jerked on the dusty road. Some peasants came over to them and one said to the gendarmes in broken Hungarian: 'I saw two more partisans there, over the road. They're hiding in the bushes.' The other peasant looked at him with scorn. The village was Croatian and had been annexed to Hungary after Yugoslavia was partitioned. Even the fascists among them hated the Hungarians.

"Then the gendarmes searched Fleischmann's pockets and jumped as though a snake had bitten them. Excitedly, the sergeant gave the order—'You run for reinforcements. I'll go and look for the other two partisans.' He kicked Fleischmann. 'This one can stay here. He won't be running away. You,' he addressed the peasants, 'your lives are my guarantee that he doesn't move until I get back.'

"Both gendarmes left. The contents of Fleischmann's pockets, apart from the revolvers, were strewn on the ground. They included a folded note. Fleischmann exerted himself, rolling over to reach it. He swallowed it. One of the peasants, a woman, noticed and came over to him. She whispered: 'Is there something else you want to destroy, my son?' 'Myself,' he said.

"The two lay there for a long time, Fleischmann manacled and Kallós dead, until the reinforcements arrived: intelligence and gendarme officers. The platoon descended to surround the area in order to hunt for us, while the detectives went through Kallós's pockets.

"Fleischmann was shocked and afraid; the transmitter's earphones were in the dead man's pockets.

"As I said, I knew nothing about this. Tony and I, surrounded by hundreds of soldiers with naked bayonets, were led to where Fleischmann and Kallós lay. I understood then that I'd lost the game.

"They took us to Szombathelyi, the gendarme headquarters. I won't tell you what they did to me. It's hard for me to understand how I remained in one piece and didn't lose my mind. I've heard many horror tales about methods of torture, but I had never imagined that people could be so cruel. Do you remember in Cairo, we went to see 'Mission to France'? Colonel Simmons had advised us to see the film. We were annoyed with him. 'What did you want?' I asked him. 'To scare me?' Nobody could withstand such torture. But the torture and suffering in that film was nothing compared to what I went through. No imagination could dream up what they were capable of doing. They tortured me for two days trying to find out where the transmitter was. I denied everything. I knew nothing of any such instrument. Suddenly they showed me the earphones, telling me they had been found in Fleischmann's pocket. I went through an agonizing crisis—should I accuse him or confess? Had Fleischmann not taken the earphones, I thought, they would never have imagined that we had the transmitter with us. But I couldn't bear the thought that he would pay the price for it. He had endangered his life for me and for our mission. I had brought the transmitter and I would have to take the consequences.

"I didn't know the earphones had been with Kallós, and had I known I would have laid the responsibility on him. He was dead already.

"Under heavy guard, they led me off to find the transmitter. I saw Tony and Fleischmann next to the village guard post. Only two days had passed, but it was impossible to recognize them. They looked inhuman. My God, I thought, do I look like that? They had pulled Tony's curls out by the roots and I saw fresh wounds on his head. He had no teeth left. I saw they had been tortured even more than I had.

"When we came to the place, I saw the corn had been trampled down completely. Searching for the transmitter, they had destroyed the entire harvest. A car drew up and from it jumped an officer carrying a suitcase with the transmitter. They'd found it without my help.

"There was another great danger facing me. A book of French poetry was the key to the code. I had to get rid of it, whatever happened.

"I was lucky. The officer of the guard did not know that the transmitter without the key to the code was useless. He didn't know that a book of poetry could hold something more important than poems. He sent us manacled and under heavy guard to Budapest. On the way to the station I 'forgot' the book in the car. Nobody noticed. Perhaps some lover of lyric verse would now enjoy it.

"But in Budapest they knew the value of the transmitter without a code key and they wanted to know what the key was. The torture started all over again. Sometimes the sound of Fleischmann's and Tony's wailing reached the basement. They revealed nothing—after all they knew nothing about the code. I only repeated: 'The code was next to the transmitter.' I claimed that the key was a table of numbers, but they did not believe me and continued their torture.

"Then I made a serious mistake. You, perhaps, will understand me—many probably wouldn't. A person comes to a point where he or she can't keep quiet any longer. You have to say something to make them stop for a moment. They lashed me continuously to make me tell them my real name. I gave them a false name, and they let me be. Two hours later I was again taken to that terrible room. They had found out I was lying and their anger was a hundred times worse. I thought—why not give them my real name? My mother wasn't here anymore. After all, they had promised me before we left that our parents would be out of Hungary before we got there, and months had gone by since then. Mother was surely in Palestine already, and my brother, Gyuri, had arrived there before I left. I couldn't do any of them any harm.

"I told them my name. After an hour I was put into the adjoining room. Mother stood facing me. It's impossible to describe that moment. Strange, mixed feelings passed through me. The first feeling was one of pain, as though I'd received a terrible blow. Suddenly, I was flooded by a wave of happiness—my mother. I shouted it, 'Mother!'

"But in the middle of my happiness, my world grew dark. I'd brought disaster on her! It had been criminal to tell them my name! But once more my heart swelled—Mother! I forgot where we were, forgot the torture and the imprisonment, forgot everything—there was only one word left—Mother! I broke away from my guards and rushed over to kiss and embrace her. It was a rare moment of happiness. I felt as if I'd died just then, the world around me disappeared, there were just the two of us, two souls hovering in space. I felt I was suddenly light, safe, just as I used to feel when I held her hand and nothing on earth could make me afraid. I was in a magic world in her arms, as though evil would never again overtake me.

"I don't remember what I said or what she said. I uttered meaningless sounds and words, like a baby who doesn't know how to speak.

"'Anniko'—that's what she always called me—'how did you get here? What's happened to your face? You've been beaten!'

"I came to my senses, came back from my imaginary world, back to prison. She trembled in my arms, Mother, and all around us stood the cruel interrogators. Only then did I understand the full enormity of what I had done. This was the moment I had so feared.

"I had no words to explain to her why I'd done it. Why I'd come. She wouldn't understand and I couldn't explain. All I wanted was her forgiveness. My eyes filled with tears, I wept, I sobbed: 'Mother, forgive me, forgive me!'

"Rózsa separated us. He was the senior officer who had inter-rogated me, and now he warned: 'I hope this meeting will revive your memory and you will talk. If not you'll never see your mother again.' And turning to Mother he said, 'Convince your daughter that it's for her own good to tell us everything' and he left the room.

"We were left alone, with only a detective keeping guard. We sat facing each other in silence, only our eyes communicating. Could Mother understand from the fire in my eyes what was hap-pening inside me?

"'Why did you do it, Anniko?' she asked in a trembling voice, 'for me?'

"'No, Mother, no! You're not to blame. The day will come when you'll understand why I did it.'

"'Look at your face! And your tooth! Anniko, did they torture you?'

"'No, Mother!'

"A tear fell to her cheek. Mother's so strong, so wonder-ful. How she controlled herself! She stroked my cheek and bent to caress me, but the detective jumped up and shouted: 'No whisper-ing here!'

"The door opened and in came Rózsa and his whole entourage. 'I have permission to arrest your mother, but look how generous I am! Madame,' he addressed Mother, 'you're free to go home. If you tell anyone what you've seen here, your daughter will pay for it with her life. I repeat—everything depends on how your daughter be-haves. If she persists in her obstinacy, this will be your last meeting.'

"She went. Without a word. Are there any more mothers like her in the world? She didn't sob, she didn't weaken me, didn't tell me, 'Talk, tell all, just so I'll see you alive!' She went mutely, her silence encouraging me as though she had spoken: 'Hannah, do your duty!'

"When the door had shut after her, Rózsa said in a friendly tone: 'I'm sorry I resorted to extreme methods with you; after all you are the daughter of the great writer, Bela Szenes. I regret that I caused your mother sorrow. Such a refined woman. I can see how much you love her. You have committed a great sin against your homeland. But you can still put it right. Reveal the code and you'll have made up for it. If not, I'll execute your mother in front of your eyes. They'll kill her and afterward they'll kill you. The choice is in your hands.'

"'No,' I shouted, 'no, don't touch Mother. You can't do that.'

"'In front of your eyes, I'll have her executed,' he said, stressing each word with a satanic smile.

"I broke. That was the first time I cried under interrogation. I burst into hysterical crying and screaming. 'Kill me, torture me, curse me, just don't touch my mother.'

"'The code,' his voice pounded at me.

"'Mercy, mercy . . . '

"'The code.'

"'Mother, mother, mother . . . '

"'Your mother's gone, miss. I'll give you three hours. If you talk you can see her again, if not . . . they'll carry out the sentence you imposed on her by your silence.'

"I was taken back to my cell. I sat immobile as if dead. The officer's words now took on a terrifying significance. I was faced with the choice of becoming a traitor or condemning my mother to die. If only I could commit suicide. It was the only solution. Once, in Szombathelyi, I had managed to tear away from the gendarmes, and I ran up the stairs in order to get to the third floor, to jump out the window. Actually, I didn't know then that I'd have to face a situation like this, but I already understood that death was the only way out. But I failed. I fell and they caught up with me. From then on I was tied up. Every movement of mine was watched in my cell too. The door was left open and a guard sat facing me, never taking his eyes off me. Lieutenant Rózsa was afraid I'd solve the problem in the right way.

"I knew that even if I let them have the name of the book, they would probably fail. They would certainly try to transmit false information so as to lead our bombers into a trap of anti-aircraft fire, whereas I knew that they weren't expecting information of that sort over there, and the whole thing would be suspect. I also knew that my opposite number was well trained and that he would be able to tell in a moment that I wasn't the sender. Yet I knew that it wasn't entirely out of the question that the false information transmitted would be believed. Hundreds of thousands of lives would be in danger; planes and pilots meant to strike the enemy and shorten the war would be lost through my betrayal.

"What's more, if I were only a traitorous spy, it would be bad enough. They would despise me universally. But I was more than that—I was the representative of a people. We had been sent in the name of the Jewish community in Palestine. Our steadfast resistance was that of the whole community—our betrayal would be theirs, too. No, I could not turn traitor. I must not reveal the code.

"But what about my mother? Would I be condemning her to die? To kill her with my own hands? Was there anyone in the world who faced such a satanic choice? Everyone loved their parents, but I . . . everything I held dear in life began and ended with her. Country, ideals, came second to her.

"The time they had given me to consider the offer came to an end. They came for me. I gathered my remaining strength and clenched my fists to conceal the trembling of my hands. I went along with them stonily, frozen. I had determined that I could not do it. I could not destroy her with my own hands. I had decided to reveal the code. I—I was unimportant, nothing. If they didn't kill me, I would put an end to my life. I would not be able to live after such a deed. But she had to remain alive for Gyuri's sake. And they would understand what had made me a traitor. There wasn't a single person in the world who would say—I would have chosen to kill my mother.

"Rózsa asked: 'What have you decided?'

"Is it true that nobody would say so? I continued thinking. But there was—there was one person who would—Mother. Had I asked her, she would have said, 'You have to sacrifice me.' I heard her voice ringing in my ears, 'Don't turn traitor.'

"'I have nothing to say,' I heard my voice saying. 'I left the code beside the transmitter.'

"Rózsa jumped from the table. I saw his body twist like a snake, and the wall behind him billowed above his shoulder. I looked for something to lean against, but found nothing. I was suspended in the air, and the light went out.

"Consciousness returned to me in my cell. I wasn't taken for interrogation for a few more days. Terrible days and nights followed. I ate nothing. My eyes flowed with continuous tears. I heard one sentence ringing in my ears all the time: YOU KILLED YOUR MOTHER. Sometimes it was a whisper. Sometimes it was a mighty laugh. Sometimes it was thunder: YOU-KILLED-YOUR-MOTHER!

"I wanted only one thing: To die! I felt as if I were losing my mind.

"When they took me for interrogation again, one of the 'domestics' whispered to me, 'Look through the window.' Mother was in the opposite cell.

"By means of this sort of pressure, they almost managed to drive me crazy. It took me a long time to get my strength back. They hoped, in vain, that Mother's imprisonment would break my spirit. It was now clear to me that the fact that I hadn't turned traitor had saved my mother's life and my own. If I had revealed the secret, they would surely have had no further need of us."

Hannah ended her story. "You know the rest. Now it looks as if we'll get out of this thing alive. My one serious worry now is about my mother."

"No harm will come to her," I consoled her. "In a week or two, maybe we will all be free."

"Now tell me what happened to the others."

I unfolded the tale about Peretz and myself. When I finished we sat in silence. The sergeant arrived and indicated that we should separate, and so we went into our cells. Just before she went inside, Hannah turned her head and said to me: "In the end, we failed. Perhaps others could have succeeded, but we failed."

She disappeared into her cell.

It was hard for me to decide—was she right or not?

The next day they transferred the whole group who had been in Gestapo hands—including Stipa and the Canadian parachutists—to the military prison on Conti Street, which had a very bad reputation. But we hoped that the imprisonment would last only a few days.

Tony had some fat left from a parcel he had received from the French Consulate. He shared the treasure with us on the journey. We ate it at once without bread. Since my arrest, this was the first time I had tasted fat, and it seemed like the greatest delicacy. I felt refreshed and my mood was very good.

We arrived. It was a big, dark brown building and it loomed over us in a deserted street. Laborers were doing maintenance work on one wing of the building that had been damaged by a bomb. The gate was locked and the guard rang a bell. The other guard stood some paces away from our group with his gun. The driver was behind the wheel. Had we run in all directions they would have hit one or two of us at most, and the rest could have escaped.

"Are we making a run for it?" Tony asked with a gesture.

Why run? I thought. In a few days the war would be over. The guard was not making any political reckoning. He knew only that he had to guard his prisoners. He would shoot and not miss. Some would manage to get away, but there would be casualties. If we had come this far, it would be stupid to die like that.

Tony shrugged. His experience had led him to different conclusions. He had made seven escapes. But he did not embark on individual action. To run on his own would have been suicide.

An officer appeared at the gate and announced that only Hannah was to be imprisoned there. There was no room for us. We parted from her sadly. She put down her small brown suitcase and gave her hand to each of us in turn.

"I'll be seeing you," she said. "Come and visit me at my mother's house, 28 Bimbo Street. If the house has been destroyed, ask for me at number 30."

"Be seeing you," we said to her and got into the car.

She stood at the open gate, following us with a happy expression and a warm smile. Then the car moved off. She raised her thumb with a mischievous laugh.

That was the last time I saw her.

Chapter 8

Waiting

✴ **O**UR HEARTS WERE NOT HEAVY when we arrived in prison on Margaretta Street. We were taken to a spacious room where we were received by a man wearing a white jacket. At first I thought he was a doctor, but when he took down our particulars on a white card, it emerged that he was a clerk. Gustave the Canadian, Peretz, and I were the last. The clerk pleasantly asked us: "Palestinians? Were you members of *Hashomer Hazair?*"

"How do you know about that?"

"My name is Non, Gyuri Non. I had friends in that youth movement who went to Palestine. We're going to be friends. You'll see. Meanwhile, go to the lock-up until they get a place ready for you. Actually it is written here, 'Strict Isolation,' but I'll interpret that to mean strict isolation as a group. OK?"

"Will we be together?" Peretz asked.

"Yes, in the nicest cell we have. We have orders to treat you as captured officers."

"That's better," we told one another.

"I'll help you with everything," Gyuri Non added. "I want you to know that I am a prisoner here too."

We went into a filthy cell, packed with prisoners. From time to time more were brought in: industrial workers who had been sentenced to five or six years for not giving their utmost to their work. Their sentences were passed after trials lasting a few minutes, without testimony from any witnesses. There were also soldiers accused of desertion, theft, striking a superior and such—all in terms of a general clause, "Unfaithfulness to the Homeland." The traitors, Communists, and pickpockets all reviled the regime.

Suddenly a bugle sounded. Everyone stood up and a wave of emotion swept through the cell.

"What's happening?" we asked.

"They're fixing two guys."

"What do you mean 'fixing?'"

"What planet have you fallen from? Executing!"

"On what grounds?"

"Two Jews who masqueraded as officers," came the answer. The sound of shots followed, terrifying us.

We stood at attention. An old Christian began silently praying: "Our Father who art in heaven, hallowed be Thy Name . . . "

My face turned to stone. My heart was bitter. László, you sang well, go in peace on your last road.

When it grew dark, we were taken out into the corridor and organized into two rows. We heard a call.

"The British parachutists!"

The three of us stepped out. The crowd of prisoners gathered in the passage looked at us with excitement. Till now they hadn't known who we were.

Where were the rest?

The three smugglers, the two Jews, Stipa, and the Frenchman had also been put with the group and had become "honorary parachutists." All of us, ten in number, were placed in a spacious room with ten beds that had new mattresses, fine blankets, and clean sheets. The room was whitewashed and looked very pleasant. We were given supper, after which we quickly lay down. No sooner had we done so than the light went out. Silence fell. I could not fall asleep. The day's events had their effect on me and I was very disturbed. I hadn't been in close contact with anyone for three months, apart from a few moments. Continuous isolation changes a person. Against his will he becomes accustomed to withdraw into himself, to think slowly and weigh every detail.

After three months of being alone, a person acquires the habit of talking to himself to the extent that it seems almost superfluous to be in the company of others. Still, the reunion, the sound of living voices, the bustle, elated me. I was particularly excited at being with Stipa. The time had come to clarify what had happened, why we had been arrested.

Peretz and I moved our beds closer to Stipa's and we began to question him. This is what he told us.

After we had left him at the inn, Stipa returned to Yugoslavia. He found Gustave there, a Hungarian of peasant stock who had immigrated to Canada as a youngster and had become a successful butcher. He had volunteered for espionage in Hungary. With him, Stipa set out again for the town on the Hungarian border. Although the partisans had again not brought their people for the sabotage training course, Stipa still trusted them. They handed him a note in my handwriting, or so it seemed, instructing him to bring the suitcases and hand them over to them. He was very pleased that we had crossed safely and didn't notice that the agreed password did not appear in the note. We had arranged that if the word did not appear in any communication, he should understand that it was either a forgery or written under duress, that is, that we were in enemy hands, in which case he was to notify the nearest British contingent.

We saw Stipa in all his stupidity and pettiness at that moment. Possibly when it came to blowing up trains, he was the greatest of his generation, and he had also been great in the battlefield. In his uniform—the Gestapo outfit with the Tito hat and red star and bearing his rank as major as he sat astride his white horse— he had made an excellent impression. Now, small, broken, ragged, and unshaven, we saw before us a simple, naive peasant who barely knew how to read and write, and who was quite distraught.

Had it not been for our exhilarated mood, I would have beaten him soundly when he answered how he had not seen that the note was a forgery: "Well, you see, I've just remembered the word, but then I forgot."

Gustave the Canadian had also gone to Pecs and the detectives, of course, had been on his heels. That was on June 23, 1944, the day Peretz and I had managed to evade the detectives in Budapest. They had then decided that Gustave should be arrested before he also managed to vanish from the scene. However, they allowed Stipa to return to Yugoslavia and bring the suitcases.

On June 26, Stipa was arrested at the inn when he handed over the suitcases to the Hungarian "partisans." Six men had fallen upon him and, bewildered at the force of the attack, he had not even the chance to draw his revolver.

Now it was clear how the transmitter had fallen into the hands of the police. One link was missing, and only now did I have the opportunity to ask Peretz how he had been arrested and what had happened to him.

"After we parted at your flat, I went home with Margit," Peretz said. "I had accepted the decision that I was to leave Hungary, but I didn't want to go back to Yugoslavia. I decided to try and reach Romania. But the people in charge of smuggling put me off with all sorts of excuses. I understood that they didn't trust me. Our unexpected arrival had shaken them. Our story of having come from Palestine as British parachutists was too far-fetched and they were suspicious of it.

"Kasztner suggested that I join the train that was supposed to be going to Spain. I wanted your advice; that's why I sent Margit to find out if everything was all right with you, and if it was possible to come to you. I walked thirty or forty paces behind her. I saw them going into your building, and then I noticed two cars parked outside, with the R.R. markings on them—the military police sign. I carried on, walking past the building so as not to arouse suspicion. I knew that they had come to arrest you. About two hundred meters further, I came to a standstill, and I stood helplessly, waiting to see how things would end. I saw you come out under escort and get into a car. Then I saw Margit come out—also under arrest.

"My first reaction was to run. To get out of this city, out of this country. If they had found you, they would find me, too. I couldn't help you, and if I was caught your position would be even worse. They would cross-examine us and use one against the other.

"I hurried to Kasztner and told him about your arrest. We conferred and decided that I should leave with the convoy for Spain. Kasztner drove me to the camp run by the SS where the inmates, on the face of it, were due to be sent to a death camp. The Germans took great care to keep the Hungarian authorities from discovering their deception. The Hungarians knew nothing about the plan to smuggle Jews to Spain.

"In the camp I was caught in a terrible predicament: there were many friends and acquaintances who would surely recognize me.

Do you remember Shoshanah, the blonde, the one I was once interested in? I met her in the yard. She was amazed. She stared at me and
cried, 'Peretz!' I looked at her like a stranger, not daring to say a
word in case my voice would shake and give me away. She passed a
hand over her eyes, like someone brushing away a dream, and said:
'Sorry. You look so much like someone, a childhood friend . . . but
he's far away from here, he went to Palestine ages ago.'

"I breathed a sigh of relief. If she hadn't identified me, nobody
else would. With pounding heart, I walked around the camp, exam-
ining everyone I passed. You see, my parents were there. I couldn't
make myself known to them, but I wanted to see them. Can you
imagine what I felt when I suddenly saw my father? My tall, upright
father was walking stooped, looking broken, his clothes hanging on
him. I stood, holding my breath. I knew I should hide from him, but
my legs wouldn't obey me and I stood unable to move. He passed in
front of me, stood stock-still, opened his mouth to say something,
and raised a shaking hand. But his hand dropped at once and with a
bewildered face, he walked away. After a moment he came back and
turned his head in my direction, while I stood there motionless,
completely frozen. He left. He hadn't recognized me. I decided to
reveal myself to my parents only when we were in a safer place, further away.

"It became dark. I spent a night of horror. I imagined you being
tortured by the murderers. Would our comrades have the strength
to rescue you? The train was due to leave the following day, and it
was supposed to arrive in Spain three days later. I would get back
home, but what would I tell our comrades, what would I tell them
at home? That I had left you when you were in trouble, saving my
own life?

"I had agreed to leave Hungary on your orders! But was this
still binding under the circumstances? Certainly not. I had to stay
and do everything I could to help you. I would have to stay even
if I couldn't rescue you. Who would take your place, if not me?
Who knew why Hannah was taking so long to come? Perhaps she
wouldn't come at all. Perhaps some disaster had befallen her? I resolved to stay.

"Kasztner arrived in the morning and I heard that all my worst
fears had come true. You were being held by the Hungarians. The
house of cards you had built in your talks with the Gestapo had
caved in. The Germans knew more about us than we had assumed

and they had told Kasztner quite clearly—the train would not go to Spain but to a death camp if he, Kasztner, did not find me and hand me over to them. You can imagine what I was feeling. I'd come here to lead a Jewish rebellion only to end up with no choice but to hand myself over to the Gestapo. Wasn't this some sort of betrayal of the oath I had taken? The knowledge that my parents were among those whose fate would be decided by my decision was unbearable. I couldn't work out to what extent I was objectively weighing the matter and to what extent their fate influenced my decision.

"Finally I decided and chose what was really the only possibility—I'd do as Kasztner said.

"I wasn't strong enough to leave the camp without kissing my mother and father. I won't tell you about that meeting minutes before our ways separated, theirs to Spain and Palestine, mine—straight into the arms of the Gestapo. It's hard for me to describe my feelings. My parents were in shock. I told them our coming back to Hungary was related to the departure of the convoy. I tried to calm them and told them that we were holding two Germans hostage and that they would be released only after our return to Palestine.

"If only you could have seen my father at that moment! His eyes were full of tears and his voice shook as he said: 'You're a soldier, my son, and you must do your duty! Good luck!'

"Mother cried quietly. She clung to me. But she didn't plead with me to come with them. It would have been easier for me had they confronted me with words, or an outburst.

"From the hiding place in which we'd met, I watched them walk, supporting each other, through the gate of the camp. The Jews had all left the camp when I, too, walked out of the gate.

"The detectives were waiting for me outside. They grabbed me by the arms, made sure I was unarmed, and pushed me into the car. You know the rest."

I followed his story with growing shock. In the end I couldn't control myself and asked: "Could Kasztner and his partners really have handed us over in cold blood?"

Peretz contemplated for a long time before answering.

"There's no simple answer to your question. It seems that Kasztner imagined he was manipulating the strings, without understanding that he was a puppet being controlled by other hands. Have you heard what became of my parents? Do you know where they sent the train?"

"No," I answered softly.

"I haven't heard either," Peretz continued. "I try to comfort my-self with the hope that I rescued them. I'll judge Kasztner in terms of what happens to the people on that train. If they were rescued from this hell, I'll be able to accept what I did too."

✳ ✳ ✳ ✳ ✳

It was now Tony's and Fleischmann's turn to describe their way to Yugoslavia and back. They told how they had acquired the smugglers' address from Schwartz—himself a Hungarian Jew and one of our new cellmates, whom we now met for the first time. Af-ter they had crossed the border—they were eight men and one woman—the smugglers left them beside the Drava, promising to return the next day. They hid next to the river. They waited eight days for the smugglers, who never came. They decided to proceed under their own steam in the direction of the mountains, which they succeeded in doing.

In Yugoslavia they joined a fighting partisan brigade, with the exception of the two Frenchmen, Tony and Paul, who wanted to reach de Gaulle's forces. One member of the group, known as Albert, who wore glasses with clear lenses and dyed his hair, was trying to establish contact with the British. He claimed he was a diplomatic messenger and had in his possession secret letters from the man who had been prime minister in Hungary until he was ousted when the Germans invaded—Kállay. According to Albert, Kállay was hid-ing in the Turkish consulate in Budapest and was planning a pro-British rebellion.

"We hoped to make contact with the British contingent through Albert," Fleischmann continued. "When we were taken to the British, we met Captain Gary [Reuven Dafni], who interro-gated us thoroughly. A woman officer, Hannah Szenes, though we didn't know this yet, and another fellow with dark hair and brown eyes [this must have been Yonah, Peretz explained] offered us the chance to go back to Hungary to work under the woman officer's guidance.

"We agreed and set out. The woman officer was given the pa-pers of the girl we had brought into Yugoslavia. When we were over the border and about to enter the village, Kallós expressed his fear of what would happen if we were questioned and they found out that the women officer couldn't speak Hungarian. She had spoken only

English with Kallós and French with Tony. She hadn't spoken to me at all, because I don't know any language other than Hungarian.

"'Don't worry,' she said in good Hungarian, 'I'll manage in Hungarian too.'

"That was a surprise. We blushed because we had used some expressions not usually used in the company of women."

When the story came to a part I already knew from Hannah, I stopped them with the question: "How was Schwartz arrested?"

"The smugglers were caught and they divulged that Schwartz had sent us to them."

The smugglers with us in the cell protested. They had not turned in anyone. But I was sure that one of them, Kantorovi, had informed on them. I had not liked him from the beginning.

One of the smugglers, Szécsény, who had been quiet the whole time, exclaimed despairingly: "But who turned me in? I'm innocent!"

"What are you crying about?" Peretz rebuked him. "You're not being interrogated."

"I want them to let me out of here. I'm not guilty. I was only selling eggs."

We burst out laughing. "Eggs?"

"Yes, two hundred eggs."

"And they arrested you for that?"

"Yes, and they said they're going to hang me. Honestly, only two hundred eggs. I sold them dirt cheap."

"He's right," said Sipos, the other smuggler. "He was only selling eggs."

"So why was he arrested?"

"Because Kantorovi said there were three of us, and the whole village knew that Szécsény was a smuggler and so they arrested him too."

"But there were only two of you," Fleischmann interrupted.

"That's right, but we signed a statement saying that there were three of us."

"They'll hang me," sobbed Szécsény.

Air raid sirens sounded and immediately the bombers were flying overhead. Searchlights came on and we heard powerful explosions. Prisoners streamed into the shelter.

"We're likely to be hit," Schwartz explained. "There's a gas factory in the vicinity."

A hellish symphony began. I do not know how many planes were attacking, but it was the biggest air raid I had experienced during the entire war. The sound of the explosions blended into one continuous thunder. It seemed as though the planes were stationary. The rumble of their engines never stopped. We all lay on the floor, looking up at the sky in great tension. Szécsény was the only one to get hysterical: "I don't want to die! I've got a wife and children!"

He attacked the cell door with his fists. We could not calm him. The guard opened the door and asked roughly: "What's up?"

"I want to go to the shelter," Szécsény answered.

Indeed, only the lives of murderers and pickpockets had any value here. The attack lasted for six hours. My nerves became accustomed to the thunder and I fell asleep.

* * * * *

They brought us breakfast the next morning. We sipped the thin soup, ate our 200-gram portion of bread—the day's allowance—and remained hungry.

We were taken for a medical examination. Only the doctor's assistant was in the clinic; his name was Totovits. He was a youngster in his twenties who had been sentenced to death, but this had been commuted to life imprisonment. Four years earlier he had blown up a German military vehicle, killing over twenty soldiers. He whispered to us: "See that one of you is sick every day and I'll be your contact."

We returned to our cell. We began to receive visits. A tall man with a movie star mustache came in and introduced himself.

"Schneeweiss. German. Life imprisonment. I'm a clerk here. What do you need? Cigarettes! You'll get some at once."

He turned to the corridor and called to someone thin, with a refined face—a man of about thirty.

"My name's Johnny," he said in English. "Berlin correspondent for the *Daily Telegraph*. I was sentenced to death, but my sentence was commuted. We'll look after you. For the time being, take this!" He took a box out of his pocket with about a hundred cigarettes in it. Then the two of them left.

We pounced on the box. For months I had been smoking cigarettes made of sawdust and newspaper. The world suddenly looked good. We sat in a circle enjoying the rising smoke. The door opened again and in the doorway stood a gray-haired paunchy man in uniform. When we saw the colonel's rank on his shoulder, we stood to attention.

"I am Colonel Babos," he said, "the public prosecutor."

We did not say, "Nice to meet you." We were silent. He surveyed us one by one and suddenly asked: "Which of you is the major?"

Stipa, small and miserable, who had been standing behind one of the smugglers, answered tremulously: "I am."

The colonel was most surprised.

"Are you a major?" This was not how the Hungarian junker had imagined him. An officer, according to the standards of a Hungarian military man, would be educated, a man of culture, of good family and bearing.

"What did you do before the war?" he asked.

"Laborer!"

The colonel winced and then burst out laughing.

"A laborer?! Ha-ha-ha! And a major? Now I know what the partisan army's worth! You wouldn't even be a simple soldier with us! With one company of cavalry I'd wipe out every partisan together with your Tito—and in less than twenty-four hours!"

"In spite of all that, I am a major!" insisted Stipa. Peretz was unable to restrain himself and burst out laughing.

"And who are you?" the colonel asked.

"Lieutenant Goldstein," he answered.

"A Jew, eh?"

"Yes!"

"You've come here to stick a knife in our back! And we treat you well." He started walking to and fro, very angry. "Beds! Sheets! Do you deserve them?"

"If courageous Hungarian parachutists were caught on English soil, they'd be treated in a more decent manner," answered Peretz, "except that you haven't got such people!"

Colonel Babos flushed.

"Insolence!" he roared. "A Hungarian jumps wearing his uniform, weapon in hand, and he never relinquishes a post he's conquered! Whereas you, you spies, you come like thieves in the night, Moscow's hirelings! You and your Churchill. Try Communism in England, not here! You'll be up to the neck in blood, but there'll be no Communism here!"

"Blood calls to blood, Colonel," said Peretz.

"Swine! Shut your mouth! I'm not afraid of Roosevelt the Jew! I'm not afraid of anyone on earth. I'll show you what I can do! Filthy Jews, traitors!"

"Colonel, sir," I addressed him politely, "you're mistaken. With you, the traitors are in government and the patriots in jail."

He strode toward me, fists clenched and eyes burning, but he changed his mind, turned around and left the cell, his face promising evil. At the door he looked back and screeched: "Swine! You'll remember me yet!" and slammed the door.

We broke into boisterous laughter. It was a marvelous release from the continuous sense of oppression and distress we lived with. We relished our victory. We were certain that his threatening fist could not harm us. He would not dare. When Hungary surrendered, Nazi collaborators would face vengeance.

An hour had not gone by when the door opened again.

"Pack your things! You're moving out!"

"Where to?" we asked.

"Somewhere you'll be less happy!"

An uneasy feeling descended upon us. Perhaps we had overstepped the mark. We went up two floors, where we were put into a narrow room one-meter-sixty wide and six meters long. It was dirty and empty except for blankets. We stood waiting. Hours passed and nobody came. When it grew dark, we began banging on the door.

"You've forgotten us here!" we told the guard.

"To hell with it! This is your new cell," the guard snapped.

"What?! But there's no room here to stand or lie down—there are ten of us! How are we supposed to sleep? On the floor?"

"If there's no room for you to sleep, hang yourselves!" the guard laughed.

"And supper?" Szécsény demanded.

"No supper. The colonel's orders are only two meals a day from now on."

We were shocked. Was this how the colonel, the public prosecutor, was taking revenge on us? But never mind, we said, he would not break us like that. In fact, it was a sign of weakness. He had no other way of getting at us.

We discussed how we should sleep: lengthwise, only nine could fit in; crosswise it was impossible to lie straight. We finally decided that all the short ones—seven in number—would lie across the cell and the remaining space would be for the three tall men. The blankets would serve as both mattress and covering.

* * * * *

The days crawled by. We sat all day long on folded blankets, our backs against the cold wall, telling stories in order to take our minds off the night. There was only thin soup to eat in the morning and a spoonful of soup with vegetables at noon. From morning to night each person battled with himself over the portion of bread. We divided it into three thin slices that did nothing to assuage the hunger that tormented us. The bread became a yardstick of character. Those lacking self-control ate it all at once. Others didn't touch it until evening, when they ate it under the gaze of hungry eyes that followed every movement of the mouth. This bread, kept till evening, held our thoughts through the whole day.

Our cell had a special lock in addition to the usual one. It could be opened only in the presence of the officer of the guard who kept the key. This did away with the hopes we had pinned on our friends, Non, Schneeweiss, Johnny, and Totovits. They would not be able to help us. The guards were crude and foul-mouthed. They could not forgive us for refusing to address them with the words "we humbly request," as required by prison rules, so they cursed, threatened, and humiliated us. Nor did they allow us to remove the slop pail. When it was full we all banged loudly on the door and finally we urinated through a crack in the door. This roused a storm. They reminded us what we could expect under emergency laws: on charges of treason, sabotage, espionage, and such, the accused were tried in a court that had the power to hand down the death sentence or a verdict of not guilty. But we knew that the accused had to be brought before such a court within eight days of arrest, and sentence had to be carried out within two hours. If this period passed, the court order was cancelled. So to this threat we answered unanimously: "We were arrested three months ago!"

Our only comfort came from the doctor's assistant. One of us went every day for a medical examination, returning full of information. While treating the "patient," Totovits managed to convey a summary of the day's news: the Russians were getting closer and closer. Battles around Szeged, Szeged taken, Kecskemet under siege—it was a good lesson in the geography of Hungary. Fleischmann and Schwartz drew a map of Hungary with boot polish. We would spend hours studying the map, checking distances, making imaginary trips to the battlefronts that were so close. Sometimes one of us would raise a finger: "Shhh!" imagining the sound of cannons, then shaking our heads at the mistake. Our mood, which had been high at the beginning, grew increasingly worse due to the difficult conditions in the cell and the endless anticipation. We could not understand what had happened, why Hungary had not yet surrendered.

On September 29 it seemed that there was a turn of events. The news came, as if borne on the wind, that Hungary's army was on emergency alert. The guard was not changed, visits to the doctor were canceled, as was the walk in the exercise yard, and prisoners were forbidden to congregate. We sensed that something was about to happen.

That night there was a light tap at the door. One of the guards whispered, giving the Social Democratic greeting at the beginning and end of his message: "Friendship! The Fascists tried to take over the government, without success. Tomorrow—surrender! Hungary will be out of the war! Friendship!"

We passed a sleepless night. But when day came everything was back to normal, as though nothing had happened.

In the morning we were taken under heavy guard to the military court building in the prison yard. There was a notice on the door: "Emergency Court. Do not disturb!"

I contracted my muscles so that the guards would not sense the tremor passing through me. We were all as white as chalk. We had deluded ourselves. We would be tried without a lawyer, without any defense, in a special court which, even under fascist law, was illegal.

They called my name. I was surprised when I entered to see only an officer and a sergeant sitting at a table decorated with icons of the crucifixion. Could it be that a mere sergeant and an officer had been given power over human life?

"My name is Captain Simon. I am your prosecutor!" said the officer, indicating a chair.

The sergeant read my name from a document and asked if I was the person.

"I have to present the case against you in the military court," the prosecutor began. "The charge is clear, but some details will have to be checked. I don't know how much time will be taken up by additional interrogation. You have the decision in your own hands: either to be judged at once or to postpone the trial. If your trial is held now, there's no doubt that you'll be sentenced to death, but they may decide to grant you clemency. But you can drag it out and maybe you won't have to stand trial at all."

I thought for a moment. If the prosecutor was talking like this, there was probably a chance for a pardon. But what did I need the trial for? And if someone, simply out of neglect, forgot to sign the pardon? I would be executed! It would be better to postpone the trial and maybe in the meanwhile, there would be an armistice. I chose to postpone and he agreed.

Peretz did the same. We were both returned to our cell and our spirits revived.

* * * * *

The military prison on Margaretta Street was a gray and dismal four-story building. It had been built for 300 prisoners, but 2,400 people were incarcerated at that time. There were 89 Jewish prisoners crammed into the cell next to ours. Jews were held in special cells. Jews and Aryans were allowed to be together only in our case—in the "English" cell. Conditions in all the cells were terrible. There was no room to lie down and people took turns sleeping in sitting positions. Jews were discriminated against in food allocation, resulting in fights in their cells. Whoever was left without the smallest of portions would go wild and blame the prisoner in charge of the cell. The guards would sell the prisoners the missing portions of bread for shoes or clothes. In a short time many were barefoot and naked. Every night the cries of the Jewish prisoners could be heard: the pail intended for 6 was used by 89. Water supplies ran out. A prisoner who died was left in the cell until morning. "Keep him till roll-call. He's still on the list of prisoners. Then you can bury him," the officer of the guard replied when they begged him to remove the corpse from the cell.

We suffered from the dirt. For months we had not changed our clothing and had showered only twice. I felt the need to scratch, but I was ashamed. When I couldn't bear the itch any longer I removed my shirt and began searching the seams. I found three lice. I furtively squashed them between my fingernails and lied to the others. "No, I didn't find anything!"

The itch did not stop. I fought with myself for a few hours and then undressed again. I examined my shirt closely and found more lice. My comrades observed this activity with revulsion. I consoled myself that I had pushed them into the task as well. If I had lice on my skin, they certainly weren't exempt. The others did not follow my example. We'll see! I thought. I was well rewarded by a good night's sleep: I was not at all bothered by hunger since I had simply lost my appetite.

I stripped off my clothes and underclothes twice a day. I spent many hours a day like this, checking for lice. It was something to keep me busy. Tony joined me three days later in this and then everyone else followed. I was not embarrassed any longer. The lice hunt became routine, part of the daily order. Hour after hour we would sit next to the wall, crouched over every seam in our clothes. Squashing lice between our fingernails was disgusting to all of us. We soon found a system: we emptied our haul into an empty bottle. The layer of lice rose steadily inside the bottle.

One day we heard names being called in the Jewish cell. It was visiting time in the prison. We knew there was nobody to visit us, but we listened to every sound, trying to catch news of events from the outside.

Fleischmann, who had outstanding hearing, placed his ear to the crack and suddenly leaped up in excitement: "They're calling Andre Kallós! It's our Kallós's brother!"

He went back and peered through the crack and saw the ones who had been called walking past.

"It's him! Andre Kallós is here!"

An argument broke out between Schwartz and Fleischmann as to whether he should be told that his brother was dead. In the end it was decided that he should be told. This Kallós was in great danger, without a doubt. In their testimony, Fleischmann and Tony had placed the blame for the transmitter on the dead Kallós. The detectives had reached the conclusion that Kallós was a British spy, an intelligence man, and they were searching for his brother who had disappeared. It was his luck that he had been imprisoned for another "crime" all that time. They had searched for him everywhere but in prison.

Our "patient" told the "patient" from the neighboring cell that Kallós should be sick the next day. That same day I also received notice to be sick. Somebody wanted to see me.

The following day we turned up, two "patients," Schwartz and me. When we joined the two rows in front of the clinic, waiting for our turn, a thin, dark man approached me and asked my name. I told him and he held out his hand, saying: "I have the same name."

It emerged that we were relatives—distant cousins. We had not known each other until then. He told me what had happened to his family. His wife had been deported, together with their little boy and the rest of the family. He had met my sister some time before the German invasion. He knew nothing about my parents. He had escaped from a labor camp and had worked forging Christian documents, until he was caught a few days ago. He expected to get the death sentence. His crime was twofold: deserting the army and forging documents. But he hoped they would not manage to put him on trial.

In the meantime, Schwartz had told Kallós about his brother's tragic death. The man was completely broken. His brother's wife had visited him only yesterday, telling him she was pregnant. Both of them had been sure he was in Yugoslavia, perhaps even in Palestine.

A pleasant-looking blond lad with a mustache, dressed like a cadet, listened to our conversation and asked if we were the captured Englishmen. He introduced himself as Vajda, Gyorgy Vajda, and told us he had been arrested for anti-war propaganda. He had an escape plan: his friend, a lawyer, would visit him and hand him his permit to enter the prison. With this document, he would walk through the gate. The guards knew his friend well and would not ask to see the permit when he left.

"But they'll notice your disappearance within five minutes," Schwartz said to him.

"Maybe they will, but I'll be home by then. I'll change my clothes, take some money and get out. My parents' house is a few steps from here, at number 30 Bimbo Street."

Both of us stared at him in amazement. We remembered Hannah's words: "If my mother's house has been destroyed, ask for me at number 30 Bimbo Street."

"Do you know the Szenes family?"

"Of course. But only the mother is at home. Gyuri and Hannah were my childhood friends. Hannah went to Palestine a long time ago, and Gyuri went to France. Who knows what became of him."

"Gyuri reached Palestine six months ago," I said, "and Hannah's in the prison on Conti Street. She was the fourth person in our group."

Vajda was shocked. He could not believe his ears.

"Hannah, a parachutist? She's here? It can't be!"

It was our turn to go into the clinic. We were the last ones.

* * * * *

It was October. Cool nights and misty, wintry days. We shook with cold at night, and we were forced to close the window during the day as well, leaving only the round chimney hole for ventilation. Apparently there had once been a stove in this cell. Our hunger increased and tormented us. Our only conversation was about food. We were all very tense and quarrels naturally broke out. Each suspected the other of having received a larger portion of bread. Tony would divide the bread with painstaking fairness. This was what we would do—the one handing out the bread would stand with his face to the wall and call out a name, then he would put his hand behind him, take a piece of bread and give it to the one in line. Nevertheless, one always felt discriminated against.

Bombers circled overhead, dropping pamphlets undisturbed by the anti-aircraft guns. We scrutinized them and saw that they were German planes. We wondered what the Germans were doing with pamphlets. Weren't the radio and newspapers enough for them? That evening the guard came, the one who was a member of the Social Democratic party, and he told us that military vehicles were also distributing leaflets throughout the city. The Germans were urging the Hungarian people not to surrender but to carry on fighting, and warning that the Russians were approaching.

Indeed, we had been hearing the sound of cannon for some days. It came from a distance, but seemed to be coming closer. There was no doubt at all now: it was Russian artillery!

We knew very little about events outside. News was sporadic and it was impossible to know what the real situation was and what the prevailing mood was in the army and among the population. To us it seemed that the whole country was waiting for the Russians to come. Perhaps this was only an illusion, stemming from the tension that was rife throughout the prison: when would the day of liberation come? We found it hard to imagine that the Hungarians were prepared to see their country turn into a battlefield, bearing all the hardships of a war against the Soviet Union. We were sure that the Germans were nearing their end.

On October 12 I declared that the next day would bring the event we were all longing for. Everyone wondered how I knew this, and I explained: on March 13 Hannah jumped into Yugoslavia, on April 13 we made our jump, on May 13 I left for Papuk, on June 13 I crossed the Hungarian border, and tomorrow was October 13. Obviously the Hungarians would surrender tomorrow!

They laughed, but everyone awaited the coming day with anxiety. It is easy for prisoners to become superstitious. How bitterly we were disappointed when the day came and went and nothing happened.

Two days passed. On Sunday, October 15, there was a sudden knock at our door. The guard raised his fist in the Communist salute and cried: "Freedom, brothers! Horthy has declared a cease-fire!" He ran on spreading the news. In a moment, a joyful hurrah resounded from every corner of the prison. The guard opposite our window, on the roof of a small church, waved his cap at us. The doors were flung open and all the prisoners except me went out into the corridor.

The sergeant, who was the officer of the guard on our floor, came around with a request: "Gentlemen, please stay calm. The order to release you is due any moment. But don't forget that there are criminals here too, and I'm sure you don't want them to escape and go scot-free. Be patient."

"He's right." The men agreed and stopped planning an immediate rush out of the prison. How sweetly the sergeant's words rang in our ears: "The order to release you . . . " Our imagination began to work: "We'll go to a good hotel and soak in a hot bath. We won't get out until the tailor arrives with a new suit and clean underwear!"

"We'll dine at the Ritz or the Gundel. Roast chicken, white rolls, coffee, and a cigar."

"Certainly, Tony, and wine, real champagne!"

And before we did anything at all, we would fetch Hannah.

And tomorrow we would begin our hunt for the detectives, especially Rózsa.

The warders were asking the prisoners to return to their cells, to avoid contact with the new prisoners—the fascists. At this news, happiness reached its peak. They were bringing the fascists here already! Hungary had indeed changed its face.

We were all talking at once. Everyone was excited. Nobody was able to control his feelings any longer. Tony was the only one to cast a hint of doubt: "I'll believe this only when I've had the first sip of that champagne."

"Get away, you owl. Great things are happening and you're sour!"

"Don't forget, I've been a prisoner for five years. I'm used to disappointments!"

"Leave him alone. He only likes escapes. It's beneath his dignity to be handed his release."

Peretz and I sat facing each other. We had not spoken Hebrew for months. It was impolite to use a "secret" language in front of our companions in misfortune. Now the cord had slackened and we returned to Hebrew. It was so heart-warming, so evocative of home, of freedom.

"What's it going to be like when we get back home?" I said. "What will the comrades say? We've probably been given up for dead long ago."

"Our return's going to give someone or other an unpleasant surprise," Peretz joked. "And the kibbutz has probably settled on its permanent site by now; we won't recognize it. The children have grown. Where's Yonah? Perhaps he's back home already."

Then Peretz began talking to Fleischmann about his immigration to Palestine, trying to prepare him for life on the kibbutz. Fleischmann had inherited a rubber goods factory from his father. Peretz had decided that Fleischmann would come with all his equipment to establish a factory at Maagan, our kibbutz.

The day ended and nothing happened. We consoled ourselves with the reasoning that, in the chaos following the surrender, there had been no time to attend to the release of prisoners. We would look forward to the following day. Only one thing troubled us; we again heard the sound of cannon fire. Apparently there was still some local resistance and the Germans were possibly trying to clear a way for their retreat.

We waited for our informant, the guard, and he came late that night, but he said nothing at all. We banged on our door in vain— he stayed clear of us.

We heard suspicious noises—explosions, shots, machine-gun fire—close at hand; the sounds of battle within the confines of the city! One by one the inmates awoke. The entire prison was tense and alert. The din stopped and a deep silence fell. We held our breath and strained our ears for the slightest rustle or murmur.

Snatches of conversation and isolated words reached us from the guards' conversation with their replacements: "They've taken the bridges. . . ." Fleischmann swore he had heard this clearly. But who? The Russians? The Hungarians? The Germans?

The hum of an engine rose from the yard. Swift footsteps clattered on the corridor paving. A cell door was opened. We could hear excited conversation emanating from the cell, but the words were fragmented in the void of the passage. We could only catch an incomprehensible mixture of syllables. Then that cell door shut noisily, the barred gate creaked closed, and the footsteps retreated into the night.

Had the release begun? When would it be our turn?

Shots echoed again. We sat tensely, identifying the type of weapons being used outside: machine guns, rifles, hand grenades, and dull bursts of explosives. Then we heard the loud rumble of tanks in the streets. Many heavy tanks.

"The Russians, perhaps?" Fleischmann guessed.

Nobody answered. There was fear in our hearts. Something was not as it should be in the streets. Tanks were coming without firing a shot, nor were they being shot at. The rumble of their engines and the clatter of their tracks aroused no response. If they were Russian tanks, they would have been met with either fire and resistance, or with cries of triumph. What was the meaning of that silence out there?

"They released the captain in 28," the guard called from the corridor to his friend on the roof of the church.

We were stunned. He was a new prisoner, brought that same day, a fascist who had been arrested when the surrender was announced. Now he had been released! It was obvious. The tanks in the street belonged to the Arrow Cross.[13] It seemed that with German aid they had rebelled against the surrendering government and were now in control—the captain's release proved this.

There was total silence in the prison the next morning. Prisoners were not let out for their walk, and breakfast was carefully served with not more than one cell opened at a time. Visits to the doctor were not permitted. We were absolutely cut off from the world. A cold, threatening air seemed to emanate from the faces of the guards. They were as wary of us as if we had the plague.

In the afternoon the guard was doubled. Indistinct information filtered in somehow: there was a new prison commander. We also heard that Szálasi, an unsuccessful officer, had appointed himself the nation's leader in place of Admiral Horthy, who had been imprisoned. Hungary was rallying the people for total war against the enemy.

We became fully aware of the change that had taken place on the following day. The new prison commander began his rounds. The door opened abruptly and a gaunt, evil-looking major with piercing eyes behind pince-nez glasses came in. We received him standing. He turned his head and in an expressionless voice asked, "Who are these?"

"The English parachutists, sir!" the officer of the guard replied from behind.

The major did something unexpected: with a sudden motion he mimed the hangman's noose around his neck and exclaimed, "Krrrrak!" Then he pointed at us: "You lot!" he said, and left the cell.

We stood there dumbstruck, but when our glances met we burst out laughing. He really was too ridiculous.

That day they made the prisoners swear loyalty to Szálasi, the new head of state. An amnesty was promised, but only to those prisoners who had sworn an oath of allegiance to the new regime.

Bad news reached us bit by bit. Many new prisoners had been brought in and they told us that there had been a Jewish uprising on October 15, which had been brutally suppressed. Hundreds of Jews were being concentrated in the city squares and members of the Arrow Cross were shooting them down. Columns of Jews were being made to walk in the direction of Vienna, but they were being killed en masse on the way.

We also heard that the military court, which had been virtually canceled recently, had been reestablished and would begin functioning energetically the following day. We understood that the major's display had not been merely to frighten us.

We expected the Allies to intervene. They surely could not quietly accept the renewed takeover of Hungary by the Nazis, not when Hungary had at last dared to shake off the German yoke.

We waited twenty-four hours a day for the bombers to come and rain down fire on the criminal city, but nothing happened. The city was completely paralyzed. Even in the distance there was no cannon fire. It seemed as if the whole world had accepted the fact that Hungary had returned to fascism, more fanatically than before, and as for the remaining Jews in Hungary—their fate was sealed!

Chapter 9

How Hannah Fell

✳ ON OCTOBER 20 Gustave, Peretz, and I were called to the prison office. The prison commander asked our names. The warders answered for us.

"Jews!" shouted the commander, "and where are your yellow badges?"

"These are the English parachutists," explained an officer standing on the side.

"Stupid dogs! Get them out of here before I shoot them!" the commander fumed.

"It's too good a death for them. We'll hang them one by one!"

We were used to such scenes. Since our arrest, we had been threatened with various gruesome deaths, but this time it was particularly unpleasant to hear.

Once again we were taken to the court, where we were made to stand in the corridor with our faces to the wall and our hands behind our backs. We went into the room one by one. I was last.

An investigating officer, a stenographer, and a guard who stood behind me were also in the room. The officer had a red band under his rank insignia, denoting that he served in a military court. He read to me from a sheet of paper bearing numerous signatures. This was a summons to trial under special emergency laws. I knew what this meant—the death sentence, to be carried out within two hours. But I also knew that according to the same law, the accused had to be brought to trial within eight days of his arrest, whereas I had been in prison for four months.

"Am I to be executed?" I asked.

"And what do you think? We'll give you a medal? Do you know what you caused us? The Russians are killing our sons, raping our women, and destroying our country!"

"What have I to do with the Russians?"

"They're your allies."

"Are you making me personally responsible for the Anglo-Russian agreement? I didn't sign it."

"Your insolence goes too far. We'll see if you can keep cool facing the firing squad."

The stenographer looked at me with strange dreamy eyes. I'll never know whether she was amusing herself by imagining my execution or crying in her heart for the young man about to die.

"That would be unpardonable murder. Even under your laws it would be illegal and it would make you a war criminal. You won't get away with it, you can be sure."

He gave me a long look. Then he stood to his full height. I thought he was going to strike me, but he turned to the guard and stenographer, saying, "Get out. I don't want to fix him in front of you."

They left the room and the officer drew his revolver. He came over and stood facing me, as if standing at attention. I saw a handsome man, towering head and shoulders above me. He inclined his head slightly and said, "Lieutenant, sir, I am very sorry. I know that the order I'm going to give is against the law, and perhaps I'll pay for it dearly, but I have received an order and I cannot go against it. I am obliged to stand you against the wall."

"And they'll hang you for the murder."

"Perhaps I'll manage to escape. Nobody will know what happened to you. Meanwhile, I must think of my children."

The guards now collected the prisoners and we returned to our cell in silence. The comrades surrounded us, asking questions. It wasn't easy to answer. Each of us was occupied with his thoughts and his own world. Peretz and Gustave, like me, were deep in introspection. Finally, the Canadian told what had transpired.

The cell was silent. Everyone shrank into his own corner, not daring to look his companions in the face. Suddenly, ominous noises rose from the yard. Someone was again being taken for execution. After an interval of several weeks, the court had renewed its activities. We followed every movement and sound with bated breath. We heard the click of rifles and the clang of the condemned man's chains as he walked to the corner of the small church. The echo of the firing squad's footsteps struck us like hammer blows. The command came: "Aim!" followed by a clear voice: "We'll meet again, murderers!" It was drowned in the volley of shots.

We stood frozen. The voice of the victim echoed among the walls.

The three of us had moved our bedding close to the door, in order to be together. We noticed that our presence was hard on the others. They avoided our eyes, as if the smell of death emanated from us already. We were dead in the world of the living.

I sat immobile, my jaws clenched and my eyes fixed on a red stain on the wall, a reminder of a squashed bug.

Only Gustave was not quiet. The curses flowed as he wished his Hungarian motherland death and destruction. Then my eyes left the stain on the wall to drift around the room until they fell on Peretz's face. He was sitting calmly, his gaze seeming to penetrate the walls and coming to rest somewhere far away. A warm smile hovered about his lips. He was accepting his sentence heroically. Peretz did not want to die. He had never given up hope of returning to that life he had barely begun to taste. He had never wanted to be a hero. However, when brought face to face with death, his spirit was wonderfully serene.

We sat thus, waiting. They would come and put chains on our hands and feet and take us to separate cells. Our chains would be removed only after our deaths.

It was a wintry day at the end of autumn. The cold in the prison no longer bothered us. We felt an inner cold that froze our blood and our thoughts. Only one thing troubled us: our anxiety to have the sentence carried out soon, while we were still able to face it bravely. Suddenly we were overcome by a frenzied wish to impart our last will and testimony. It was Gustave, the Canadian, who started, and we followed suit. We drummed into our cellmates' ears details such as our address: Maagan, Kinneret, Palestine, and we repeated everything that had happened to us, detail by detail, and I told them

Lucy Nuzbacher, Palgi's sister, who perished in Auschwitz with their parents.

the name of the girl I loved, and her address. I asked them to send her my greetings and to tell her I loved her, and that she must find someone who, if possible, would love her as much as I did.

As evening fell we heard the tramp of the firing squad's boots once again. Lipót Jellinek, a Jewish fighter, was facing his murderers. When the sentence was read he shouted: "I die because I believed in a better future; you will die because you didn't believe in it!" The command "Fire!" was given before they had finished reading the sentence.

Two days went by. Twelve people were put to death in forty-eight hours, but our turn had not arrived yet.

When the lights were put out, it was possible to relax. Nothing would happen for the next twelve hours, twelve hours that were all mine. I dived into a world of dreams. Sweet, beautiful dreams of joy and splendor. Father, mother, and my sister came back to life, caressed my hair. Feelings of love from childhood days revived in all their delicacy. I sailed home to my country, Palestine. Tears of happiness flowed when I felt I was with my friends again. From time to time I would awaken and then my imagination, so fertile in hope and illusion, shattered.

Suddenly they were calling names—our names. I jumped from my blankets and was blinded by torchlight. They had come for us.

"Cool! Cool!" I drilled into myself. It was time to show that a Jew from Palestine knew how to die.

We went out to the dark corridor. We said only two words to our comrades: "Be well!" There was no point in saying, "Till we meet again!"

We went down the dark stairs behind the guard. We could not understand why this was being done at night. According to prison custom, executions were carried out during the day.

We were taken into a room. A young, splendidly dressed man rose to greet us, told us his name, and said that he was from the Red Cross and had gift parcels for prisoners of war. He asked if we wished to send messages to our relatives, and asked for our addresses. In shock, we returned to our cell loaded with good things and a spark of hope in our hearts: they knew about us.

The great joy with which we were greeted on our return cannot be described. We were like people back from the dead. But not as ghosts—we came bearing gifts of American cigarettes, chocolate, meat, milk, coffee. I could not close my eyes all night. It was better to enjoy our luxuries and divert ourselves from the thoughts of the fate awaiting us.

The days were difficult. It would have been all bad but for the parcels. The ration of bread grew less and less every day, and there were days when we had none at all. All the food we had was soup in the morning and at noon, a sort of broth of vegetables and water fit only for animals. The cold intensified and tension reached a peak. But still they did not call us. We did not delude ourselves, though. We had had so many disappointments that we had no strength to hope.

On Saturday morning they took us to the court. The trial was to be held that day, they told us. We waited in the corridor, trembling with cold. Someone standing behind me whispered that Hannah Szenes was also in court.

The three smugglers, Tony, and Fleischmann were called into the hall. Gustave the Canadian, Stipa, Peretz, and I remained in the corridor. We stood for hours with our faces to the filthy wall, under the eyes of guards bearing guns and bayonets who rained blows on anyone attempting to speak to his neighbor.

At about two o'clock our friend Non appeared. He walked to and fro until he managed to whisper, "No sentence was passed in Hannah's trial. The bastards don't dare!"

It was difficult to believe—after all, they were putting people to death without trial every day. Could they be wavering?

After an hour we were taken back to our cell. We were greeted by cheers. We found all our comrades there, too. They had not been sentenced! The judges had announced after long consultation that sentence would be passed in a week's time.

We heard from them how the trial had proceeded.

On entering they had seen Hannah sitting on the bench for the accused. She had smiled at them, fresh and confident as though they were at the theater. She listened intently to the prosecutor, making pertinent comments to her neighbors from time to time. The presiding judge was an old colonel with a title, Geró László by name, and the prosecutor was Dr. Macskás. Our friend Captain Simon was the investigating magistrate.

First the prosecutor spoke. He accused Fleischmann of treachery to his homeland through giving aid to an enemy agent. Tony was accused of being an accomplice to espionage, and the three smugglers of treachery. (The charge sheet had to be translated for them, as they didn't understand one word of their "mother tongue," Hungarian.) Finally Macskás read the charges against Hannah: treachery against the motherland and spying for the enemy. The prosecutor demanded a sentence of fifteen years with hard labor for the men and the death sentence for Hannah.

The men defended themselves only briefly. Fifteen years under the circumstances was not a punishment at all. How long would this regime last? A week? A month? It wasn't worth arguing with the judges. Only Szécsény, the smuggler, wept and pleaded that he had only sold two hundred eggs to the Jews. At an exorbitant price, yes, but one was allowed to extort from Jews. Such a serious sentence for so trivial a crime? He had only done it for the sake of his hungry children.

Then Hannah was asked if she pleaded guilty.

"No!" she said in a clear voice, rising to her feet. "I do not admit to betraying the motherland. I came here on a mission for my own country, my only homeland. True, I was born here, in this city, it was here I learned to love beauty, to respect my fellowmen, to strive for a better world. The Hungarian people were tired of anger and hardship; I loved this nation and thus I learned to love the humble and the suffering. I dreamed of a beautiful world in which the Hungarians would be compensated for their great suffering and the Hungarian nation would give the world what it had acquired in its hardship: understanding of others, aid to the weak. My father was a writer and he imbued me with the belief that good would overcome evil in the end. I was the disciple of the nation's great, of writers who taught me that humanity must fight for the victory of good. I thought that this was the spirit of the Hungarian people.

"But when I grew up I understood that I, as a Jew, had no place in this country. The peasants were rotting under the yoke of their land tenancy while the landowners incited them against the Jews. As if we, the Jews, were stealing the bread from their children's mouths. The nation's leaders decided on a policy of racial discrimination and law after law was passed against Jews. And that's how I woke out of my empty dreams, which were the dreams of my fathers and forefathers as well, and came to understand that I no longer had a homeland, a real homeland. Then came the war. This regime, which had been leading the nation astray for twenty-five years, now brought upon it the greatest disaster of all. With neither need nor any justification you joined Nazi Germany in the war. You paid for this deed with hundreds of thousands of casualties. But it wasn't your pact with the Germans that made me fight you. I remembered this nation kindly from my youth. I was sorry to see the people who had been so close to my heart sacrificed to a leadership without conscience. However, you weren't satisfied to fight on Germany's side—you turned on my people as well, and that is why I came back. I came to save my Jewish brothers.

"No, I'm not a traitor to my country. My country's over there, far away, in the land of my forefathers to which I returned. Nevertheless, I remained faithful to Hungary, my country of birth. My purpose in coming is itself an expression of this faithfulness. Every Jew remaining alive in Hungary after this terrible war will have it in him to soften the judgment of this nation, to lighten the punishment it will have to bear.

"The traitors are those who brought disaster on the people. You should not, Your Honor, add sin to crime."

Perhaps Hannah continued to speak, but the presiding judge ordered the court cleared of other accused. They waited for a long time and when they reentered the hall, the presiding judge announced that sentence would be passed on November 4.

The news spread like a brush fire: they did not dare sentence Hannah to death. It was obvious that the judges were confused. Hannah's personality and her words at the trial had influenced them. They understood the day was approaching when they would have to account for themselves.

The following day, Sunday, October 29, we awoke to the thunder of cannons. The windows rattled with shock waves. It emerged that the Russians had made a wide breakthrough in the valley of the River Tisza and were now some twenty kilometers from the city. New hope surged in our hearts. It seemed that the end of the nightmare was not to be estimated in weeks but in minutes, hours, or at most a week.

Indeed, it could be felt within the prison that something decisive had happened. Everyone sentenced to five years or less was released. They were preparing a list of prisoners who had not yet been tried, but the prosecutor had decided on a delay. In the chaos that prevailed, many Jews were among those freed. This included my newfound relative and Kallós's brother. The furnaces in the prison basement were fed with court files. The entire archives went up in flames. Information came through the grapevine that the military court was moving to western Hungary, taking some files and a number of prisoners.

The prison was almost empty of inmates. We also learned that the prison on Conti Street had been vacated. We were anxious about Hannah.

But one day and then another passed, and the freedom we were hoping for still had not come. We grew accustomed to the loaded artillery dialogue a few kilometers away. The prison returned to its routine as though nothing had happened or was about to happen. The seven days passed without the prisoners being summoned to hear sentence. Nor had we been called to trial yet. We thought: just let them not take us away from here! Transfer to a different place held new dangers and postponed the day we would be released. Rumors of the Russian advance were varied and strange.

On November 5 we were visited by Totovits, the doctor's assistant, who came with the excuse of having to give first aid to a critically ill patient. Totovits shocked us with the news that the Russians had reached the Danube, but were pushed back and there was only artillery exchange now, with no advance at all. Apparently the Russians were planning to attack from the south and the north to surround half of Hungary in a giant pincer movement.

This was borne out by the conquest of Pecs in the south and Esztergom in the north. The Germans and the Hungarians had amassed huge forces in Budapest itself and were apparently about to defend it at all costs. It was not worth it for the Russians to besiege the city—they had time—and so they were avoiding a frontal attack.

He told us they were going to vacate our entire prison. In the next few days groups would leave for western Hungary and from there to an unknown fate. The prisoners working as clerks had decided to place Jewish prisoners together in groups to facilitate escape. We had to escape whatever happened. Schwartz was going to be released. Peretz and Fleischmann would be in the first group and I in the second. Owing to a lack of transport we would be marched—an excellent opportunity for escape.

We were not very enthusiastic about this plan. Cold and hunger had weakened us. Any superfluous movement tired us greatly. We had only twice received a ration of bread in the last seven days. We were afraid of a foot march, and the chances of an escape under such conditions were poor. We preferred to remain in Budapest.

Our cell was on the fourth floor. Opposite, on the church roof, there was a guard. There were two guards in the yard, which was surrounded by a wall four meters high with barbed wire on top. We considered a plan to remove the window grating, descend one by one by means of ripped blankets, kill the guards in the yard, and climb over the wall, using a ladder that stood there. Tony, who was considered the escape expert, negated the plan from the outset. It would be better to be deported, he said, because we could find a way to escape on the road. He only hoped we would not miss the chance as we had missed the other opportunity two months ago.

The cold intensified by the hour. The water froze in the bucket at night, and we slept on the floor, our only covering a torn blanket.

November 7 was gloomy and overcast. We crouched in silence on our folded blankets, leaning against the wall, tightly huddled to preserve the little warmth in our bodies.

There was the sudden sound of a shot or two. It came from the yard. What was happening? Perhaps they had executed someone again? Impossible. We were well versed in all the details of the ceremony: the tramp of the firing squad, the sentence being read out loud, followed by a prayer and a bugle call. This was how they honored the condemned prisoner on his last journey, ending in the gray yard under our window. Sipos, the smuggler, climbed up to the window and peered out. "There's a table with a cross on it out there, but you can't see a thing." At that moment we heard the voice of one of the sergeants, hurrying the prisoners working in the yard to gather the straw because it was going to rain.

Had a bullet accidentally been fired by one of the guards? The echo had led us to believe two shots were fired. No wonder, we thought—they had recruited new guards, old men who did not know how to use a gun properly.

Close to noon, Schwartz went to the doctor. It had been a long time since any of us had managed to leave the cell. We waited with extreme tension for him to return. He came half an hour later. He was pale, weakly clinging to the wall. With his right hand, he slowly removed his hat, his gaze wandering above our heads, as if he could not see us.

"What happened?" Fleischmann asked.

"The shot we heard was the shot," he stammered in a choked voice. "They killed Hannah . . . an hour ago . . . "

We stood petrified. Hannah? It couldn't be! It was a mistake, a mistake, a mistake! Why her and not us?

A mistake, a mistake—I repeated to myself. "A mistake"—I mumbled over again—"A mistake!" Tony pressed my hand with his steel fingers, whispering, "Calm down, brother, be cool!"

Fleischmann pounded at the door. The head guard came and asked roughly: "What's up?"

"We want to know who was executed an hour ago!"

"What's that got to do with you? Shut up!"

Fleischmann broke.

"Sergeant, sir, we humbly request, kindly tell us: who was executed?"

That was the first time this cruel man had heard any of us speak in this manner. Even he revealed a spark of humanity. "A young girl. A partisan. They say she was a British spy."

It was Hannah, then.

I felt I had to say something, but the words stuck in my throat. I saw everyone's eyes on me. Finally I managed to utter, "She was the most wonderful person I ever knew."

Everyone whispered after me, as if in prayer: "She was the most wonderful . . ."

We rose to our feet and stood at attention for a very long time. Then we sat down without a word. The tears that would not flow, as though they had frozen, were searingly painful. I was like a man who had lost his mind. I was unable to summon a single thought. I could only repeat to myself what Schwartz had said: They killed Hannah . . . Hannah they killed . . .

I heard about Hannah's last day some time later, from the doctor's assistant, Totovits, and from Gyorgy Vajda, who had been her childhood friend and was now a clerk in the prison.

They had brought her from the prison on Conti Street early in the morning. The last of the prisoners there had been removed that morning. She was put into cell 13, "the cell of tears," which was the condemned cell. She was in high spirits and did not sense what was going to happen. "I spoke to her through the door," Vajda told me. "She was overjoyed to see me. She said she was proud that I, her childhood friend, was here as a prisoner and not a jailer. I hadn't the courage to tell her the meaning of the cell she was in. My heart filled with horror to see her, so fresh and young, joking and unaware of the death hovering over her."

About an hour after her arrival, Vajda recalled, Captain Simon came and said to her: "Hannah Szenes, you have been condemned to death. Do you wish to ask for a pardon?"

"Condemned to death? No! I want to appeal. Bring me a lawyer!"

"You may not appeal," Simon answered. "You can ask for a pardon."

She did not flinch. She stood erect, and with glowing eyes said in a ringing voice: "I was tried before the court of the Commander of the Hungarian Forces, Grade B. I know I am entitled to appeal."

"There is no appeal!" was the answer. "I ask again: do you or do you not wish to request a pardon?"

She flung at him: "A pardon? From you? I will not beg murderers and hangmen. I will not ask for mercy from you!"

"If so, prepare to die! You are allowed to write parting letters. Hurry, because we will be carrying out the sentence in an hour from now."

She was left alone in her cell. She sat for a long time without moving, staring at a point on the wall. We will never know what she was seeing.

She asked for paper and pen. She wrote two letters. One to her mother. Nobody knows what was written in it, because it never reached its destination.

The second letter was to Peretz and me.

When the letters were taken from her, the lawyer who had undertaken to defend Peretz and me, Dr. Firi, went to the court. He was a good-hearted man who was respected by the court because of his past as a military judge. He had resigned from that position, not wanting to be party to the activities of that court over the recent period. Now, hearing of Hannah's sentence, he went to Captain Simon and said: "Don't execute Hannah Szenes. Let her be!"

"She held to her denial all the time, but in the end she confessed," said Simon, taking a letter from the file and reading a sentence. "Carry on with our task. Don't flinch. Carry on with the war till the end, until the day of freedom, the day of victory for our people!"

Dr. Firi was silent. He knew that people like Captain Simon would never understand the meaning of those words.

Simon folded the letter, stood up, and buckled his sword.
"Is everything ready?" he asked his second-in-command.
"Yes, sir."

Just then, Hannah's mother knocked at the door of Captain Simon's office; only a clerk was there. She said she had come to see her daughter.

The clerk looked at her and perhaps the sight of this broken mother stirred some humane instinct in him. He said, "You'll find Captain Simon in Margit Körut Boulevard. Hurry over there, madam, or you'll be too late."

She did not know what his words suggested, but she hurried to get there as fast as she could.

The hour Hannah had been given passed. At ten in the morning, Captain Simon entered and silently indicated that she should follow him. Two soldiers escorted her to the yard. Next to a gray brick wall, at the corner of the small church, was a wooden structure filled with sand that was saturated with victims' blood. A post was thrust into the sand and Hannah's hands were tied to it, behind her back. She looked straight into the eyes of the soldier and the officer.

Captain Simon approached her with a kerchief for her eyes. With an emphatic shake of the head, she pushed away his hand.

Her mother arrived at the prison office. "Captain Simon?" she inquired.

"He's busy at the moment," the clerk answered. "He'll be in in a moment."

She sat and waited. I'm not too late, she thought.

Hannah did not allow them to bind her eyes. Perhaps she wanted to see the sky, stretching above this cursed prison, for a few more moments. Or perhaps she wanted to fix her burning gaze on this officer and his three soldiers standing ready to shoot her, so that her blue eyes would follow them as long as they lived, giving them no rest.

The captain gave the command in a hoarse voice. The soldiers fired. She sank, bleeding, to the sand.

Captain Simon returned to his office. Two blue eyes, the same eyes, the same look that he was trying to forget, met him when he entered.

The mother rose and made her request. She had the right to see her daughter. She was a mother.

"Don't you understand, madame? Your daughter was executed a half an hour ago."

He dared not look into those blue eyes.

A heavy silence fell on the cell. We honored her memory in silence. We sat immobile.

What was there to say? What more? Neither despair, nor curses, nor fury—there was only the silence of the grave.

That was how November 13 found us. We suddenly became aware that they were reading out long lists of names at the cell doors. Our door opened and a guard announced: "Fleischmann, Peretz, Schwartz, and the three smugglers, get your belongings at once. You're being sent to western Hungary."

The six of them took their blankets, their only possessions. Stipa was in the hospital. The interrogation at Pecs had turned him into a broken man. The rest of us stood at the door: Gustave the Canadian, Tony the Frenchman, and I. We extended our hands to those going. With a warm clasp of the hand, I bade farewell to Peretz and the others.

"I promise to escape!" I said. "Till we meet again, comrades!"

The door closed.

There were three of us left in the cell.

Chapter 10

The Escape

THE NEXT DAY, Gustave came down with a fever and was taken to the hospital. Tony and I were left.

Silence prevailed in the prison. On our floor, fifty prisoners remained out of a thousand. The guards were not afraid of us anymore. For a few American cigarettes—which I had cherished like diamonds, smoking sawdust instead—they would open the door for a while, allowing us to stroll around the corridor. On one of these walks I met General Kiss, a high-ranking officer from the Russian front, and Bajcsy-Zsilinszky, who had been freed from German captivity and rearrested after the Arrow Cross rebellion. General Kiss, supported by Bajcsy-Zsilinszky, had been planning a daring operation: an attack, coordinated with the Russians, in which the Hungarian army would drive a wedge deep into Russian lines and instead of continuing to fight them, the Hungarians would open a gate for the Red Army behind German lines. The plot was discovered. They were brought to trial. A few days after we met they were executed.

The man who had been Hungary's prime minister when the Germans invaded, Miklos Kállay, was in solitary confinement. He had taken refuge in the Turkish consulate in Budapest until a "mob"—actually an organized gang sent by the rulers—broke in and dragged him from hiding. I looked into his cell and saw the old politician, with his gray hair and white mustache, imploring, extending his plate. I was shocked to hear him say: "Sergeant, sir, I humbly request a little more."

"No seconds," the warden flung at him, with obvious enjoyment.

We exploited these walks to become thoroughly familiar with the prison building. We were determined to escape. We had thought more than once that it would be better to jump from the window and be hit by a guard's bullet than to face a firing squad or go to the gallows.

The nights were misty and cold. Perhaps the guards would not overcome us; perhaps they would not react swiftly because their fingers would be too cold. We decided to get tools to carry out our plan. We approached the guard with the story that we were artisans and wanted to work—we were bored. He laughed: "They won't put you to work!"

Once we were lucky. They took us to the washroom. It was the first time since we had arrived that we had been allowed there. On our return, walking in two rows with the rest of the inmates on our floor, we passed some prisoners sitting in a ring around a big pot, peeling potatoes. We stepped aside and sat with them. We were given knives and began to peel.

Suddenly there was a shout: "Five men, over here!"

I made sure I was one of the five. I relied on Tony to make the best use of whatever he could get there.

Guarded by an old man, we were sent to the court, where we were ordered to clean some rooms. I was engrossed in collecting "treasure." I put everything I could lay my hands on that would be useful in our escape into a pail. We were working on the second story. The windows overlooked a busy street. I figured that if I were to jump from this height, I would break a leg.

I slipped away from the guard, went down to the first floor, and opened one of the doors. The room was full of people. I apologized and got out of there. I opened another door—someone was lying there. The third room was empty. I darted over to the window, which had white-painted panes, and opened it wide. To my great disappointment I found that it was barred! I went unseen back to my work.

I returned to my cell with my booty: two books, a screwdriver, and a short, thick iron bar hidden in my shirt.

Tony smiled and displayed his find—a strong, sharp shoe-maker's knife.

They did not come for me in the afternoon. Apparently they had found that I was not among those allowed to work.

We decided to escape on the first overcast night.

The plan was not practical. We would have to tear the blankets into three pieces, but it was unlikely that they were strong enough to bear a man's weight, so we would still have to jump from a height of six meters. Nevertheless, we clung to this stratagem, since we had no other.

The following morning we were transferred to a large hall full of people, where we learned that we were to be moved to the west at dawn the next day.

They had just put out the lights when a heavy air raid began. There were over sixty prisoners in the hall, people from every walk of society and every corner of the earth. There were about twenty miners with us, who started singing a gentle lullaby permeated with sadness about generations of miners who often met their death in the coal mines. It was a wonderful song in which the desire for life and hope were woven with fear of the twists of fate and an acceptance of death. Another group began singing when they had finished, after which someone stood and recited a poem, followed by another declaiming part of a play, and finally old Békeffy, one of the great men of the Hungarian stage, rose and recited the poem "Flames" by Jozsef Kiss, the Jewish poet. The sound of the explosion outside accompanied his thunderous voice. It was an enchanted, dreamlike night. The words of the poet came alive in the gloom. Perhaps some spirit remained in mankind. Perhaps they had not succeeded in trampling everybody.

Early in the morning of November 22 we went down to the basement to receive our confiscated belongings. Everything of mine had been stolen except for my watch, a present from an American Jewish pilot whom I rescued after he had jumped from his burning plane over Yugoslavia.

They announced that they were not returning money and valuables, so I had come down to the basement for nothing. There was a sudden loud announcement. "Drivers, mechanics, fall in."

I stepped forward without hesitation. A sergeant asked me if I had a good understanding of cars. I said yes. He escorted me to a yard where a Mercedes they could not start was standing. I tinkered with the engine, found the problem, and fixed the car.

"Can you drive?"

"Of course."

He asked my name, wrote it down, and said: "You're the driver for this car."

My heart pounded: an opportunity, and so unexpected, to escape.

I began working feverishly on the car. I gave it a thorough check, cleaned it, and polished it without a break.

"What are you doing here?" I heard from behind me. I turned my head—Captain Simon.

"I'm cleaning the car."

"You're out of luck, friend," he said with an ironic smile. "This is my car. Did the idiot choose you of all people? Get back to your cell!"

End of the dream.

At noon we were all taken out to the yard. We were 300 prisoners, all "politicals." We were arranged in fives, in alphabetical order. Tony and I managed to get into the same group by changing places.

We were loaded onto trucks and taken under heavy guard to the railway station. We had become friendly with a group of youngsters and we tried to stay close to them. They were Communists, among them three Jews, caught as Soviet parachutists. We wanted to have people around us who, like us, were prepared to escape. The station was almost entirely destroyed by air raids. The big waiting room had taken a direct hit. A strong guard was waiting for us, not old like those who had guarded us till now, but young and violent. All 300 of us were made to stand against a wall, and we were warned that anyone daring to turn his head or make a suspicious movement would be shot. And we stood with our faces to the wall hour after hour, tired and freezing, while the guards dealt vicious blows to anyone who made the slightest movement.

It was misty when they began loading the prisoners into the train cars. The prisoners were in five cars and the guards in two, one in front of the prisoners and one behind.

When we climbed into the car we looked for a place next to a wall. We examined it: not very encouraging. The wood was soft, but it was about five centimeters thick and all we had was a shoemaker's knife and an iron bar.

Taking care to keep our strategic position, we turned our attention to the other prisoners, wondering what they were like. There was one group we did not like: Romanian Kulak peasants, who had been arrested as hostages in the villages conquered by the Hungarians. And there was a Jewish leather factory owner we had been warned about while still in the prison. He had been arrested for profiteering and manufacturing faulty shoes for the army, but had secured good conditions in prison by acting as an informer.

We were pleased to find Stipa in the car, together with a group of five Yugoslavian partisans. We took him into our confidence. He agreed with the plan and also promised his group's cooperation as its superior officer. One of his partisans was friendly with the Communists and Jewish-Hungarian-Russian parachutists, of whom about ten had come into our car. We allocated tasks among ourselves. It turned out that they were also equipped—they had two pocket knives.

Two went to work at once, even before the train moved, and the others stood across the car, not allowing strangers to approach. It was pitch dark. We began to sing in order to cover the sound of sawing. We sang rousing Hungarian songs with all our might, banging when we heard the sound of the iron bar's blows. Before the train started, a sergeant came in and conducted a check by torchlight, but he saw nothing.

"To hell with you," he muttered instead of a good-bye. "Thank God we're rid of you. From now on Goering himself will be taking care of you."

The train moved.

It emerged that we were going to Komárom, in western Hungary, a journey of six hours. We estimated that we could cut a man-sized exit hole in two or three hours. If the train was not delayed en route we would escape in the vicinity of Tata, the miners' city. There were a few from this city among us. According to them, the entire city and its environs were hostile to the Nazis. They were sure we would find cover there until the storm blew over.

But the train stopped over and over again. We had just left the station when an air raid began. We saw Russian fighter planes right over our heads. We passed close to the artillery batteries.

Through the barred hatch we could see flames bursting from the cannon mouths.

The train took a roundabout route, since the main lines were either blown up or occupied. Because of our movements back and forth, we lost our sense of direction and time. It seemed to me that we had been in the car for hours already. Tension mounted every time the train came to a halt, because the guards would then jump out of their cars and inspect the prisoners. The halts increased, but, fortunately for us, they did not manage much since the train immediately moved on and they had to get back to their cars. The work on the hole in the wall continued with all of us taking turns at it.

Our throats were raw with shouting and wild singing by the time we heard the sound we had all been anticipating: the crack of breaking wood. The hole in the wall was ready and cold wind burst through, chilling us to the bone.

Very tense, we gathered around the break, ready to leap. We all knew that it was first come, first served. We were ready and equipped for our escape. I was wearing two suits, one mine and the other a present from a prisoner who had taken pity on me when he noticed me shivering. I had a few portions of bread in my shirt and gloves I had sewn from strips of blanket. Tony had only one suit, but he also had a sweater and hat with which he could make his appearance among people without looking like an escaped prisoner. Thanks to Tony, who had hidden a razor blade, we were shaven. I had an important treasure that I had guarded the entire time: pep pills for pilots and parachutists, which could refresh even the most tired person for hours at a time. I had also kept the tiny compass.

The two who had broken through the wall went part of the way out, but did not dare to jump. We pleaded with them to jump or make way for others, but they only slid down between the wheels of the train when it came to a halt. One of them was not careful enough, touching the link between the two cars and causing a loud clang that echoed a long way off. At that moment the guards opened fire from all directions. We heard a groan—one of the men was wounded.

At the sound of the shots, we all jumped to the opposite end of the car. Nobody wanted to be caught near the hole in the wall. I threw away my gloves and the bread as though I had nothing to do with the matter. The shots became regular: they were using rifles and submachine guns, but, fortunately for us, the train moved on before the guards managed to find out if an escape was in progress or whether their ears had misled them.

Before I could recover, Tony grabbed my hand. "Come on!" he whispered. I quickly searched for and found the gloves, the bread, and another small parcel that did not belong to me. I shoved everything into my shirt and hurried out of the opening after Tony. We stood on the platform between the cars, not sure what to do. The guards were firing on both sides of the train as if they had gone crazy. It would be impossible to jump without being hit.

An iron ladder was next to the hole. It was used for climbing onto the roof of the train. Tony started to go up and I followed.

The roof was smooth with a layer of frost. I slipped and lay flat on the curved roof. The train was going fast and the wind cut like a lance. We started to crawl. The wind blew Tony's hat off; he tried to catch it and almost fell off the roof. I turned my head and saw that the partisan shoemaker, the one who had brought the pocket knife, was crawling after me. We reached the other ladder and went down and then up again to the next roof with the intention of reaching the regular passenger cars so that we could mingle with the crowd. We would get off at the first station, we decided in a whisper.

We came to the guards' car and climbed to the roof. We were out of their line of fire, because they had to take care not to shoot any of their comrades. Then the train slowed, so we hurriedly climbed down from the roof so that we would be able to jump before the guards discovered the hole and our absence.

My jump was not successful. I had earlier received a blow to the thigh and so could not leap as far as the ditch beside the tracks. The train stopped and I rolled under the car to hide. I heard a door opening above and people jumping out. It was the first car, the one the guards were in.

Cursing loudly, the guards ran toward the car from which we had escaped. They never imagined I was beneath their own car.

The guards did not manage to get to the prisoners' car before the train began moving again, and they returned to their car. I lay between the wheels, completely flat and burrowing into the gravel. The train passed over me with a stunning clamor. I lay for a few more seconds after the last car had passed. I could not believe the miracle had happened. Afterward I stood up and fixed my gaze on the little red lamp hanging from the back of the last car that was receding as I watched.

I waved at the departing train and burst into wild laughter.

I was free.

I lowered myself into the ditch with great care. The thunder of cannons reverberated in the air, and from time to time rockets and explosions illuminated the whole surroundings. I stood dumbly in the darkness and tried to discover the whereabouts of Tony.

Suddenly the sound of a high-pitched whistle pierced the air. It was the French song Tony was always whistling, usually causing me to beg him to stop as it irritated me. This time the tune was amazingly sweet. I walked as lightly as a cat to where he stood and we fell on each other's necks. It was so good to be together. I knew at that moment that I had formed a friendship that would last forever.

I took out my little compass and we tried to establish where we were. We decided to get away from the railway tracks. Even if they did not search for us, the tracks were well guarded and we were likely to be caught. We estimated the direction in which Budapest lay and began walking through the fields.

We came to vineyards and made our way among the vines. The ground was wet and it was hard to make progress. Every three or four minutes we were obliged to lie down in the mud when rockets lit up the area. We advanced this way for a few hours until there was a sudden, tremendous thunder of cannons. We were in the zone of the artillery entrenchments. If we continued walking, we were likely to fall into a weapons installation, and we decided it would be better to hide until daylight. Perhaps we would then be able to find out our position and plan our next moves.

We looked for a storeroom or packing shed and, after some exertion, found one: a small structure of river stones. We broke the lock and went in. It was a wonderful hiding place. There was a pile of cornstalks next to it, which we arranged as a mattress, and lay down to sleep. We had to renew our strength.

We were asleep quickly out of sheer fatigue, but not for long. The cold disturbed us. When we first came upon this hiding place, we decided: this is it! We're not budging from here! The Russians were getting closer and there was a chance they would arrive within a day or two. The best thing to do was to hide and wait, rather than endanger ourselves on the way back to Budapest. However, during the night we found out that since the cold penetrated our bones, it would be impossible to stay here long. We jumped around to warm

up. Hunger and imprisonment had eroded our strength so much
that we couldn't bear such cold.

The morning of November 23 arrived in a faint, overcast light.
The horizon seemed unwillingly to reveal itself, but somehow we
made out a village with a church not far away.

We decided that one of us should go down to the village in order to investigate the situation on the roads. At a slight distance, we
noticed a streetcar. The Budapest district was not well known to us,
but we knew that the streetcars went about thirty kilometers beyond the city. If so, we realized that we were very close to Budapest
and therefore could take a streetcar, which were not subject to the
same stringent security checks as trains. But we had no money for
our fares. We could have sold one of my two suits, but we didn't
know how much to ask for it. We hadn't the slightest idea what market prices were and were afraid to arouse suspicion and expose ourselves to arrest.

Tony spoke only halting Hungarian, and his look betrayed that
he was a Frenchman. I spoke fine Hungarian, but could arouse suspicion: what was a young civilian doing in a village that had become
a front line? I decided that Tony should go to the village priest and
try to get information from him regarding conditions on the road
and also enough money to get to Budapest. We could see from the
church that the priest was Catholic. Since it was a known fact that
nearly all Frenchmen were Catholics, we hoped that the priest, even
if he would not help, would not inform on us.

Tony went to the village while I waited impatiently. I surveyed
the surroundings and dozed for a few seconds. Suddenly a pup appeared, barking and sniffing—it had sensed strangers. Hopefully
the peasant had no valuables in his shed and would not be alarmed
by the sound of the dog's barking.

The thunder of the cannons never let up for a moment. The
sound of the shots was sweet to hear! The thing we yearned for was
close!

It began to snow.

At last Tony came. With his strange smile—he was toothless
after his "treatment" by the gendarmes on the Yugoslavian border—he showed me six coins.

"The priest was alarmed when he heard I was a prisoner of war.
He handed over his loose change and told me that there's a streetcar

leaving for Budapest in two hours' time. There's no inspection as a rule. He asked me to leave quickly; if not, he'd call the police. I was careful and took a roundabout route to get back. We have to get going at once, in case he has already informed on us."

The previous night had damaged our appearance, which in any case had not been the peak of elegance after five months of wandering and hardship. After we cleaned our clothes as best as we could, trying to create a good impression, we went down to the station.

I chatted with the passengers, to cover for Tony's poor Hungarian. During the conversation I learned that the Russians had crossed the Danube in the north and the south, and there was the "danger" of their surrounding Budapest. I feigned alarm and said we had to fight to the last drop of blood and not surrender. We looked like good patriots. Tony supported my stand. "That's it!" He could say these two words in a perfect Hungarian accent.

The journey passed without incident. We reached the heart of the city. We had enough change left for one more streetcar ride.

Chapter 11

Refuge

＊ **A**ND NOW, WHERE TO?
　　　To Kasztner? Heaven forbid. To Elisheva Kurcz?
　　　Doubtful, but worth checking. To Hansi's flat, where
I had been arrested? Certainly not. If they were to search for me,
that would be the first place they would go. In any case, four months
of blood had passed since I had last seen any of these people, and
who knew what had happened to them, or where they were? And
we had to be especially cautious. It was dangerous to move about
the city in our condition, and without anyone to guide us. We could
not do anything foolish, however slight, that would go against law
or custom, even things that a bona fide citizen could do, like jay-
walking or littering.

"Come with me," Tony decided. "We'll try our luck at the
French Embassy. Perhaps they'll grant us protection for an hour."

We took the streetcar to the embassy, which officially was the
representative of the Vichy government, but the deputy military
attaché, Captain Roise, was a de Gaulle supporter. We stood waiting. One of Tony's acquaintances had gone into the building and after a half hour came out. This was a sign that we could go in without
danger.

We rang the bell and the gate opened. The gatekeeper asked what we wanted.

Tony introduced himself and, in an accent borrowed from the south of France, said we had come for help. We had just fled one of the country towns recently conquered by the Russians.

The gatekeeper turned to me and asked for my name too. Tony answered for me while I mumbled "yes" and "no" at intervals. It never occurred to the gatekeeper that I was not a Frenchman. We were permitted to go upstairs. Tony went into one of the offices on the fifth floor while I waited in the corridor. A passing clerk asked me what I wanted. "I'm waiting for my friend," I replied in English.

Ten minutes later Tony indicated that I should come inside, and I went into a large room. It was furnished in good taste and had a fireplace that spread warmth and a homey atmosphere. A tall, lean, pale man standing beside a desk introduced himself as Lieutenant Cotin. He extended a hand to me. "Welcome," he said.

An officer gave orders that a warm room and a bath be prepared for us, arranging to provide clothes and a good meal as well. In no time, we were sitting in a comfortable attic room, clean shaven and dressed in new clothes. Cotin entered and was startled; he hardly recognized us. He gave us some money and documents. My document stated that I was a prisoner of war with permission to remain in Budapest so that my familiarity with important professions in the Hungarian war industry could be exploited. I was surprised: somehow he had acquired a photograph of me.

He laughed. "The moment you came in, I noticed the strong resemblance between you and one of our clerks. This is a photograph of him."

I could be his guest as long as I wished, Cotin said, but I was to be cautious and keep away from people. My French was admirable, but I would not be taken for a Frenchman, nor a Belgian, as my documents now stated.

Barely twenty-four hours had gone by when Captain Roise, the deputy military attaché, informed me regretfully that I had to leave at once. The Hungarian police had come to arrest the military attaché. He had managed to escape, but the embassy could no longer be regarded as a safe place. The way they had forcibly removed Prime Minister Kállay from the Turkish consulate indicated that the police could break into this building and conduct a search. He promised to keep in touch with me through Tony and to do what he could for me.

I left the building feeling bitter. I did not believe the captain was being frank. I suspected that he wanted to be rid of me.

I began wandering around the city looking for a place to stay or a familiar face. I went to several hotels in vain. At one of the hotels I noticed a woman listening to my conversation with the concierge, a suspicious expression on her face. The broken Hungarian I had adopted in order to appear foreign did not, apparently, please her. She intervened, asking for my papers, and then gave some sort of sign to the concierge, who promised to find a room for me and told me to return at four o'clock.

I kept a close eye on their movements, ready, should they call the police, to hit them with the bronze table lamp and escape. I thanked them, paid in advance for a week, and left, never to return.

The city had undergone a complete change since last I had seen it. Many houses had been damaged. The bridge over the Danube was ready to be blown up and the Margaretta Bridge had been destroyed, either by sabotage or carelessness.

There were hardly any men my age in civilian clothes. The streets were full of uniforms, and most of the young people were in those of the Arrow Cross.

In one of the streets I came across a column of about 200 Jews being herded along by guards with the Arrow Cross armband. The Jews, dressed in tatters, looked tormented, weak, failing.

Pedestrians stopped and watched. I also stood, shocked and not daring to ask anything. Apparently this was a common sight. Cries of mockery and contempt were heard. A woman wearing furs ran toward an old woman who was lagging behind the others and pummeled her in the face with her fists. I heard shouts from the crowd, berating the guards for neglecting their duty and not getting the Jews to "lift their feet."

"Perhaps they'd rather be going by car?" somebody taunted. But I had learned something: there were still Jews in the city. I went on my way in confusion. I was afraid to follow the column lest I arouse suspicion.

Most of the houses in the street where I had been arrested were now piles of rubble. I found a corner under the stripped staircase of one of the houses, protected from the wind and the eyes of passersby. After making a careful note of the place, I went to the cinema. I spent two hours there, safe and warm. At the end of the film I returned to my corner.

I passed a hard night, almost freezing and afraid to move around to get warm so as not to draw the attention of pedestrians and the many guards patrolling the city.

When morning came, I went to a public toilet where I washed my hands and feet, refreshing myself a little. I wandered around the city again. I looked for the few houses whose addresses I knew, but they had all been bombed. It would not be wise to inquire after people. Who knew where such questions might lead?

I phoned Makkai, the man who had been an anti-Semitic member of Parliament and who had been released from prison a few weeks earlier. He was in Switzerland, so I went looking for his driver. Makkai had given me his address, assuring me that I could get help from him, but nobody answered the doorbell.

I found the name in the telephone book of the old man who had looked after me at the beginning of my hardships and who had saved me when I tried to commit suicide. It turned out that he was a man of standing, with a city apartment and a country villa listed under his name. I dialed the number and a clear young voice answered. I said I wished to talk with the owner of the house.

"On what matter?"

"I have regards from Paris," I answered.

"Really, from whom?"

"I'll convey that personally."

"Come, come, Mr. Pinter"—that was the name I had used—"be our guest for lunch and you'll see father."

The son was at home. "My son is a soldier," the old man had told me five months ago.

I dared not go there—who could tell how the son would react when he found out who I was? And anyway, how could I put my life in the old man's hands? There is a great difference between promise and deed when it comes to endangering one's life for another.

I was left with one more address: 30 Bimbo Street.

This was the address of Gyorgy Vajda's family, Hannah's neighbors in her childhood. Gyorgy had been Hannah's friend. Surely, his father could not refuse to help me.

I phoned, but he was not at home. He would be back in the evening.

I came to Bimbo Street at six o'clock. Charming villas stood in beautiful gardens on the slopes of the mountains. Here was num-

ber 28, a small, attractive house, modestly tucked away in a wonderful garden. Hannah's house. This is where we would have met to
celebrate victory. I wondered what the mother's situation was,
whether she was still alive.

When I came to number 30, I rang the bell next to a brass plate
that stated "S. Vajda, Engineer."

The old man opened the door. He bore a remarkable resemblance to his son. I asked if I could speak to him in private. He led
me to a room and closed the door behind us.

I told him who I was and why I had come. He asked me quickly:
"Did anyone see you come here?"

"No, I was most careful."

"I am very sorry, but there is no way I can help you."

"I am speaking of a day or two—just until I can make another
arrangement."

"I can't. The place is full of fascists. I mustn't endanger my
family."

"Sir, your only son is also, perhaps at this very moment, pleading for shelter from a stranger. Would you like them to turn away
your son as you are turning me away? They'll be throwing him into
death's arms as you are doing to me now."

"My son is imprisoned in Margaretta Street. He didn't escape,
and may God protect him. But I want you to get out of here. I am
not prepared to endanger my family."

I returned to my hiding place in despair.

The next morning I met Tony. There was nothing new. They
had not searched the embassy yet, but it could happen at any moment. Captain Roise sent his regards and promised to help me. I had
to be patient.

Tony chased about with me all day with the aim of finding
friends, but we achieved nothing. Apparently all those who had
once been innocent and honest had now estranged themselves, and
we discovered that it was pointless to trudge the pavements.

After two days I felt that I was losing my strength. I was forced
to lean on walls when I walked in the street. I had a fever and coughed
constantly. I was afraid my coughing would draw the attention of
the guards. As I lay worrying and in pain under the stairs, I had the
thought more than once that I had no choice but to give myself up.

Only when morning came did I feel some relief, setting out
to roam the city again. Tony, whom I met every day, did much to

encourage me. I waited at the alternative time that evening—we arranged two meeting times every day, in case the first did not work out. I was on the point of despair. Had Tony also left me to fend for myself?

But he came, giving me a note with the message: "23A Narcissus Street. Ring three times."

"Captain Roise asks you to be there at exactly ten o'clock."

I gripped his hand with intense feeling. I knew that I was more indebted to Tony than to Roise. We parted warmly, arranging a meeting the next day.

At ten o'clock I was standing outside a double-story villa in a fine garden. I checked the note—I had not made any mistake. This was number 23A. I read the nameplate, "Dr. Bela Antal, Secretary of State."

I rang three times and a tall, broad-shouldered lad appeared in the darkness. He was followed by two gigantic dogs. Without a word and without looking at me, he opened the gate. I was wrapped in pleasant warmth as I entered a large room, divided into a dining room and salon. Four men were seated around a table, and three extra plates indicated that they were expecting guests. A beautiful red-haired maid was serving the meal. The diners rose to greet us. A tall man who bore a strong resemblance to the lad who had opened the gate was first to extend his hand. "My name is Juszt," he said.

His companions introduced themselves one after the other. A short man whose every movement bespoke decisiveness introduced himself with a click of the heels as Lieutenant R. After him came a young man with a child's face, golden hair, and blue eyes to match. "Lieutenant Van der Vass," he said, adding when he saw my wondering look, "Holland." The last of them was a muscular, stocky man with reddish-brown hair and mustache. His penetrating blue eyes had an expression of friendliness. This man never hesitates, the thought flitted through my mind.

"Tim Barker," he introduced himself, inviting me to be seated.

The maid removed her apron, also shook my hand, and sat down near the man who had opened the gate for me.

"What would you like to drink?" asked Tim, as if this were an ordinary visit.

"With your kind permission," I answered, "I would first like to have a hot bath."

Leaders of the Zionist youth movement in Cluj, Romania. Top row, left to right: Yonah Rosen, Palgi. Bottom row, left to right: Yosef Lazar, Rivka Bar-Yosef, Meir Barkay.

Tim showed me the way to the bathroom. Everything was ready for me: a bath filled with hot water, towels, soap, and clean underwear.

"You're a magician," I told him.

"No, I just know where you came from," he answered and shut the door.

Dinner passed with lively conversation. I was asked many questions and I answered them in turn. I knew they were testing my reliability. I learned that the owner of the house was away, but had given these people the run of his place.

Tim, a RAF man, had been captured at the beginning of the war, when he jumped from his burning plane over Germany; he had escaped about a year ago. Since that time he had been in Budapest. Van der Vass, also a former prisoner of war, was head of the Dutch underground in Budapest, whose members obeyed him as though he were a general. Marta, the house maid, was Jewish. Juszt was a Hungarian writer of German extraction. R. was the owner of an estate in northern Hungary. He had come to take everyone there. He had built a bunker on his property where they could all stay until the Russians arrived.

According to their estimate, the area would be conquered in three to four days. They were, of course, willing to take me with them.

"I want to stay here," I said. "I think I still have something to do here."

"As you wish. The house is at your disposal."

The conversation continued till after midnight. In the end, Tim and I were left. We went to make ourselves some tea in the kitchen.

"Are you really going to stay?" he asked.

"Yes, from what you said, I gather that you are the last British officer in Budapest. When you go, I'll take your place. You can hand over your duties to me."

"There's nothing to hand over. The Russians will take the city in a few days' time. At any rate, they'll surround it. You haven't got a transmitter and there is nothing to transmit. Actually, there remains only one duty that I will hand over to you. It's something we have to do as human beings: help the Jews in every way you can, because the Germans are annihilating them."

I was filled with admiration for Tim, who said this while tending the kettle. It was good to hear such words. I couldn't contain myself and clasped his hand in gratitude.

He looked at me in amazement.

"What are you thanking me for? I have given you a difficult job. But I am sure you will cope, since you are a Jew from Palestine. I want you to know that I also did my best."

I could barely restrain tears.

We drank our tea. As we were about to go to bed, he said, "By the way, Van der Vass will put you in touch with some people who will be pleased to see you: people from the fighting Zionist underground."

The next day, I went to the city with Tim. I asked him what documents he was using and he showed me a revolver. He took a position near the steps when we were on the streetcar, ready to jump at a moment's notice. When I heard him ask for a ticket in Hungarian, a chill ran down my spine. Any fool could tell he was a foreigner. And he had lived in this city for over a year, roaming around from morning to night without knowing Hungarian or German. He was fluent in one language, English.

Tony did not come to our morning meeting. I was a little worried when he did not turn up at the alternative meeting either. I walked around and, in the evening, met Van der Vass. I heard from him that there had been a search at the French Embassy and many had been arrested, Tony among them, possibly.

I went to the International Red Cross office with Van der Vass.

After a short while, we were taken to the manager's office. A broad-shouldered young man with a blond forelock—a typical German—rose from behind the large desk.

"Mr. Sampias." Van der Vass introduced him.

I looked at him. I had seen this person somewhere before. I remembered it: with Kasztner and Peretz. But this was Rafi. Rafi Friedl.

"Rafi," I exclaimed in surprise.

He looked at me as though he could not believe his eyes.

I had reached safe shores.

I heard about the situation from my companions until late that night. I had difficulty catching up. Two days ago, Kasztner had gone to Switzerland for the third time. The negotiations with the Germans were still going on. This time, they were demanding money, in American or Swiss currency. The Gestapo officers wanted to have good money in hand when the day came for them to run for their lives. They were also looking for contacts to help them evade punishment.

This was the inside view of the negotiations, whereas on the surface, they were interested in carrying out a population exchange. In Russia and Russian-held Romania were hundreds of thousands of Germans, and the Nazis were suggesting that these be exchanged for Jews. A ghetto had been established in Budapest, where 80,000 Jews were concentrated under dreadful conditions, and in the meantime the Nazis were bringing more Jews. The column that I had seen had been on the way to the ghetto. There had not been another expulsion, mainly for lack of trains. The project for forging Swiss documents was collapsing—the authorities had noticed the forgeries. It was no wonder: over 100,000 such documents had been distributed,[14] when the embassy had issued only 8,000 genuine documents.

Apart from the ghetto, over 20,000 Jews were concentrated in special houses, under the auspices of the Swiss government. The authorities had requested that all genuine Swiss citizens be put into such houses in order to differentiate them and the people holding forged papers. Some 3,000 Jews were hidden in Red Cross establishments, mostly children. Close to 3,000 people were in embassy buildings. Tens of thousands were living under forged Aryan certificates, prepared instead of the Swiss documents, which were losing their viability. A heavy responsibility was carried by the Zionist movement, particularly the leaders of the Pioneer Youth. The members of the movement bore the burden of feeding and clothing tens of thousands of Jews, as well as providing them with papers. Among these were thousands of children and even babies entrusted to them by their parents. There was increasing recruitment every day. The number of people released from the obligation to serve was decreasing. More certificates were required to prove that the bearer was released from service, and most of the members were occupied with supplying these documents.

There were sharp discussions regarding the methods adopted by the rescue project. Nashka, a slim blond girl who came from a Ruthenian village, was one of the central figures in the movement. She had placed herself in the International Red Cross offices, distributing certificates to anyone who wished. Many knew that there was a helping hand there. But some of the comrades thought that, in her enthusiasm, she was creating more danger than possibility of rescue. There was no doubt that her activities would be discovered by the Gestapo in the long run. But Nashka clung to her opinion that only a chosen few could find salvation under the system of a careful underground operation. She objected vehemently to this sort of selection and to limitations on her activity.

I settled down in the Glass House, a spacious four-story building on Vadász Utca, near the Swiss Embassy in Budapest. The Glass House was, at first glance, part of the embassy—the Swiss flag flew over it and there was a guard near the gate, and so it was considered Swiss territory. Actually, the building served as the Zionist operational center and hundreds of activists had taken refuge there.

In the early days of my stay in this building, I learned what was going on around me and understood that negotiations between Eichmann and Kasztner had been conducted all the time I was in prison, but without concrete results. The activities of the pioneer movement, on the other hand, had been most fruitful. I had no doubt that the thousands of Jews who were helped by the forged document project, the thousands successfully moved over to Romania or back into Slovakia, and some 3,000 children being sheltered in the Red Cross houses had all remained alive by the daring and dedication of the handful of fearless young leaders and hundreds of rank-and-file members.

The highly complex rescue project was based on the fact that the mass murder and annihilation was being carried out legally in terms of Nazi law. The greatness of the underground people lay in their ability to read the minds of the murderers, and they saved the victims from their clutches by apparently legal methods. However, as the Russian pincer closed from the north and the south of Budapest, the regime's system was shaken. The streets of the city were filled with armed gangs wearing the Arrow Cross badges on their sleeves. They robbed, looted, and murdered anyone who crossed their path or who, in the opinion of the gang leader, was suspected of desertion, Communism, evasion, spying, or simply of being a Jew.

The certificates, whether real or forged, were of no use anymore. The system of houses protected by the Swiss, Swedish, or Red Cross flags was collapsing. The Swiss consul, Carl Lutz, and the Swedish consul, Raoul Wallenberg, were still able to call the police every so often, via the Hungarian Foreign Office, to forcibly eject the gangs of murderers, but this was becoming more and more infrequent. Bad tidings came one after the other. However, this condition of lawlessness also created new ways of response and rescue: if an Arrow Cross gang could take the law into its own hands, breaking into a protected Swiss building and removing those who were sheltered there, leading Jews to the banks of the Danube to kill them, what was to prevent any other group, a stronger one, from getting those same Jews away from the gangs and leading them elsewhere? Thus, another band came into being. This was the group of tough Jewish youngsters, strong and resourceful, who looked in every way like gentiles, dressed in uniforms, well-armed, and with officer's insignias, walking around the city, foiling attempts to murder Jews. Sometimes they used force and at other times deception. They would respond to calls from Red Cross children's refuges to chase out gangs who had broken in; they provided a cover for suppliers of food to these houses and would also steal supplies for them.

It is impossible to give a complete description of what went on in those days. Every hour, information streamed into headquarters, and following every bit of news a runner in a group would set out to clarify what had happened, to estimate the extent of the disaster, and to suggest ways of handling the situation. However, on too many occasions the runner himself was robbed or the reinforcements that were sent failed in their task, were trapped, or disappeared. The faces of some of these young people were engraved in my heart. Many have remained nameless—underground fighters who chose pseudonyms for themselves when they were sent into action, so that I never knew their real names. Many fell, but many remained alive, and I want to mention at least some of them: Diósi, Auslander, Moshe Weisskopf, Yosef Meyer, Tibor Rosenbaum, Tzelka, Willy Izzu Jowkiz, Yosef Schaffer, Moshe Alpan, Kahana, David Gur, Kepes, Eli Shlomowiz, Lila, and many more.

One day we were dealt a very hard blow—Zvi Goldfarb disappeared. He was devoted to establishing bunkers and assessing weapons for the final stage, when no strategy would be of any use and all that would remain would be to fight to the last bullet and to die with honor. Zvi Goldfarb's disappearance was significant, because he was about to keep an important meeting with some people who were involved in acquiring arms. It emerged that every one of those who was supposed to be at the meeting had disappeared. A comrade on the lookout informed us that they had fallen into an ambush. News flowed in: one of the bunkers was surrounded and the thirty young men and women in it had fought with what weapons they had, but all had fallen into enemy hands. Some had been wounded, and most were taken to an unknown destination. Nashka had also disappeared, as had little David, the expert document forger. There was no doubt that an informer or a traitor had betrayed the network and we had lost the best of our people and our fighters.

Meyer Karpati, one of the most excellent, enthusiastic, and also level-headed youngsters, arrived in a panic. He had witnessed the battle between the army and a group of comrades who had been in the second bunker to be discovered. He followed those who had been captured and saw them taken to the prison on Margaretta Street.

We sent runners ordering all bunkers vacated. There was now no doubt that we were being betrayed and it was impossible to know who else would be affected.

We decided to try to rescue our friends who had been captured. We discovered, via connections with the Communists and Social Democrats, that a large group of our people were being held in the prison where I had been so badly tortured.

I vetoed at the onset a plan to break in and rescue them by force. Perhaps we could get together the force for the actual break-in, but we would surely not have the strength to hold the prison until we could gain control. That would require taking it floor by floor and investigating each cell in order to find our comrades, whose where abouts we did not know. We also had no up-to-date information as to the number of guards, their weapons, and their means for calling for reinforcement.

Instead, a different daring strategy was adopted. Comrades, dressed in Hungarian uniforms and with an officer at their head, went to the prison. The officer presented an order—forged, of course—to take the prisoners whose names were listed on an attached sheet, correctly signed and stamped, and execute them on the banks of the Danube. They were handed over without argument. All were present.

The "officer" played his part well. He ordered his men about and abused the prisoners in Hungarian, and made it clear that they would pass through the gates of hell very soon with his assistance. The comrades bade one another farewell, sure that their end was near. When they crossed the river without anything happening, they were bewildered. And when they reached the Glass House and the gates opened to embrace them as well as their captors, who then broke into a mighty roar and threw their caps in the air, they were stunned, unable to believe the miracle that had happened.

The rescued comrades were hard to recognize. In the few days that they had been in the murderers' hands, they had become broken remnants of themselves. Zvi and Neshka, the strongest spirits now weakened by torture, burst into tears. Little David, the greatest document forger ever, leaned against the wall and looked around in wonder and confusion with bloodshot eyes.

Our comrades gave us the names of others they had met in the prison. The "officer" and his men set out again. By now it was late at night. They rang the bell at the prison gate, but nobody answered. They fired a round of bullets, but still nobody appeared. They threw a few grenades into the yard. Only then did the old guard poke his head out: "There aren't any prisoners left. They have taken them all." "Where to?" roared the officer. "To the prison on FA Street."

But there, too, nobody opened the gate. Because of the continuous pounding the Russians were carrying out against the city, the guards had abandoned the prisoners in their cells and were hiding in the basements. The "officer" broke the lock of the gate, entered the prison, and found some guards. Threatening them with his submachine gun, he forced one of the guards to release the prisoners on his list, thus saving the lives of another seventy-two comrades.

Crowds of Jews massed outside the gates of the embassy, all deeply distressed. Their lives and the lives of their dear ones were hanging in the balance, and they were seeking help to save them. Inside, comrades whose own lives were no more secure than those begging for assistance worked from morning to night in rooms thronged with people. Stenographers recorded details of horrific deeds. This material was being collected as historical testimony. Anyone who listened for hours to these stories apparently became indifferent to the fate of individuals. Lives were not going to be risked for the sake of one Jew anymore, because inevitably there would be reports that a thousand Jews, or hundreds of children, were being led to the slaughter. For these, it was worth taking risks.

Fate is blind. More than once it happened that precisely those who only dared now to come out of hiding for the first time were casualties, while others less fearful, who moved around pursuing their mission, were spared.

We were organized as a headquarters, but had no control over the course of events. The most active people would suddenly disappear, never to be heard from again. The operations center was like the captain's cabin of a ship foundering at sea: there were no lifeboats, all that could be done was to block the ruptures in the hull that were breaking through at an increasing rate, and everyone knew that sooner or later the ship would sink.

It was obvious that it was only a matter of time till hostile forces would break into the Glass House. The houses sheltered old people, the sick, and those Zionist activists whose appearance or accent gave them away as being Jews, preventing them from moving around freely on the outside. It was here that an unending stream of escapees came, snatched from the clutches of death as the Gestapo, Arrow Cross, gendarmes, police, or gangs attempted in these last moments of fascist control to annihilate Jews who had managed to escape the fate Hitler had decreed for them.

Apart from the problem of logistics and sanitation, we were very much concerned with the added danger of centralizing so many people in the nerve center of the underground and rescue operations. But at this stage we could only plan what we would do when the ruse—the guard at the gate and the Swiss flag—was discovered.

The building adjoining the Glass House had the offices of the Hungarian Football Federation, a most respectable body, which had won the World Cup several times. The house was deserted in those days. We constructed a few well-hidden outlets into the Federation which, on its other side, shared a common wall with a five-story house that had a gate leading to the next street. The plan was that, when the commander of the Glass House decided the time had come to scatter, everyone would go through the hidden entrances into the Federation building, closing and camouflaging the escape exits afterward. If it became clear that the enemy planned to break into the Federation as well, holes would be blasted through the wall to the next house with dynamite, and everyone would make a dash for it. All the inhabitants of the Glass House had been provided with forged papers for this eventuality. There were some, indeed, who played with the idea of defending the house, but it was obvious that with four revolvers, a few hand grenades, and the personal weapons of a handful of individuals who used to walk around dressed as members of various armed forces, we would not succeed in holding the house. But we could gain a little time to allow the escapees to get some distance from the scene of the attack.

A lone policeman at the gate signified the protected status of the Glass House and underlined the prohibition against attacking neutral Swiss territory. The government headed by Szálasi, head of the Arrow Cross fascist movement, who held power through German strength, wanted very much to win international recognition, which was how certain diplomats, such as Lutz and Wallenberg, had managed to keep their building's immunity. The rescue workers who used their badges also managed sometimes to stay immune.

But the day came when the guard at the gate, a significant symbol, disappeared. One of the comrades in policeman's uniform took his place. A few days later, however, some policemen who had been guards in the past offered their services. They had deserted from the police force, having reached the conclusion that, in the last days of the present government's rule, the best place to be was with us. An even greater surprise was the arrival of a platoon-sized detachment of Hungarian soldiers under the command of officers of the Hungarian nobility, requesting asylum. We received them willingly. They reinforced the viability of our ruse and added to our strength. Nothing better symbolized the chaos of the times than these phenomena. The border between the hunter and hunted began to blur, and it was becoming a free-for-all.

The trains to the capital had stopped running long since, apart from military transports. This represented a reprieve for a considerable number of Jews who would otherwise have been forcibly evacuated to Budapest. Even though many thousands were interned in the brick factory in the southwestern part of the city, the expulsions had come to a halt.

In our closed world, the fear of death seemed to be closing in on us. There were days when we thought that we had reached the end of the road, but the following day convinced us that our situation had in fact worsened.

We expected that the main preoccupation of the Nazi leaders in those days would be with their own survival, given the imminent collapse of the army. But to our amazement we learned that Eichmann had returned to Budapest at the head of his command to organize the transfer of the Jews to the West. On the surface, these Jews were going to be employed in rebuilding the new lines of defense on the Austrian border.[15] In fact, they were being transported to extermination centers. In the extreme cold, tens of thousands of Jews were made to wait in long columns, without food and with no shelter during the night. Dysentery and typhus spread, and whoever fell ill on the way was shot. Stragglers were bayoneted and their bodies flung by the roadside.

One of our comrades, K., who used to pose as a subaltern in the Arrow Cross, succeeded in a daring and brilliant plan: he presented himself as a doctor to the minister of health and requested that a hospital be allocated to him for treatment of members of his organization. He was given an abandoned hospital and began gathering wounded members of the underground there. "Doctor" K. and his aides would also go where the Jews were concentrated, select the ones who were sick and destined for execution, and remove them to his hospital.

But the wonderful rescue operations and the spiritual power of the rescuers were dwarfed by the magnitude of horror of the Holocaust. Whatever they did with their fervor and courage was meager compared to the destruction. Forty thousand Jewish men and women set out on a 250-kilometer march from Budapest to the Austrian border. Ten thousand perished along the way. Nobody even bothered to bury them. Their corpses, strewn along the road, bore witness that the Nazis were not abandoning their dream of the "Final Solution," and would not rest until the last Jew was annihilated, even though the Reich that was to have lasted a thousand years was now entering its final death throes.

Just before Christmas, it became known that for a few days there had been no forced marches of Jews to the West. Had the intervention of neutral governments, the pope's appeal, or Kasztner's meeting with Himmler brought this about? Or had they taken pity on the guards and decided not to spoil the holiday for them? One way or another, there was something almost tangible in the air. On Christmas Eve everything fell silent, and there was a sense of foreboding—there was a silence in the streets, a threatening silence.

At five in the morning we heard the shriek of a shell and an explosion very close by. A shell had hit the dome of the big church named after St. Stephen. After some moments of shock—as if to allow time to digest the significance of the event—a hellish fire broke out on all sides. A heavy bombardment began, reminiscent of the magic night in El Alamein when the Eighth Army started its rout of Nazi Germany.

It soon became clear that the city was surrounded; nobody could leave or enter. The two Russian armies had met in western Hungary, closing the ring of the siege.

If the rule of the city had been unstable before, its encirclement caused further collapse and the relinquishing of all restraints. In the besieged city, there were now 120,000 German Wehrmacht soldiers trapped together with 30,000 horses that had served for transport since petrol ran out. Rule in the streets passed absolutely into the hands of the Arrow Cross gangs, without any centralized control over them.

Under heavy bombardment from the air and mainly from a thousand cannons and a hundred rocket launchers, the city was being totally destroyed, street by street, house by house, spreading like brushfire and leaving nothing untouched in their path.

People were burrowing into basements and cellars until hunger and thirst drove them into the streets to scavenge for food and water. Between one explosion and the next, they would dart out, take cover, look out for their next stop, and then jump to it, sometimes getting wounded in the process.

Bodies were not buried. In the beginning, there were some who would carry the wounded or the dead to the entrance of a destroyed building, but such acts of humanity were dangerous. People learned to ignore the corpses that lay about, and tank drivers did not hesitate to crush them beneath the treads of their vehicles. Only when a horse was hit and fell did men and women converge on it from all sides, like a group of hyenas, tearing at the meat with knives or bare hands. And in a matter of minutes nothing was left but the bones, and sometimes the bodies of those who had been hit by shrapnel or wounded in quarrels over the last bits of meat.

Our organized strength had weakened and our operation began to collapse. We still had some supplies in hidden storerooms here and there, but transferring them to the children's houses was dangerous and sometimes impossible. More than once, the comrades trying to deliver supplies were attacked and robbed, and if they did arrive safely, they found that a gang had overrun the house, murdered the people in charge and even the babies, and stolen the food. The rescue fighters, who had seen so many horrors that their hearts had hardened till they considered themselves immune, cried at the sight of the small corpses. It had cost them so much effort and blood to bring the children here, and now, meters from the frontline, a moment before the end of the terror, they had met their end. Ofra, Agmon, and Yosef Shefer, wearing uniforms of the Fascist Youth, took three children who had by a miracle remained alive and moved them to another children's house, only to find, the next day, that the same cruel fate had overtaken the children of that house.

Gangs overran the "protected" houses, which then became traps for the Jews there. If previously the Jews had been taken to the banks of the Danube under cover of night, to be murdered on the spot so that the river could wash away the bodies, now nobody cared that Jews were being murdered in broad daylight with their bodies mounted in piles, even serving as protection for people trying to cross the road between one explosion and the next.

Makeshift loudspeakers announced the coming of mysterious German armies, about to advance from the West and liberate the besieged city. Detachments of the Arrow Cross spread out among the ruins and cellars, catching whomever they came across and transporting them to the front to fight the Russian invader, to hold the city until these so-called liberating forces arrived. In Freedom Square, the central square in Budapest, a young Jew was hanged. Mendel was his name; he was born in Safed and raised in Hungary, and his body hung for a week with a sign attached: "This Jew threw a grenade into the Party building."

Even young boys endangered their lives in rescue activities. Many of them served as contacts. One youngster, a member of the Mizrahi movement,[16] arrived at headquarters and with his last strength delivered a note, then swayed and fell. The doctor who confirmed his death found that he had been hit by three bullets. He had continued running until he completed the task he had been given. The note had stated that Komoly, the engineer, chairman of the Zionist Federation and Kasztner and Brand's Rescue Committee, had been caught and taken to an unknown destination.

Uniformed comrades went out, despite the danger, to comb the usual trouble spots: the Danube area, the party center of the Arrow Cross, the secret police, the Gestapo, but without success— Komoly had vanished without a trace.

The following morning we received a frightening piece of information: the Gestapo commander was organizing a force for an operation due to take place on January 6. This was the final destruction of the ghetto. The force would blow up the remnants of houses with their inhabitants, and all approaches, bunkers, and hiding places were to be sealed, to erase all memory of the deeds committed by the Gestapo in that ghetto.

The last member of the Rescue Committee, Aharon Biss, took it upon himself to conduct an additional final negotiation with the Gestapo. He presented himself to the Gestapo officer who had remained in the city and made a deal with him. In exchange for a cancellation of the decree to blow up the ghetto, the commander would receive a large sum of money, forged papers, and the assurance that when the time came, Biss would testify in his favor and save him from the death penalty.

Perhaps the soldiers of the Wehrmacht who continued to fight and die in the battle for the city believed that a German army was advancing from the West, and would shortly lift the siege, but it was clear that the Gestapo commander knew the truth. The army was the figment of Goebbel's imagination. The commander made the deal in the hope of saving his skin.

The ghetto and its 80,000 remaining inhabitants were thereby saved!

Chapter 12

Liberation

✳ THE RED ARMY'S METHODICAL FIRE, which was forging the way for the advance, intensified. It became absolutely impossible to move about in the streets.

I was completely cut off from headquarters in the Glass House. I lived in a large five-story building that stood at the edge of a spacious park known as the Városliget (a well-known park in Budapest). We rented the five-room apartment from its Christian owners, who had fled in fear of the bombardment and Russian invasion.

The apartment had served as the center of document forgeries for a long time. Comrades who usually visited there were mainly in uniform. Pil, who had lived there before me, proudly went around in the uniform of a railway worker. Little David, who had lived there with him, wore the uniform of the Fascist Youth movement, and the third, Yosef Meier—who looked so tough when he was not smiling his charming smile—was dressed as a field security officer. I had been given documents that described me as a member of the secret police serving in the war ministry. When I came to the flat I found only Pil's sisters, Shoshanah and Esther.

Two streets away from us, Zvi and Neshka were living with a woman named Margit. Like the Margit who had taken Peretz in, she was a gentile and deeply loyal to us. Willy was also living there, but was home only rarely. He was always on the move in the city in case he came across somebody needing help.

On January 12, I tried, without success, to reach headquarters. When I returned to the building, I found the street closed off by a barrier of stones. I crawled to Margit's house. It took me two hours to cover a distance that usually took me eight minutes. I found Willy there, gaily recounting the day's events. Fascists had caught him on suspicion of being a Jew.

This was not the first time in his life he had been miraculously saved. He grew up in the Carpathian Mountains in a district that had been torn from Czechoslovakia and annexed to Hungary just before the war broke out. There was a warm, traditional Jewish community of mountain farmers in the area. When he was thirteen, a campaign to cleanse Hungary of "undesired" elements was organized, and 28,000 Jews were transported by the Hungarians to the Polish border, as though to send them over. When they were near the border, the Hungarians opened fire with their machine guns and then covered the piles of corpses with tons of quicklime. Willy and his whole family had been rounded up in the operation. By a miracle, Willy had not been hit, but his instinct to stay alive led him to lie still among the corpses, and only after nightfall did he force his way out of the mass grave. Taking leave of the corpses of his parents and brother, he then returned to his village, leaving the nightmarish forest behind him. There was no place for him in his village, and he went to Budapest. The memory of that night was never to be erased.

Willy became one of the important activists in the defense and rescue network. He was indefatigable, always planning sabotage, making contacts with smugglers, training the comrades to use weapons, forging documents—and when asked why he did all this, he would respond with a look of amazement. After all, it was obvious: the purpose was rescue. Had he not seen with his own eyes how Jews were being killed? He did not want Jews to die, not without resistance.

He had been arrested six times. Once, when he was being taken by the SS from the border to the capital, he jumped from the train and got away. Another time, he escaped from Hungarian police who had caught him with a case full of forged documents. Yet another time, when he was riding a motorcycle, he was recognized by two members of the secret police. He knocked both of them down and escaped on his motorcycle. In the fourth instance, he demonstrated how to escape from a streetcar. The detective who had caught him was taking him by streetcar to the secret police headquarters. When the streetcar was filled to capacity, he jumped without hesitation from the rear steps, but immediately ran after the same streetcar and mounted from the opposite side. The detective, with some of the passengers, jumped down after him but never found him; he had stayed on the streetcar. The fifth time also involved a miracle on the streetcar. He was negotiating with a soldier to buy a hand grenade, but one of the passengers noticed and alerted the others. He punched his way through the crowd, jumped, and, as he did so, threw a grenade back into the streetcar. Many were injured, but he stayed alive.

More recently, he had been driving a motorcycle with Zvi as a passenger to a meeting with the steering committee. As they approached the meeting place, they saw Neshka with two strangers. They understood that she had been arrested. At first, they drove on as though they did not know her, but when Willy heard Zvi say, "I can't desert Neshka," he turned the motorcycle back in the direction they had come from. They fell straight into a trap. A military vehicle was blocking the road. They tried to turn back, but another vehicle cut them off from their retreat.

That was the sixth time Willy was arrested. Eventually he was freed by comrades. He was rather hurt—it was beneath his dignity to escape with the help of others.

Now he told us how he had been arrested for the seventh time. When he was caught he protested vigorously at being taken for a Jew. The fascists dragged him into a yard and closed the gate. They ordered him to drop him trousers. This time, he thought, he was lost. Six armed men surrounded him. The fascists examined him and decided he was . . . pure Aryan!

He laughed uproariously. Here was a striking example of the existence of miracles.

Willy's gaiety infected us as we sipped the champagne he had managed to acquire when even water was in short supply. We were probably the only ones in the entire quarter who did not go down to the basement despite the heavy bombardments. We were not comfortable in the presence of the other tenants. But the walls suddenly shook. Two rockets that had been fired by a diving plane had penetrated the room through one wall and left through another without exploding. The three of us were in the kitchen at the time and so nobody was hurt. We saw that the danger was growing. The whole building could be destroyed any minute. Our nerves were on edge and we felt we could not bear the siege much longer. We had the feeling that we would all fall at the last moment.

Willy suggested an astounding plan, but one we all accepted. He would prepare a forged document, and, dressed in Hungarian officers' uniform, he would go out and request a cease-fire for two hours to allow the dead to be buried. We would then cross over to the Russian lines with white flags in hand.

The Russians had reached the adjoining house the day before, but they had been repulsed. We no longer had the spirit to wait. We could see that the Germans still had considerable power. German transport planes were dropping supplies and the Germans would be able to hold the city for a long time yet.

I went home to get my uniform and to inform Esther and Shoshanah about the plan.

It took me more than an hour to cover the 300 meters to my house. I crawled all the way because of the machine gun bullets from the air and the ground that were whistling all around me. It was almost evening and there was not much chance of the Russian snipers hitting me. I was forced to traverse the crossing on the street leading to the wood, which was apparently being held by the Russians. Strong fire was coming from there. I advanced at a slow crawl in the slushy snow. Every so often I would touch a warm corpse lying in its own blood. The street I lived in, Damjanich Street, was partly protected from ground fire by the church at the edge of the woods. Sodden with sweat and slush, I arrived at the solid building where I lived. It stood in place in spite of the many hits it had sustained.

I noticed that in my absence, numerous telephone cables had been put up over the yard, which was full of Wehrmacht men. One house had become the regional command. This was a reason for us, finally, to go down to the basement too. It made no sense to stay in the flat with two beautiful young women in the vicinity of the regional command, buzzing with German officers.

Taking blankets with us, we went down to the basement. There was almost no furniture left in our splendid flat. We burned pieces every day to warm ourselves. We were already considering tearing up the floor boards for firewood.

In the basement, we squeezed in among scores of hysterical tenants. There were regular explosions, setting up a ceaseless noise that made the few remaining windowpanes rattle shockingly.

By the miserable light of a candle, we settled down for the night. Some neighbors brought the latest news: the German army was streaming in. All nearby houses were packed with soldiers. Tanks filled the empty lot beside the house. An attempt was to be made to chase the Russians out of the woods. It was likely that the attack would begin from our side of the street—our house served as officers' quarters.

There was a sudden silence. Our ears had grown so accustomed to the sound of explosions, the wail of katyushas, the hum of bullets and shells, that the abrupt silence was frightening. We held our breath. Then we heard a loudspeaker: "Soldiers of the Hungarian army. Citizens. Patriots. Stop serving the Nazis. Rebel against the traitors. Your city is destroyed. The German army is not coming to liberate you. If you carry on resisting you will multiply casualties. You will die of hunger, plagues, shells. Surrender and save what still can be saved."

"Enough. Enough," one of the women shouted. Others shouted back, "If only the Russians would come." Those in charge ran about whispering in the ears of the ones who had rebelled, pointing furtively to us in our officers' uniforms. Our camouflage was good, obviously. They were as afraid of us as we were of them.

The candle went out and we fell asleep.

Shoshanah woke me toward morning. It was quiet in the basement, and outside as well. My heart pounded. What would the silence bring? We lay with bated breath, listening to every rustle. Something was about to happen. Then dawn flickered. We stood up to peer into the yard and see what was going on. Suddenly, an old woman came in and announced with a wail, "The Russians are here."

The inhabitants of the basement had apparently been lying awake straining to discover the meaning of the silence. When the old woman's words were heard, they rose as one, as though an electric current had passed through them.

"Get Esther awake quickly," I whispered to Shoshanah, "and let's get out of here."

We had no time to lose. The streets could pass from hand to hand again, and I did not want to fall into the murderers' clutches. Indeed, the miracle had occurred.

I could have roared with happiness. Weights rolled off my heart. My head spun. A great thing had happened, but I knew I had to slow down and control my feelings. One had to maintain a cool head. Perhaps the old woman had made a mistake, and heaven help anyone showing his true face too soon.

We had to hurry. My disguise—a secret agent of the defense ministry—had been useful, but now it could become an obstacle. It would be enough for someone to point at me and scream, "Fascist." Before I could begin to explain who I was, they could smash my skull.

The battle resumed by the time we reached the gate. The bullets came from the opposite direction this time. Apparently, the Germans had decided during the night that it was not worth defending our street, which was held at one end by the Russians. They had fortified themselves at the other end, where they had control over the side streets that gave them access to supplies and allowed them movement.

While the German guns were still rattling ceaselessly, we saw the spearhead of the Red Army among the islands of rubble. Soldiers in strange-looking clothes—short, thick jackets that seemed to have been made out of blankets and brown hats with a fur rim—all looked short and fat and ponderous, but hearty. From the gate of one of the houses, an old soldier surveyed the street where the Germans had barricaded themselves. A few soldiers were rolling a light field cannon.

We got up and ran to the other side of the road with bullets shrieking around our heads, while the old man waved his hand and yelled at us. But we could not hear what he was saying because of the noise of the battle.

We reached Zvi and Neshka's house. Together the whole group ran in the direction of the wood. The Russians paid no attention to us. They were busy with the battle and were probably accustomed to people running away from danger zones.

We moved among trees and bushes, single file in the spacious wood, ploughing our way through deep snow. There were seven of us: Esther, Shoshanah, Zvi, Neshka, Willy, and Margit, with me in the lead.

At times we were alarmed by the screech of the shells and jumped into foxholes or lay flat on the ground. More than once, shells hit bushes and trees right next to us. We were furious: would we be hit now, now of all times? The Germans still had their hands out for us, but we would escape nevertheless. We had to escape, no matter what.

When we were close to the other end of the wood, a bullet passed so close to me that I was almost dazed. I flattened myself and another bullet passed beside my ear. Those behind me had also flattened themselves, and we advanced like that, at a slow crawl, for several dozen meters until we reached thicker bushes. Then we lay there for about half an hour, after which we continued at a running crouch with stops and starts.

I was grateful to the Russian sniper for being less than perfect at his task.

Finally, we reached the end of the wood where we were protected from bullets. We looked in the direction of the city and knew the battle was still raging there. We breathed sighs of relief.

I was deeply excited. I embraced my friends. We laughed and tears flowed from our eyes. We had been saved! Despite all the killing and murder, tens of thousands of Jews were still alive in Budapest, many of them by virtue of the courage and self-sacrifice of those who had risen to take their stand against the extermination plot.

My mission was at an end. A thought went through my mind: strange, but the same fateful date was repeating itself. It was January 13.

The Final Reckoning

HEN NIGHT FELL, row upon row of Red Army soldiers marched in procession, their white furs engulfed in the screen of steadily falling snow. The echo of their marching was lost in the thick layer of snow underfoot. Everything had a dreamlike quality. The soldiers appeared as pale figures gliding in the void of the city.

We stood at the paneless window of a small house in the suburbs of Budapest, our bodies shuddering with cold, but our hearts full of gratitude and love for the Russian people. We felt that we were partners in events that would be engraved in history.

The ghetto had been liberated and the whole eastern sector of the city was in Russian hands. The guns still roared, and the hundreds of windows in the Royal Palace high on the mountains was illuminated by flames and sparkled proudly above the city as in the days—now remote as legend—when receptions for the rulers of the world were held there. Here and there, shells from the last German outpost were still falling and the rattle of machine guns had not come to a stop. The battle raged, but the majority of the surviving Jews were on this side of the lines.

Many had shed their assumed identities and seemed to come back to life as Jews. Jewish women removed the crosses from their necks, and the hats and coats that had given them a gentile appearance vanished. The tension abated. Fear subsided, but only to be replaced by expressions of grief in the eyes. The Jews who had survived were broken, starving, frail, and sick. I saw them dragging themselves along the streets in search of their homes and destroyed worlds.

The city was in flames. The Red Army was wreaking its fury. Its revenge was as great as its rage. Shops, houses, women—they regarded all as booty for the frontline fighter. The men were taken to prisoner of war camps. Wherever one turned there were ruins, flames, human bodies, chattel. The destroyed roads were deserted but for black-clothed women darting across the streets, hurrying to avoid the eyes of the Russian soldiers, to hide quickly in basements and niches. A million and a half inhabitants of Budapest were sunk in filth and despair.

The people who had treated us so cruelly were reaping their punishment. But as fate's bitter joke would have it, the Russians' fury and desire for revenge hurt the Jews more than the gentiles. The Jews who saw the Russian army as savior and liberator were the ones who dared go out into the streets and were thus more often harmed. The enraged Russian fists did not differentiate between the enemy and his victim—they were incited by anything that came their way.

There was no food in the city. Transport was disrupted. All vehicles—horses as well as carts—were confiscated. The last of our own stores which were used to support the children's houses and the ghetto were plundered. We were starving. The nightmares of the prison returned, where every dream centered only on food.

The Jews had broken out of the ghetto. We felt released from the yoke of concern for the Jews of Budapest. Each man would take his own fate in his hands. But we felt responsible for the abandoned children, the orphans. We swore to rescue them and take them to Palestine.

We turned to the command of the Second Ukrainian Army, which had conquered the city. They shrugged; it was no concern of theirs. They were only concerned with wiping out the enemy and were not obliged to worry about the population that had collaborated with the enemy. But the Jews were victims of the enemy, the remnant of a murdered people—what was to become of them? "Wait until a civilian government is in power," came the answer. And, indeed, a civilian government was established. The Russians had apparently decided that they would not interfere with internal affairs at that time. The civilian government would restore order.

The commissar in charge of supplies to the civilian population was a Jew who had suffered greatly, having been condemned to death and saved from Horthy's clutches only by the wide-scale protest of unions all over the world. He had spent sixteen years in jail. Was it possible that he would not be deeply concerned and affected by the fate of the babies, the children of his own people, possibly the only survivors left in Europe?

"I have been given the responsibility and the duty to feed one and a half million starving people," he said. "Far be it for me to differentiate between sectors of the population for good or evil. It is imperative that each and every one of us reeducate the citizens to new values of equality between one man and the next."

The Jews were hungry long before the start of the siege. They had been dying for weeks and months. They were broken in spirit and body. Continuous malnutrition and cold were wreaking havoc among them. They were without shelter, while the others were living in the basements of their houses or in the basements of houses that had been stolen from the Jews. But the most urgent problem was the children. There were thousands of orphan children drifting about without home or family. They had managed to escape hell and still hovered between life and death. At least we had to take care of them.

Explanations and pleas were of no help. The Jewish Communist shut his ears and his heart: "We must not sow the seeds of a new anti-Semitism by Jewish pleas for special treatment."

Nevertheless, the commissar gave me a signed order authorizing me to engage in the purchase of food and its transfer to starving Budapest. Formally, any food I managed to acquire was for general use, but I had his personal promise that whatever I managed to get would not be confiscated and could be allocated to the children and the ailing under our care.

We went into action immediately. The comrades, who were bound to one another in the brotherhood of fighters, felt that the only world left was the one they created by joint activity. They had looked for the world of yesterday in vain. It was slaughtered, destroyed, and pulverized. There were not even any roots left for it to sprout anew.

News of the extermination camps filtered through, and it emerged that some of the Jews were still alive. And then the first people to return from the death camps began to arrive. Dressed in rags and tatters of prison garb, skin and bones, with faltering steps and eyes sunken deep, deep into their sockets, they told of tens of thousands still in the camps, without the strength to begin to walk, even though the Nazis had fled long ago and the gates were wide open.

The same wonderful group who, during the expulsion and siege, had worn itself out in the struggle, fighting resourcefully and fearlessly, now understood instinctively that they had to shoulder new missions. The rescue and aid center was revived and I found myself in the hub of an operation I would never have imagined being called upon to do. In the name of the Jewish people, I borrowed money from every possible source, signing and undertaking things I hoped would be honored by the treasury of the Jewish Agency in Jerusalem. All the activists found themselves performing tasks that they had selected according to their particular abilities.

A well-oiled machine was established. Some began organizing training farms for youth and older people to prepare them for immigration to Palestine. Some were involved in acquiring food. Some set up centers to absorb or rehabilitate displaced people, providing them with greater protection and means to enable them to continue their wanderings in search of their lost lives.

We were cut off from the outside world. There was neither mail nor telephones, but we sensed that despite everything we had been through, we had to reach Poland, the valley of slaughter. We had to give both concrete help and transport to get the few out who remained alive. We organized a delegation and sent it on its way. We dispatched emissaries secretly to Bucharest in the hope of establishing contact with the outside world.

With our own eyes, we saw how terrible the wreckage of the Holocaust was and also in some cases the super-human spiritual strength that had kept the wick of life burning and that tore like a taut wire when the liberation came. The strong desire to witness the routing of the Nazis, to see the revenge taken, also cracked. Terror

and nightmare did not pass with victorious fanfare, nor with a renewed surge of life force, but with a sense of spiritual emptiness and
a lack of will to live. Even the babies held on as if in the hope of
the mothers' return, and when they failed to come, the infants died
by the score. In the first weeks after the liberation it seemed as if the
number of the dead exceeded the number of victims of the Nazis'
last rampage.

Those with the strength to take the long way back arrived in an
increasing flow. At times it seemed as if exaggeration and manic
delusion were behind the horror stories of furnaces—after all, Jews
were coming, and coming, and every day brought more than the
day before. I would go twice a day, looking for acquaintances in the
camp. In my heart of hearts I was hoping to find my sister Lucy, my
mother, my father, to see them as they were engraved on my heart
on the day I left for Palestine, standing at the station lovingly calling after me with choked voices: "Till we meet again!"

One day, suddenly, the flow of returnees stopped like a dying
river, and the following day the camp was at a standstill: there were
no more over there, no more living Jews.

About a half-million Hungarians and Transylvanian Jews
would never return. We learned that the information about the extermination camps and the mighty Nazi machine that was meant to
ensure that no Jew would remain alive on earth was the bitter truth,
and not a mere horror story.

The remaining few were regaining their strength bit by bit in
the transit camp we had established. They were equipping themselves for the road to their childhood landscape, to what had been
home to them. But all they found there was destruction and death,
and they began to understand that the life they once had was no
more, and that, though they still breathed, they, too, had died over
there in the furnaces. It was then that the loneliness, more terrible
than any suffering they had endured, struck them. They began to
try to build a new life on the grave of all they held dear.

Fleischmann was among the last to return. He had been transported to Germany from the prison, on foot most of the way, marching in the fierce cold, in snow up to the knees, wearing summer
clothes, weakened by imprisonment and continuous hunger.

Peretz and Fleischmann had stayed together the whole way,
supporting each other, while behind them like milestones the bod-

ies of their fellow sufferers dropped by the wayside. Those whose strength failed were indeed shot where they fell, and nobody bothered to give them a burial, just as we had heard earlier. Peretz hoped to muster his strength till the end, but he was afraid the Nazis would kill him even in the last minutes of the regime since he was a Jew and, in their eyes, a British spy.

On December 8 Peretz and Fleischmann had arrived in Oranienburg, a big industrial city north of Berlin. They were made to stand in front of a factory that manufactured the Heinkel bombers. "Mechanics forward," a German officer shouted. Peretz and Fleischmann stepped forward. Peretz had adopted the name of one of the non-Jewish prisoners who had weakened and was shot after the last identity parade. He was taken with a group of prisoners to work in the factory. Fleischmann was taken to another part of the factory.

That same day the factory was heavily bombed. Fleischmann was transferred to another place, and he had neither seen nor heard about Peretz since then. Nor did he remember the name Peretz had assumed.

I sent comrades to Oranienburg to search for Peretz, but they found no sign of him. Yet I hung on to the last shreds of hope that he was alive. It was true that there were only a few coming back, but perhaps Peretz would still turn up.

While I was still feverishly involved in the desperate effort to save those I could, a British sergeant found me and informed me that a British military delegation had arrived in Budapest some time ago. The brigadier general was furious, wanting to know why, contrary to all instructions, I had not presented myself before him. I presented myself and explained that I was totally absorbed in a humanist and Zionist operation. He declared that I was a soldier and subject to orders. And his order was to get into uniform, join the British delegation, and get back to my base in Cairo on the first plane.

I told him I could not do so. I would not leave Hungary until I found out what had become of my parents and my sister. I had to get back to the cursed city where I was born and raised and from which my family was expelled so that I could investigate their fate.

The general warned me that I was ignoring his order at my own risk. He would not personally prevent me, but his Russian colleague knew about me and neither he, the general, nor His Majesty's government could help me if I fell into Russian hands. All his attempts to find out what had happened to the Swedish consul, Raoul Wallenberg, who had repeatedly endangered his life during the most difficult days in order to rescue Jews from death, had come to nothing. He was convinced that Wallenberg was in Russian hands, though they denied it. Who knew whether they had not killed him?

Following my meeting with the general, I decided to go underground. I went into hiding in the apartment of a wonderful couple, Marta and her husband, who served faithfully as my contacts with the outside. I knew I would be able to remain in Budapest for only a few days, but I did not want to leave until I was quite certain I was leaving behind well-organized Zionist and communal bodies, and until somebody was sent from Palestine to take my place.

Then I received a transmission from Zvi Yehieli: "The British are putting pressure on us to instruct you to leave at once for Cairo. They claim that your presence in Budapest is liable to complicate their relations with the Russians. On receipt of this message you are to report at once to the British delegation and place yourself under their orders."

I had no choice.

We set out on the road leading eastward.

I was equipped with the Russian certificate Willy had arranged for me, hoping it would stand me in good stead if I got into trouble. The roads were full of barriers and guards and anything could happen. The main danger was being caught by the Russians and sent to do hard labor in Russia. I took as a driver the brawny, taciturn fellow who spoke Russian with a Carpathian accent. I chose to travel on side roads and, as we approached the border, we turned onto a dirt road.

We passed the road blocks without incident. In the early hours of the morning, in the middle of our journey, we had a flat tire. An early-rising child came out to watch the tire being changed. He was gaunt, filthy, his body wrapped in rags, and he looked like a gypsy, one of the unfortunate people who had shared the fate of the Jews.

I asked the boy what had happened here during the war. "When they locked up the Jews there"—he pointed to a big building at the end of the street (only then did I notice we had stopped near a large synagogue)—"all of us children came and pulled their sidelocks," he said proudly.

I was silent. Was I to take revenge on him?

We carried on along the main highway. From here on I knew the road well. I recognized every house, every tree. Nothing had changed since I last passed this way, seven years ago. I sat still in the speeding car and sank wide-eyed into the experience—a visit to the city of my birth. I was not longing for my city, but I did not want to leave Europe without seeing it. I knew I would not forgive myself if I did not pay it a visit, but I had delayed doing so until I was about to leave Europe. Damned Europe.

The mountains of western Transylvania were in front of my eyes. Every village, every town, roused memories. Here in the middle of this wonderful valley, among rocky cliffs soaring to the sky, I had attended scout camp; here, besides this stream, I had kissed a girl for the first time; here, I had formed the bonds with all my soul that bound me to that group with whom I had shared dreams of a new world we would build on the banks of the Jordan. Where had they all gone? Some had immigrated to Palestine where they were fulfilling our youthful dreams, but the majority—where were they?

Peasant houses sped past. Here was the house on the farm belonging to Yonah's grandfather. Yonah, my comrade on the parachute jump. I turned my head and sank into my memories.

The city streets dozed in the gray light. My heart was beating heavily and I had difficulty holding back my excitement. There was a bitter taste in my mouth after the night's journey. It seemed as if I had entered a dead city that had pounced on me from ancient dreams. Here was the street corner where we used to meet every day after school. This was where I had waited for her, the only one, full of youthful joy. Here was the market, unchanged. Perhaps I had dreamed a bad dream; perhaps there had been no war. Jews were not expelled, perhaps my immigration to Palestine also was nothing but a dream, and my life on the kibbutz only my imagination, and I was home. Here was the street leading down to our house. I'll ring at the gate, the window will open, and mother will sleepily ask: "Who is there?" Then she will see me, pass me the key to the gate with a shake of her head, and say, "At this hour, son?"

"Here," I cried, and the driver stopped the car with a screech of tires.

The little house on the side street slept on as I sat dazed, sat looking at that house, without the strength to get out of the car.

No, it was better not to know the truth. I would go back to Budapest, go back to Palestine, and delude myself; my parents and sister had returned. They were sleeping innocently. I was at that gate, but did not go in.

"We're going back to Budapest," I said to the driver. I did not look at him, lest he notice my flood of tears.

"Budapest? Aren't you going into the house?" the driver asked in amazement.

Yes, I had to go into the house. Had I lost my mind?

I went down to the gate. I rang the bell, once, twice. Nobody answered.

A family of Swabians, that is, of German extraction, used to live in our neighborhood. Such Germans were a Fifth Column preparing the way for the Nazi invasion. I remembered them as decent neighbors, but who knew what they had done to my parents with the Holocaust at their doorstep?

Suddenly a window opened in the neighbor's house. "Who are you looking for?" a woman asked me. It was the same German woman.

I stood mutely, leaning against the wall, my legs trembling.

"For God's sake," the woman burst out, "but it's you." Her head disappeared and she opened the gate of her house. She fell on my neck, crying and kissing me. She pulled me inside and in the midst of endless tears began to spread out clothes, pictures, and a few valuables whose memory was carved on my heart. My parents had entrusted these things to her, and she had looked after them. Nobody had returned. Nobody had come for them.

She opened our house with a key she had, leading me from one room to the other—here was the furniture, the pictures on the wall, the ashtrays—everything in place. It was as though they had simply gone out for a short walk, to return in a while. But a chill wind blew in the orphaned house.

Who knew better than I that there was nobody to wait for? The miracle that had not happened till now would never happen.

I felt breathless. A spirit of death, a sense of loneliness, its name orphanhood, was choking me. My head was spinning.

I knew I could not stay another moment in that house, that city. I had to run, get far away, as far away as possible so that I could weep, weep.

"Good-bye, I'm leaving," I said to her and turned to go.

"Where to?"

"To Palestine."

"What shall I do with your property? Can't you wait a bit? They will come back. They will certainly come back."

"Look after everything for awhile, and then give it to anyone you like," I called to her loudly from behind the door as I ran to the car.

"Drive," I ordered the driver, unnecessarily, since he was already behind the wheel with the motor running.

The city awoke, windows opened, and shop doors yawned. The market was full. I looked in vain for faces from my childhood. There were strangers, strange women all around.

The whole city was strange to me, hateful. It had changed completely, to the point of being unrecognizable.

It was a city without Jews.

On January 20, 1945, exactly one year after I had arrived in Budapest, we—comrades bound deeply one to the other by destiny—gathered for a candlelight dinner. I looked at the faces around me. They were boys and girls in terms of age, but men and women prematurely old with scarred souls, burning with a mighty flame of self-sacrifice and dedication to the pioneer ideal. Those who were left had come now to part from me.

These friends and many, many others had lately been saved and were feverishly engaged in rescue operations: they obtained food and medicine for Jews who had remained alive.

They were setting up centers throughout Hungary for orphans who by miracle or by their own ingenuity and will to live had not perished. In a kind of rage they were orchestrating illegal crossings of the new borders, leading the confused and stunned survivors to the coastal countries, to the sea. There was no doubt in our hearts that the sea would not continue to be a barrier between the abyss behind and the one hope that still made life worthwhile.

Not everyone came. Some of the comrades had already gone to the Polish border, where they were organizing a transit point and a first aid station for the displaced people who were streaming back from the valley of slaughter. Others had gone to assist refugees who were seeking to flee Europe by sea, either with the help of the soldiers of the Jewish Brigade who had joined the *B'richa* (Operation

Escape),[17] or through the *Mosad l'Aliya Bet* (Organization for Immigration), which was secretly dispatching the Jewish survivors to Palestine in boats.

Many, many others were not there to take leave of me, having vanished in the terrible storm without a farewell, snatched without trace, so that we would never know what had befallen them.

In my heart I parted from each and every one of them: those I knew would never return, and those remnants of the camps whom I still hoped would suddenly appear out of the ruins, frail and broken, but alive.

The plane took off, circling the destroyed city. I pressed my face to the window, taking a last parting look. I breathed freely.

From the distance, my country called to me in all its wealth of color and its glowing sun.

I had completed my task.

We flew over a still, green park. The white of marble glinted through the leaves. A cemetery . . .

The Jewish cemetery on Kereszturi Avenue.

There among the other graves was Hannah's.[18]

In the distance rose the chimney of a bombed factory, like a warning finger. Do not forget.

No, I had not completed my task. I never would.

It was impossible to forget them—the living or the dead.

Epilogue

MY PLANE LANDED WITH A JOLT on the runway of the El Mazar airport, near Cairo. One of the tires exploded. The undercarriage collapsed and the plane came to rest on one wing, rotating like a giant pair of compasses, with a deafening, grinding screech as parts disintegrated and flew into the air.

Bruised, we broke through the emergency exit before the plane caught fire. My commander, Colonel Tony Simmons, welcomed me with a hug and a pat on the shoulder and then took me to the apartment where we had lived while waiting for departure.

"Have a rest tonight," said Tony, "then come tomorrow so that I can debrief you." He patted my shoulder again. "You've done great work for your people," he added emphatically.

The large apartment was empty. I could not but think, in the silence that enfolded me, of those with whom I had dreamed the dreams of a Jewish revolt, those who had not returned.

I went down to the teeming square and walked in the warm night streets of Cairo, as humming with life as ever. Anxiety gradually overtook me: what would happen tomorrow? What should I tell or not tell when I gave my report to headquarters? What was

Tony implying when he emphasized that I had served my people? Would the British officers understand why I had gone to the Majestic Hotel, to the Gestapo headquarters, or would I face a court-martial? And Peretz? Could I tell how he had come to give himself up to the enemy? And Kasztner? What should I tell about his part in these events? I did not close an eye all that night.

In the morning, I entered Tony's room, saluted, and said, "I can't make any report until I have reported to an authorized representative of the Hagana."

Tony stared at me for a long time and then said, "All right, I'll get in touch with your people." The next day Zvi Yehieli arrived.

I sat with him for days and nights. I told him everything: about Hannah, about Peretz, about everything that had happened to us. I learned from him that Yoel Brand had been imprisoned by the British all the time we had been receiving those encouraging telegrams in his name, sent by the Immigration Establishment in Istanbul. The British authorities had been deceiving Moshe Sharett of the Jewish Agency and the people running the Immigration Establishment, who were doing their best to investigate every faint chance of rescuing Jews.

Zvi concluded, "We mustn't tell the British the whole truth behind Peretz's arrest. They wouldn't understand. They might use it against us. Tell them everything that happened to you personally, without hiding anything. But don't tell them what you heard from Peretz."

I agreed, and thus related a false version of how Peretz came to fall into Gestapo hands, a version of events I presented in the first edition of this book, which was published while the British were still ruling Palestine.

A week later I was home, a discharged soldier. I was welcomed with warmth and admiration by everyone. They wanted to hear what had happened over there, yet my story about the horrific fate of Jews forsaken by man and God found no echo in their hearts. They wanted another story, about the few who had fought like lions to sanctify the name of the Jewish people. Wherever I turned the question was flung at me: Why didn't the Jews rebel? Why did they go like sheep to the slaughter? It was soon evident to me that we were ashamed of those who had been tortured, shot, thrown to the flames. A consensus was being formed that viewed the victims of the Holocaust as the dregs of the people. Unknowingly, we were accepting the Nazi viewpoint that the Jews were subhuman. "Soap," they were called. Yet we were excluding ourselves from this definition. History was making bitter fun of us; we were ourselves placing the six million on the bench of the accused.

Those whom fate had allowed to observe the Holocaust from a safe distance gave themselves the right to judge, dividing all Jews simplistically into two categories: the people who had allowed themselves to be led to the slaughter and the few, the heroes. Others divided them into martyrs and traitors, since it was not possible, in their opinion, that a disaster of such magnitude could have struck the nation without traitors within.

Those who had not been tried in the flesh in the valley of slaughter gave themselves excitedly to tales of heroism that were to influence the education of generations to come. They clung to the glorious heroic deeds of a few, but failed to understand the mute heroism of masses of Jews who were caught in a situation with no solution and were annihilated without a fight, nevertheless retaining their humanity through all the tortures of hell until their last breath.

I withdrew into myself, while the feeling strengthened within me that I had returned from another planet and that those who had sent me there, as well as the girl I had come back to, would never fully understand. They would not understand, because they had not been there. And as for those who had by blind chance survived the killing fields, they were condemned to eternal isolation. For we all use the same words, but meanings are absolutely different.

When I was on my way back to Palestine, I met Moshe Sharett in Cairo. During a conversation with him I expressed the view that the Hagana should investigate the events in Budapest and that Kasztner should face a Hagana trial, and that he should until then be suspended from all public positions. My suggestion was accepted. A role assigned to him in the World Jewish Congress was subsequently withheld from him. The trial was conducted during the first World Zionist Congress held after the war, in December 1946 in Basel.

It was difficult to recognize Kasztner. He was a broken man. There was no trace of his self-confidence. In response to my claim, Kasztner unfolded the whole affair of the Budapest Rescue Committee and tried to prove that his motives had been impeccable. If he had erred, he said, he would account for his mistakes, but he protested against being branded with the mark of Cain.

*Paratroopers who returned from their missions to various countries in
Europe and the Balkans, 1958. Palgi is in the top row, third from left.*

The judges were persuaded that Kasztner had had one aim—to
rescue Jews, and that he had operated to the best of his understanding and out of loyalty to his purpose. Further, they refrained from
judging each of his actions in themselves, and asserted that those
who had not been put to the test could not place themselves as
judges over anyone working in those abnormal circumstances.

I found it hard to reconcile myself to the sentence. Wounds I
had thought had healed already were opened to bleed again. The
nightmares returned. The figures of my parents and my sister, Lucy,
pursued me night and day, demanding vengeance. I was in a private
hell, because awake or dreaming, a question I could not express vi-
brated through me. Why, why had they not put them into the rescue train? In what way were they less entitled to live than those that
had stayed alive? Three hundred and eighty-eight Jews from my
city had been saved on that train. Why were they not among the
survivors? After all, some of the people who had decided on the
list—Kasztner among them—had been my friends, school friends,
companions of my sister and myself in the youth movement. Why
had they not saved Lucy? Why had they not saved my parents?

Why did they have to die? But others would have had to die instead of them had they been on the list. The more my rage mounted against those who could have and did not rescue them, the more guilty I felt for being alive, and for being incapable of rising above the vengeful feelings I harbored against those who had been my friends and who I felt had betrayed me.

Perhaps we will never know what criteria guided the selection of those to be saved, and any research into the subject will probably not get to the roots of these considerations. But what was a man to do when he had the task of deciding who must live and who must die? Was he to save himself the agony of such a decision by forfeiting the lives of close to 1,700 Jews?

Doubts began to peck at my mind. Perhaps it was my desire for revenge at what had happened to me, the loss of my parents and my sister, that had prompted me to bring Kasztner to trial. I saw a number of the leaders, at the Congress, who had abandoned their communities to their dreadful fate, taking refuge themselves over the border, and here they were, being treated with honor and respect. I had to ask myself whether this one who had stayed at his post to the end, even though he had the chance to save himself, was really better or worse than they were. I struggled with myself for a long time until in the end I came to terms with the Hagana judge's decision, and saw it as a responsible and balanced conclusion to a chapter of horror that had to be closed to allow life to go on. I also saw it as a duty to myself to assist Kasztner's immigration to Palestine and his absorption into the country.

I believed that this really closed the chapter. But fate would not have it so.

Malkiel Grünwald, an elderly Jew who had immigrated from Hungary to settle in Jerusalem, published a pamphlet containing slanderous indictments against public figures he wanted to destroy. In 1953 he accused Kasztner of collaborating with the Nazis in the deal known as "Goods for Blood." Kasztner was accused of willfully concealing from the Jews of Hungary what lay in store for them, of saving friends, family, and a group of leaders in the "Notables Train," and of foiling extensive plans for rescue. In response, the attorney general brought a charge of libel against Grünwald.

Grünwald's attorney, Shmuel Tamir, succeeded in turning the case against Grünwald into a case against Kasztner. Furthermore, he managed to turn it into a political vendetta against David

Ben-Gurion, Moshe Sharett, and those in the Immigration Establishment. He accused them of being lackeys of the British, preventing large-scale rescue of Jews that could have been carried out had it not been for the corrupt ties between the heads of the Jewish Agency, the British, and the Nazis, with Kasztner as the link between them. I came out in defense of Kasztner, in return for which Tamir accused me too of collaborating with the Gestapo.

In the verdict delivered in 1955 the judge, Benjamin Halevy, sided with most of Grünwald and Tamir's claims, establishing that "Kasztner sold his soul to the devil."

This dramatic pronouncement—drawn from the treasury of German culture, the Faust saga—still echoes and causes shudders of horror, whereas the echoes of the shots that pierced Kasztner's heart, fired by fanatics, have long since been forgotten.[19] Likewise, not many still remember that the Supreme Court subsequently annulled the verdict handed down by Judge Halevy.

This sad chapter of events, which split the nation in two camps and even caused a government crisis, embodied the ailing, tormented soul bequeathed by the Holocaust to the people of Israel.

Would it have been better to conclude this book without recalling the forgotten and awakened ghosts? Perhaps, but I have been unable to do so. For we have no contract with history, and who is to guarantee us that another Holocaust will not rage around us once again? The point in establishing the State of Israel is, perhaps, its ability to rescue Jews and prevent another Holocaust of destruction, and we are not yet free from our snare. The rule still holds:

If you go and do not return—you will be a hero.

If you go and do return—you will be judged.

If you do nothing—you will sit in judgment of others.

But a people will continue to exist as long as there are those who say: Who will go, if not me? And they go even knowing that, should they return, they will be judged by those who did not go.

Notes

Chapter 1

1. Jewish Agency: Public Body authorized by the British Mandate, confirmed by the League of Nations in 1922, to assist and take part in the development of Palestine as a Jewish national home.
2. Hagana: Clandestine organization for Jewish self-defense in Palestine, set up in 1920. Later the Hagana concentrated on bringing in "illegal immigrants,"
3. Yishuv: The Jewish community in Palestine.

Chapter 2

4. Lehi: A Jewish underground splinter group that advocated intensification of anti-British activities to force Great Britain to honor its obligations toward the Jewish people as outlined in the Balfour Declaration of 1917.
5. Irgun (Etzel): A Jewish military organization based on the teachings of Zeev Jabotinsky that supported active retaliation against Arab attacks and, after January 1944, also attacks against the British forces in Palestine.
6. According to Itzchak Ben Efraim, a fellow paratrooper whose mission was in Romania, this was probably disinformation, to conceal the real

destination of the planes. No British aircraft is known to have been dispatched to Poland at the time. (Personal communication.)

Chapter 4

7. For details on Kasztner, see the Introduction and the Afterword.
8. *Hashomer Hazair:* A youth movement deeply committed to Zionism and Jewish culture. Originally formed in 1913 in Eastern Europe, it was influenced by the Scout movement and the Wandervogel German movement, which was anti-militarist and pro-youth independence. Later *Hashomer Hazair* became revolutionary socialist in ideology, particularly in Israel.
9. The number of passengers on the rescue trains is given here as 1,686. The original Hebrew edition of the book quotes a smaller figure. In the interim further information has become available, although it remains difficult to be exact. At least five people died en route and a few others were removed by the Gestapo because they did not have Hungarian passports. In addition, some people managed to get on the train in Budapest and others were born during the journey.

Chapter 6

10. Admiral Wilhelm Franz Canaris was chief of the Abwehr, the German military Intelligence Service, which was responsible for espionage, counterespionage, and sabotage. He was, however, anti-Hitler, and secretly aided the underground of the German officers, the Black Orchestra, which made several attempts on Hitler's life. Hitler ordered his execution in April 1945.
11. The V-2 was the first rocket, father of all modern rockets, with which the Germans bombarded London in 1944, thinking that they would thus reverse the course of the war and gain victory.
12. Odescalchi is the name of a famous old ecclesiastical family from Italy that also included royalty. It is not known whether the princess had royal status in her own right or gained it through marriage. Her fate is unknown.

Chapter 8

13. Arrow Cross Party: An extreme Hungarian Fascist movement established in Hungary in the 1930s that later gave full support to the Nazis' "Final Solution" to the Jewish problem. In 1944 they seized power in Hungary and conducted a regime of terror. They were disbanded by force with the liberation of Hungary by the Soviet army.

Chapter 11

14. Consul Carl Lutz, the Swiss representative in Budapest of British and American interests and those of a number of other states, working on his own initiative and also in collaboration with the Zionist underground, issued unauthorized Swiss "protective letters" (Shutzbriefe) on a massive scale and designated diplomatic buildings as safe houses for Jews. Other diplomats took part in similar rescue measures, notably the Swedish diplomat Raoul Wallenberg, who after the war almost certainly met his death in a Russian prison.

15. At this stage, the deportation to the extermination camps had ceased. In early November some 85,000 Jewish forced-labor battalions were directed on foot toward the Austrian border. A high percentage perished on the way.

16. Mizrahi: A religious movement dedicated to the establishment of the State of Israel in accordance with the precepts of the Torah.

Chapter 13

17. During the war some 27,000 Jewish men and women from Palestine volunteered for the British army. Some 5,000 of them served in the combat unit that was set up in August 1944 under the name of the Jewish Brigade. The rest were enlisted in service and professional units. *B'richa* (Heb., "Flight") was the name given to the mass migration of Jews from Eastern Europe to Western and Southern Europe between 1944 and 1948, most of whom reached Palestine through the organization of the same name. About a million refugees came under their auspices.

18. In 1950 the Israeli government brought Hannah's remains to the military cemetery on Mount Herzl, Jerusalem, for burial. A special section there was allotted for the members of the paratroop mission.

Epilogue

19. Kasztner was assassinated in March 1957 in Tel Aviv.

A Personal Biography
of Yoel Palgi

PHYLLIS PALGI

✳ **P**ARACHUTING INTO NAZI-OCCUPIED EUROPE to rescue trapped Jewish communities was an act whose powerful symbolism transformed Yoel Palgi into a legendary figure in his own lifetime. He was also the father of my children and the man I loved. But our life together, which began after this near suicidal rescue scheme, was not one of peaceful domesticity. The historical events through which we lived dominated our private lives. History was not a backdrop. It was center stage. And for those of us who felt we had a mission in life, the personal and the public were inseparable.

Born in 1918 in Cluj, Transylvania, Yoel, culturally both Jewish and Hungarian, grew up as part of two minorities. The main options open to Jewish youths at that time were twofold: they could strengthen their Hungarian cultural allegiance through the Communist Party, or they could confirm their Jewishness through active Zionism. Yoel, whom a childhood friend described as seething with energy and bursting with original ideas, chose the latter. His parents, middle-class and secular Jews who nonetheless abided by Jewish traditions, accepted his choice but were dismayed by his neglect of high school studies and his lack of further academic ambitions.

His elder sister, Lucy, by contrast, had already distinguished herself as a student at the University of Prague. By the time he turned sixteen, the ideology of the Zionist socialist movement to end the vulnerability of the Jewish people had become his enduring core belief, and emigration to Palestine was the logical choice.

Upon his arrival in Palestine in 1939, Yoel joined a group of peers from Cluj who had preceded him. Together they set out to establish a new kibbutz on the shores of the Sea of Galilee in the Jordan Valley, which became his home for the next ten years. Almost immediately he had become an integral part of the young generation of social revolutionaries—a group that included the future leaders Yitzhak Rabin, Shimon Peres, and Moshe Dayan. The harsh life they lived in those early days was softened by the tantalizing dream of a utopia that would bring about a Jewish national home built on justice and equality. This vision demanded personal participation and unconditional loyalty to the cause. But Yoel's need for individual freedom of expression often led him to play the role of castigator and critic in his public life and work. In 1942, for instance, while serving in a Palestinian unit in the British army with duties that included driving a mobile water tank in the North African desert, he caused a stir by writing an article on the ethical dilemma of driving past lost or injured German soldiers who were begging for water.

Although he was sometimes criticized within the youth movement for retaining "bourgeois" customs, such as sending flowers to a girlfriend and taking classes in fencing, an appreciation of old world elegance continued to be for Yoel a significant and enduring theme. He confronted death a number of times in his life with equanimity, but he always wanted the actual circumstances of death to carry either grace or nobility. With the outbreak of the War of Independence in Palestine, he refused to accept the kibbutz ruling that, instead of active military service, he would be assigned to truck vegetables on the dangerous road to besieged Jerusalem. Privately he said to me, "I can't die with tomatoes."

Not long ago, a young Russian immigrant boy who had read about the Hungarian rescue mission but was unaware of Yoel's death in 1978 insisted on meeting him. Such hero worship had troubled Yoel. Beyond his personal discomfort, he feared that the concept of heroism in Israel was increasingly equated with active militarism. He was particularly concerned about the distorted value judgment projected on the millions of exterminated Jews in Europe who were

denigrated for "going like sheep to the slaughter." He maintained
that true heroism was embodied by people like his sister, Lucy, who
could have escaped the Nazis but who, instead, literally forced her
self into the deportee train to accompany her mother and invalid father, with whom she perished. He complained that his status as a
hero stereotyped and fixed him in time. He was also fully aware of
the ambivalence of hero worship. On the one hand, people need
heroes to embody what they would like to have done; on the other
hand, heroes often arouse envy. Still, I think he would have found
humor in an exchange I recently had with a surgeon who would
soon operate on me. When the surgeon commanded, "Tell me your
history," I described the onset of my symptoms. "No, no," he cut
me off abruptly. "Where did you meet Palgi?"

I met "Palgi" in Cairo, Egypt, in May 1945, just three days after his return from the hell of Europe. Cairo was then the Middle
Eastern center for Allied military headquarters and a hub of international intrigue. I was there in response to a call from the United
Nations Relief and Rehabilitation Administration (UNRRA) for
volunteers from South Africa (my country of birth) to care for
Yugoslavs evacuated from the war zone by the British army to a
tented encampment in the Egyptian Sinai desert. In South Africa I
had belonged to the same ideological youth movement as Yoel's in
Cluj and sought similar contacts in Cairo. I was led to the chief of
the Hagana (the main Jewish underground army in Palestine) for
Egypt, who initiated me into this underground organization. My
clandestine tasks were mostly connected with the smuggling of Jewish displaced persons into Mandatory Palestine.

One evening I was invited to a dance by a British air force pilot of Jewish European origin who also was secretly a member of
the Hagana. On the way he had to meet briefly with "an extraordinary person who had just arrived from chaotic Budapest." We
found Yoel sitting in the shoddy soldiers' clubroom waiting for the
pilot, but despite being told that I "belonged," he would not allow
my presence at their conversation. Sitting alone at an adjacent table,
observing him, I felt drawn to this mysterious stranger. His blue
eyes were pools of sadness, his skin was almost translucent, and his
thinness gave him an ethereal air that contrasted with the intensity
of his conversation. True to the magic of such wartime encounters
where moments freeze in time, I felt we were destined to meet again,
which in fact happened some months later. During my first short

leave to Tel Aviv I met with a senior representative of the Hagana, Zvi Yehieli, who was accompanied by Yoel. This time he behaved with charming gallantry, inviting me to his kibbutz. He was visibly disappointed, as I was, that time did not allow me to go.

Soon after his post-mission debriefings in Cairo and Tel Aviv, Yoel went home to his kibbutz still tortured by nightmarish memories of the tragedy-laden rescue mission and of the fate of his family. He had difficulty communicating with people about his experiences. Some could not bear to hear about them. Others looked at him askance in disbelief. Still others thought he was heading for a breakdown. In a blaze of energy, Yoel began to record the events of the past year, feeling keenly that his mission would not be complete until he brought what he had witnessed to the world. He owed it to future generations. He owed it to the dead, including Lucy and his parents. He owed it to his compatriot and mission companion Hannah Szenes, whose moral strength and unshrinking resolution to reach Budapest, even after the Nazi invasion, had been an inspiration to him. Her execution by the Hungarian fascists had been devastating to him. His feelings about the loss of his other companion, Peretz Goldstein, were like those of an older brother, and for years he was haunted by the memory of the obscure circumstances of Peretz's arrest and disappearance.

In December 1946, I attended the World Zionist Congress held in Basel, Switzerland, where, to my pleasant surprise, I again met Yoel, who was working with the underground organizations assembling and transporting refugees to Palestine. The Congress was the venue for a meeting of the senior emissaries who were fanned out through Europe and operating surreptitiously, in defiance of the British immigration policy. Yoel and I walked together for hours through the streets of Basel, crunching down the snow.

By that time, I had become a fully trusted member of the Hagana and was given a task: "our man" in Prague was in desperate need of money to move the mounting number of refugees gathered on the Czechoslovakian border. Since my British passport would place me above suspicion, I was chosen to make the delivery. I found myself on the famous Orient Express clutching a chocolate box filled with gold coins. Yoel, who was responsible for this operation, chose to come along in the event of a mishap, but was in another compartment so as not to be associated with me. The Allies had divided Germany into zones and passengers were checked routinely by British, French, American, and Russian border police. I was only vaguely aware that the discovery of gold coins could lead to my arrest and detention in some unknown jail. Between checkpoints, Yoel slipped into my compartment to hide the coins in a safer place. Using simple tools, he deftly opened the drainpipe from the wash basin and rapidly stuffed the coins into the pipe, which he then reconnected to the basin. Suddenly he said, "I think we must not lose each other again. Let's get married when I get back to Palestine." I solemnly agreed. The thought whizzed through my mind that I would not know how to explain to my mother and friends that I was marrying a man about whom I knew so little with so much confidence and a sense of inevitability. He left the compartment a second before the police came in. The mission was a success.

Yoel remained in Europe for a few months before returning to Maagan, his kibbutz in-the-making. I had been demobilized but returned to Egypt to complete my commitment to the Hagana. In September 1947, I left to get married and settle down to kibbutz life. Yoel met my plane, and we traveled for hours by the rickety Jordan Valley bus to Maagan. More than two years had passed from the day I first laid eyes on the pale, gaunt young man in the Cairo club, and a metamorphosis had taken place. He was tanned and healthy looking, burnished by working in the fields. He was of average height, slim, and fair skinned with a shock of light brownish hair that would soon become a rather distinguished gray. The outstanding features of his face were his slow smile and very blue almond-shaped eyes. Opening the door of his "house," a spartan one-room hut, Yoel looked at me apprehensively. But I was in high spirits. Finally I had become a real pioneer.

From time to time, Yoel would travel from Maagan to Jerusalem to knock at official doors in the fight for more economic support for Hannah's widowed mother, Katerina Szenes, who had arrived from Budapest, and for Peretz Goldstein's parents. The mission's paratroopers had waived all rights and privileges due them or their families from the British army because they wished to prove to the British that they were not paid agents but volunteers on a life-saving mission. The Jewish Agency (which represented the interests of world Jewry concerning Palestine before the British mandatory authorities) was supposed to make provisions for surviving parents of those paratroopers killed in action. But with mass immigration immediately after the war, the needs of individuals in nonroutine circumstances were often overlooked. Yoel was unrelenting in his demands on behalf of the bereaved parents of his two fallen partners and began to be regarded as a troublemaker.

On November 29, 1947, the United Nations recommended the partition of Palestine, which led to the birth of the State of Israel. When war broke out with the neighboring Arab countries, Prime Minister David Ben-Gurion ordered Yoel to establish and command a paratrooper unit. The unit's red beret and special insignia became, in time, symbols of national pride. In October 1948 our first child, Ilana, was born in an overcrowded maternity hospital in Haifa. The women in my ward were mainly evacuees from displaced persons camps in Europe, and each woman recounted her own grim story and her determination to bring a child into the world. The shadows of death under which the women still lingered were brightened now by visions of hope for the future of their newborn children and for the new state.

I was proud when Yoel, dressed impeccably as if straight from the parade ground, arrived in his jeep to take Ilana and me back to the kibbutz. He seemed the very image of the new Israel, but when I saw his expression as he looked at our infant, I realized that it was with those women that he shared both a past and a hope. He was recalling how a fascist officer in the Hungarian prison where he was detained during the mission, fearing the imminent fall of the Nazis, tried to ingratiate himself to Yoel by saying, "You'll tell your grandchildren your life story yet."

By mid-1949 an armistice had been signed with Egypt, Syria, Lebanon, and Jordan, and a quarter of a million immigrants had arrived. It became imperative to build a range of institutions as a basis for an independent democratic state. Among those proposed was a national airline, which Yoel fervently believed was essential to prevent Israel's isolation from the rest of the world, as had happened during the War of Independence. When El Al, the national airline, came into being, Yoel early on became its deputy director-general and played a historic role in the company's development. (The name El Al, "to the skies" in Hebrew, symbolized one of his youthful dreams: had he been unburdened by the plight of European Jewry, he would have striven to become an astronaut.)

Yoel's most rewarding experience during his fourteen years at El Al was heading one of the largest rescue airlifts at the time. Between 1949 and 1951 he was responsible on behalf of El Al for the air transport of 200,000 Jewish immigrants from Muslim countries to Israel. Because the Arab governments did not allow Israeli aircraft to land, the Israelis had to fly under a foreign flag and with foreign crew. With the economic straits of the young state and the pressure of time, conditions were hair-raising. To pack in as many immigrants as possible, the seats were removed from the planes and replaced with hard wooden benches, to which the new immigrants were strapped. On landing in Israel the planes were hastily cleaned, checked, turned around, and put back in the air. In order to complete the mission before the Arab governments closed their borders, flights continued seven days a week. Then one day the Israeli minister of transportation and communications, under pressure from Orthodox quarters, gave an order to stop flying on the Sabbath. Since time was running out, Yoel, ever the maverick, refused and wrote to the minister that his act was tantamount to sabotage. The minister regarded the letter as offensive and ordered Yoel's dismissal. I think Ben-Gurion finally intervened. In any case, the operation continued. Years later Yoel reminisced. "When I think about the quality of those planes and the dangerous political situation at that time, somebody must have been hovering and protecting us. Not one life was lost."

In January 1954, Yoel, fully engrossed in his work at El Al, was called to testify on behalf of Rezső Kasztner, the former head of the Rescue Committee in Nazi Budapest and the moving force behind the grandiose scheme to exchange Hungarian Jewish lives for essential equipment needed by the failing German army. The public prosecutor had charged Malkiel Grünwald with libel for accusing Kasztner of being a Nazi collaborator. Nine years had passed since Yoel left Budapest. His psychic numbing had begun to thaw, and he had the strength to keep the black shadows caged. But the trial splintered him wide open. He was forced once again to confront unresolved moral dilemmas that arose out of the immoral context of Nazi-occupied Hungary.

His memoir on the rescue mission, translated from the 1977 revised edition and presented here in English for the first time, had in 1946 been published in Hebrew to wide acclaim. During the trial, the unscrupulous defense attorney, who harbored extreme right-wing political ambitions, viciously attacked the memoir's veracity because it reflected favorably both on Kasztner and (indirectly) on David Ben-Gurion's left-wing Labor government (since all the volunteers for the rescue mission had been members of the socialist

Kibbutz movements). After the trial, Yoel went through an excruciating process of reviewing and confronting his own thoughts, feelings, and motivations during the crucial time when he was part of Kasztner's rescue plan. Yoel told me that he had been blinded during the trial by horrendous images of the past, some chaotic, others crystal clear. (Among his papers were descriptions of scenes like those he saw in the last days of the ghetto, where corpses, lifted from the muddy paths, were propped up against the wall.) He was also disturbed by his small inaccuracies, even when they had no significance for the case. Searching for documentation, he began to question people and check the inner logic of his memories. He was taken aback by the tricks his memory had played on him.

One such memory, on which he insisted in court, was that he had visited Kasztner at his pension in the predawn darkness. Even as Yoel was testifying, he felt that his memory of the meeting time did not make sense. In 1956 he wrote to Attorney General Haim Cohen about the incident:

> I was pressed hard about who fixed the appointment at such an unusual hour. I also thought that it was peculiar, but I remembered that it was still dark. Was it possible that I agreed to come to a meeting at a strange house in Nazi Budapest while it was still dark? After all, no stranger could enter a pension at that hour without being confronted by the night watchmen. . . . Suddenly the whole picture became clear to me. It had been a sunny morning. I entered the pension. . . . Nobody stopped me. Kasztner's room was dark. He was still in bed. He switched on the reading lamp. I sat down next to the bed and we spoke for a long time. It was horrifying. The tragedy of the Jews and my personal tragedy spread throughout the darkness of the room. It was under those circumstances that I learned that my sister and parents had been sent to the death camp. The background to this meeting was a summer morning in Budapest, but that was on the other side of the closed blinds, and in the room there was darkness. That picture was the one engraved in my memory.[1]

Yoel also explained in his letter that he had long struggled with his feelings toward Kasztner: "Had I the right to disparage him? Am I blinded because of my personal bitterness . . . having been deprived of a family? I came to the understanding that it was wrong for me to pass judgment." Nevertheless, his heart remained heavy

over the deaths of Hannah Szenes, Peretz Goldstein, and his own
family, but he had accepted that it was not up to him to judge Kasztner for risking the lives of the parachutists. Kasztner's purpose had
been to save greater numbers. Although Yoel was devastated that
Kasztner did not include Yoel's family among those to be saved, he
knew that he could not morally have demanded their salvation because it would have meant the deaths of others instead. After making an extraordinary effort to help Kasztner integrate himself into
Israel, Yoel wrote, "I did it with a clear conscience. . . . The human
being has strange and wonderful ways of healing a soul which is
traumatized."

Yoel was adamant, however, on one particular issue on which
the defense lawyer had attacked him. In 1946 Yoel had written that
Peretz was arrested by the Gestapo through an unlucky chance. In
court under oath, Yoel explained that his Hagana supervisors ordered him to censor the real story of Peretz's arrest. The Hagana
wished to avoid tension with the British authorities and to protect
both Peretz and Kasztner against accusations of collaboration with
the enemy. Only in the 1977 edition, when it was no longer a "state
secret," could Yoel describe in detail the event as told to him by
Peretz in prison.

I shall end this sorrowful chapter in Yoel's life in the spirit in
which he concluded his letter to the attorney general:

> I must emphasize that all that I have learned in the past months did
> not change, but on the contrary strengthened the evaluation I gave
> from the witness stand. If you ask me in which direction I lean,
> whether Kasztner was a traitor or a hero, I think that calling him a
> traitor is blasphemous. . . . As far as I am concerned, I think that in
> those days [endangering one's life for the sake of others] was a Jew's
> elementary obligation, and I think that Kasztner lived up to it.

Throughout the trial Yoel continued as usual with his work at
El Al, revealing little of his inner turmoil. By the late 1950s, the major challenge of the airline was to become commercially profitable,
marking the end of the hectic pioneering stage. A number of Yoel's
early colleagues had left, and he too felt that it was time to move on.
He accepted a position as head of the Department of Civil Aviation
and enjoyed expanding Israel's international connections by negotiating for new air agreements in different parts of the world.

*Palgi, then ambassador to Tanzania, and Vice President Rashidi
Kawawa, celebrating Israeli Independence Day, 1966.*

Then, in late 1963, when a number of countries in Africa had
achieved independence and turned to Israel for advice and material
assistance, Yoel accepted the post of ambassador to the country that
today is called Tanzania. He drew pleasure from the fact that Israel,
perceived in Tanzania as a heroic little country that had driven out
the British, was, within a decade of its own independence, able to
extend aid to others. He was also rewarded by his acquaintance with
President Julius Nyerere, a statesman of Nelson Mandela's stature
with a similar ethical stand and vision. Yoel was offered the chance
to become a career diplomat, but after mulling it over we finally decided to return to Israel. He felt strongly that our first-generation
Israeli-born children needed a permanent home in Israel. In order
to be a citizen of the world, he believed, one's primary identity must
be unequivocal.

On arriving home, Yoel characteristically sought a position
that would involve him in the harsh day-to-day struggle to meet
Israel's expanding needs. He saw as a challenge his appointment to
the nonprofit health service, Kupat Holim, affiliated with the His-

tadrut (General Federation of Labor), which at that time supplied comprehensive health service to 85 percent of the Israeli population. He served as a senior member of the Central Committee and as director of the Division of Management and Human Resources. Symbolically, Yoel had come full circle. Kupat Holim, which was built on lofty ideals and carried a romantic past, expanded rapidly because of the needs of the young pioneers in the early twentieth century who, to cope with endemic tropical diseases, had formed a mutual aid association. In the 1960s, however, the organization suffered from difficulties in adapting to Israel's developing economy and to changing perceptions of doctor-patient relations. Yoel worked to build morale among the staff and insisted on further awareness of the needs of the heterogeneous patient population.

In September 1973, Yoel had a severe heart attack from which he was still recovering on October 6, when the Yom Kippur War broke out. Then age fifty-four, he was called up to military service with eighteen-year-olds. I could not believe my eyes when I saw him putting on his red beret uniform and pushing some pills into his pocket. He answered my protests by explaining, "My life is not more valuable than an eighteen-year-old's." I did not dare to object, and he was put in charge of a convoy of war correspondents on its way to the southern front. On his return, he went straight to the hospital to prove to the doctors that, because he was still alive, he could not really have had a heart attack. They told him that he was a very sick man and that his survival only proved the power of motivation. He chose not to see a doctor again during the remaining five years of his life.

On February 21, 1978, Yoel went to the Hebrew University in Jerusalem to speak to a group of overseas students about the Holocaust and Jewish rescue schemes. While at the lectern he collapsed and died. His body lay in state on the grounds of the General Federation of Labor and then, by order of the minister of defense, he was honored with a military funeral and buried on Mount Herzl with his fallen comrades from the 1944 mission.

Shimon Peres, Nobel Peace Prize winner and senior Israeli cabinet minister, eulogized him with these words: "Yoel was by nature a dreamer with the soul of a poet who chose to act. . . . It was his dream that brought him to action and his actions that transformed him into a legend. . . . He turned his gaze outward toward his people, to their needs and yearnings, pushing aside his own inborn talents. In retrospect we see that Yoel's biography is an uncommon reflection of the biography of the revival of our people."[2]

I cannot end here with Yoel's death because this was not the end. In 2001, before starting to write this afterword, I reread his memoir. After the description of how he was tortured in prison, I felt I needed a break, and so I drove down to the neighborhood store. There I struck up a conversation with the Yemen-born owner about Yoel and the events of the war in Europe. Suddenly, I heard a woman exclaim, "I was in the same prison in Budapest, and I owe my life to Yoel." Her name was Herta Goren, and her story, like those of so many unsung heroes in Israel, is remarkable. She had survived the war with only her younger brother, for whom she had become responsible at age twelve. Her parents and other siblings had all perished. But Yoel, she maintained, was different. He need not have been there. He came from the outside to save them. He came twice. He did not make his way back to Palestine after escaping from the train en route to a certain death in Germany. Instead, he became active in the pioneer youth underground that later saved her group of youngsters from dying of starvation and exposure. With the Russian army at the border, the Hungarian fascists threw them out of prison onto the streets. She said she would never forget one night when Yoel, himself exhausted, told them that they must not give up hope. He promised that they would be sent to Palestine where a home was waiting for them. Previously, Katerina Szenes had expressed similar sentiments when she told me in Israel how Yoel had traced her whereabouts in the last days of the occupation and written her a letter that gave her the strength to continue living. He implored her to return to Pest, where he offered her his room until more suitable accommodations could be found. He cared for her, finally arranging her immigration to Palestine on the first boat after the liberation of Hungary, with her son waiting for her.

More than fifty years later in my own neighborhood, Herta and I sat in her casually comfortable home where the sun streamed in from the garden. Where did she get the strength to continue the struggle in life? "I've been lucky," she said. "I was a very beloved child and I have always met people who were good to me." Yoel, Herta, Katerina Szenes, and many others confronted so much evil. How were they able to face life again? Herta had reason to trust that someone would come to help. Katerina knew that her daughter, who had died for her convictions, had not been alone in her struggle.

Furthermore, she became a source of inspiration for generations to come. Yoel was able to live with the horror of the past because he belonged to those who loved life and were willing to risk it to save others. In his own words, "There will always be those who will be ready to go." As Ben-Ephraim, one of the other parachutists, once asked, "Can you imagine our history without this effort?"[3]

Postscript

A new book by a leader of the youth underground movement in Budapest in 1945 was recently brought to my attention.[4] I was astounded to read that as part of a last, desperate measure to prevent the massacre of the remaining prisoners in the Budapest ghetto before the Russian army entered the city, Yoel had volunteered to assassinate Eichmann, who was still in the city. He was placed in charge of this plan, but it was ultimately decided to hire two local mercenaries for the actual assassination, in order to prevent a backlash against the ghetto should the Nazis discover that a Jew was responsible. Eichmann, however, fearing that it was too dangerous for him to remain in Budapest any longer, suddenly moved out a day ahead of schedule. I contacted the author of the book and asked why the story had been kept a secret. He said, "Probably because we felt so frustrated. But perhaps it was just as well; otherwise we would not have had the Eichmann trial in Jerusalem."

I wonder what else I shall learn in the future.

Notes to Afterword

1. Unpublished letter, February 22, 1956, translated from the Hebrew.
2. Shimon Peres, memorial gathering for Yoel Palgi in the Assembly Hall of Kupat Holim, Tel Aviv, February 22, 1978.
3. Itzchak (Meno) Ben-Ephraim, *Mimazor B'aretz Layahadut N'zura* (From a land under siege to a people besieged) (Tel Aviv: Sifriat Poalim, 1996), 270.
4. Moshe Alpan, *Bain Hasa'ara* (Weathering the storm) (Kibbutz Dalia: Moreshet, 2001), 307–308.